D1334385

C90 1219275

Pulling the Strings

Pulling the Strings

My Autobiography

PETER STRINGER

PENGUIN
IRELAND

PENGUIN IRELAND

UK | USA | Canada | Ireland | Australia
India | New Zealand | South Africa

Penguin Ireland is part of the Penguin Random House group of companies
whose addresses can be found at global.penguinrandomhouse.com.

First published 2015

001

Copyright © Peter Stringer, 2015

The moral right of the author has been asserted

Set in 12/14.75 pt Bembo Book MT Std
Typeset by Jouve (UK), Milton Keynes
Printed in Great Britain by Clays Ltd, St Ives plc

A CIP catalogue record for this book is available from the British Library

ISBN: 978–1–844–88275–5

To my wife and best friend, Deborah

Contents

Prologue

4 April 2015

Two hours after Bath's European Champions Cup quarter-final against Leinster, I am sitting in the drug-testing room at the Aviva Stadium.

I'm an exile now. This is my fourth season playing in England, and with my third club. I never planned it this way. I never plan anything too far ahead. There is really only one reason for every move I've made: I want to play rugby.

Soon I'll be on the move again. Bath informed me last November that they would not be renewing my playing contract at the end of the season, and I've nothing lined up for next year. There was talk about them wanting to keep me on in a coaching/mentoring capacity for the younger scrum-halves, but I'm not ready to hang up the boots yet. Leinster could be an option, if only until January, when a number of their players will be ready to come back, post-World Cup. I'd prefer a one-year deal.

My parents, my brothers, my agent and a number of my friends are somewhere in the Aviva, but I haven't had a chance to meet any of them. The Leinster coach, Matt O'Connor, sticks his head around the corner; he has a bottle of beer in his hand.

'I'll be in touch,' he says.

I never had the chance to say a proper farewell at Munster. I left three times on loan, always thinking that I'd be coming back. But the loan to Bath led to a one-year contract, followed by another one-year deal. I'd always imagined I'd be replaced in my final game at either Musgrave Park or Thomond Park, ideally on the far side of the pitch from the main stand. I'd take my time coming off, to show my appreciation to the supporters who have made my time on the field so incredibly special. But it hadn't worked out that way.

Today, playing my first match in Ireland since leaving Munster, was a little bit like what I had imagined, but in reverse. I came on as a substitute, with a scrum on the far side of the pitch.

'They'll give you a good reception,' Dad had said.

'Ah,' I said, 'maybe a few Leinster fans will, but it won't be that big.'

'No, no. They will,' he insisted.

Dad was right. As I jogged over to the scrum, from all around the Aviva there was a big roar. Many gave me a standing ovation. I was surprised, and I'm not going to lie, it was wonderful.

It's a minor miracle that I played today. In January, after a morning training session, I went to our coach, Mike Ford, and asked: 'Can I chat to you later?'

'Yeah, no problem, I will be up in the room.'

After lunch, I walked in. 'Fordy,' I said, 'I'm not happy with the way things have been going. I haven't had as much game time as I'd like. I've hardly had an opportunity to play, so I'm just wondering if you would consider releasing me early from my contract?'

He looked up. 'I had an idea you were going to ask me that,' he said. 'Ordinarily, I wouldn't allow anybody to leave midway through an important season. But if you have something else lined up, then I would be willing to consider it.'

If I know I have under-performed, then I have no issue with a coach's decision not to select me. All you want, as a player, is an opportunity to prove what you can do. Since I was told in November that my services would no longer be required from June onwards, I felt that, in their own minds, they had written me off and wanted to concentrate on developing the younger guys who were contracted for the foreseeable future.

In February, Fordy informed me he'd had a phone call from Dai Young, the director of rugby at Wasps. I spoke to Dai. He assured me that if I moved to Wasps on loan I'd be a regular in the match-day twenty-three and would start some games. 'We can get you down here straight away, if you want,' he told me, 'and you will be on the bench on Saturday.'

I asked him for some time to think about it. In the end, I decided against the move, because I knew Wasps had signed their scrum-halves for next season, so it would only have been a temporary arrangement.

One other thing was keeping me at Bath: our quarter-final against Leinster, and a return to Dublin on ninety-nine European Cup appearances.

Another consideration was that, although I was frustrated to be out of contract and not getting a lot of game time, Mike and I went back a pretty long way. He became Ireland's defence coach in 2002 and he brought a new level of sophistication to the way we defended. More recently, over the past two seasons at Bath, Fordy has often sought my advice in European weeks. This is his first European Cup campaign as a head coach. I thought I could still play a role at Bath.

After considering all these factors I said to Fordy, 'Look, I love playing for this club and I want to stay and put my hand up for selection for this European game.' I told him what it meant to me, my hundredth European Cup game, and in Ireland. That was six weeks ago.

He didn't seem overly happy about it. 'Yeah, fair enough. Your decision.' I think he'd have been happier with a loan move to Wasps, which would have meant I'd be getting some game time and he could recall me any time he wanted. Apart from being on the bench against Northampton, when one of our scrum-halves was injured, I didn't crack the match-day squad in our other league fixtures following the above conversation.

I wasn't holding out much hope for this week. I wanted to air the subject again, but at the same time I didn't want to get on the wrong side of him.

On Monday I had the feeling he was about to announce the team. We had finished a weights session and assembled for a squad meeting at Farleigh House, the nineteenth-century Gothic Revival castle which Bruce Craig, the Bath owner, has refurbished to use as the club's training and administrative base. Fordy was standing with a few players in an area off the team room, and I sensed he was informing them that they wouldn't be involved.

I said: 'Can I have a quick word?'

He said: 'Yeah, yeah.'

'Look, what are the chances of being involved this week? I just watched the video of last week's game against London Welsh. The two lads [Micky Young and Chris Cook] didn't play well.'

He looked away, and then stared at the ground for a few seconds. I thought, *This isn't good news.*

Eventually, he said: 'Yeah, yeah, they didn't do well. I know. If you had asked me that question last week I would have said "No". The two lads would have been involved. But I'm in two minds now. I'm in two minds.' He looked a little flustered.

At that moment our video analyst walked past carrying her laptop, from which she displays the team selection on the big screen.

He said: 'Sorry, Kate, could you come here a second, please? Can you bring up that team for me?' And then he turned to me and said: 'OK, Strings, thanks very much.'

I thought: *Dammit, I didn't get a chance to make my case.*

I went into the meeting. Fordy started by saying that selection had been tough. Then Kate put up the team sheet: I was on the substitutes' bench. I am convinced that, in the moments after our brief conversation, he asked Kate to make a change at number 21, taking out Chris Cook and inserting me. If I had initially been in that match-day twenty-three, he'd have told me to my face when I raised the subject. Instead, I believe he changed his mind two minutes before the meeting.

It demonstrates the value of speaking to coaches who are prepared to listen: you can influence their decisions, they do take what you say on board, provided you don't cross the line by being too argumentative.

I hadn't really engaged with Fordy that often over the weeks since I'd raised the possibility of getting out of my contract. I'd applied myself at training and contributed in team meetings as enthusiastically as if I were the starting number 9. At times I wondered if there was any point. But I did it because at the back of my mind I knew that if there was a tight call, a coach might find himself with a choice between an enthusiastic player and one with his head down. Who will he choose then?

It has been a tough couple of months, putting all my eggs in one basket for this weekend. But all week during training I was as giddy as a kid. All I've ever wanted to do is play; now, I had a shot at playing my hundredth European Cup game at the Aviva Stadium, against Leinster, with most of my family there: Mum and Dad, my brothers George and John, and their wives, Isabel and Aoife. My youngest brother Dave couldn't make it; he's working in the Cayman Islands. And the one person I wanted most to be there, my fiancée Debbie, had committed to a friend's birthday party, which she had actually organized, so she couldn't travel. No issues there – one of the things I love most about her is her loyalty. But her dad, Paddy, and his friend Liam were there. I managed to get eight premium-level tickets in a row from our manager.

Last Tuesday night, Bruce Craig hosted a captain's dinner in the drawing room at Farleigh. The squad, the coaches and Bruce arrived at 7.30 dressed in shirts and club blazers.

Three players, Stuart Hooper, François Louw and Rob Webber, were nominated to speak about what playing for Bath meant to them and to give us an insight into what motivates them. Bruce grew up in Bath and is a committed Bath supporter, and he wanted to revive some of the club's traditions. These dinners take place only four or five times a season. They're quite grand – an old-style banquet – but very relaxed and enjoyable.

Bruce and I both live on The Circus, a circle of Georgian houses in the centre of Bath. Debbie and I rent a second-floor flat where Lord Clive, aka 'Clive of India', the commander-in-chief of British India, lived for a few years in the eighteenth century. Bruce rents a five-storey house with swimming pool for about £7,000 a month; Nicolas Cage once owned the house.

Bath Rugby employs four full-time chefs, providing three meals a day, and at Tuesday's banquet the waitresses struggled to carry the mountain of food: silver platters of ribs, chicken wings, beef brisket, pulled pork and so forth. Dessert was a chocolate fondant, but our head chef, Gerry, put together a plate of melon and strawberries for me. When it was served to me, every head turned to look down the table at me, as if to say, 'What are you like?'

Last Wednesday was also the first day of my Level 2 coaching course. It was cut short to enable me to get my kicking practice and weights done. This week of all weeks I didn't want to change my routine.

Thursday's run-out was only forty-five minutes, but at match intensity. The coaches simulate a match for the starting fifteen and it's fairly full-on.

On Friday, the squad assembled at Lambridge, the club's old training ground, to get the coach to the airport. Kyle Eastmond, our inside centre and probably my best friend at Bath, lives nearby and he collected me that morning.

I've always loved travel days. I've done it countless times, but I still get excited about being in airports. I know it's bizarre, but it just gets me giddy – even Bristol Airport!

I had my lunchbox, filled with food I had cooked the night before: three salmon fillets, a bag of rocket, a punnet of plum tomatoes and four hard-boiled egg whites. It's a disaster when I'm not in control of the food I can eat, especially at airports.

I was the butt of most of the slagging for the day. Sam Burgess, our recruit from Rugby League, joked: 'Ah, the King of Ireland returns.' At passport control in Dublin, the garda glanced at my passport. 'Welcome back, Peter,' he said.

'Ah, yeah, you don't even have to show your passport here,' said some of the lads. 'Oh yeah, just keep walking through.'

After we collected our bags, a garda showed us where our bus was parked, and he walked alongside me, chatting. 'Personal security?' said Horacio Agulla, our Argentine winger. 'Where's *our* security? It's only for you?'

The bus took us from our hotel, the Hilton on Charlemont Place, to our captain's run at 3 p.m. in the Aviva. As the barriers came down for the DART, I recalled that familiar feeling I had before Ireland games. *Ah, fecking hell, I even miss crossing over the train line.*

The same old faces were all at the door. The two security lads shook my hand and one of them said: 'Hello, good to see you back.' For a change I turned right into the away dressing room. Unfamiliar territory.

I had received a message on Facebook the night before from the head groundsman at the Aviva, Majella Smyth. We hadn't been in touch since I last played there, in 2011, so I texted him back.

When we came on to the pitch I saw Majella striding along the touchline. As I walked towards him I passed three more groundsmen sitting in the front row of the West Stand.

'Jesus, lads,' I said. 'Nothing has changed here. Still sitting down and doing nothing.' Big roars of laughter, before they all shook my hand. No handshake from Majella, just a big bear hug. He'd been here for my Irish debut against Scotland, over fifteen years ago, and for every Irish home game since. We chatted about the old Lansdowne Road and the new Aviva, and he told me he'd been keeping a close watch on my career.

We had intended to do a longer captain's run, but the coaches decided against it, worried that the stadium had numerous vantage points for potential spies. We formed a huddle and then walked the pitch, talking through different scenarios rather than actually running through our plays.

After dinner we met in the team room for a motivational video, with clips and highlights of our campaign in Europe, interspersed with images of newspaper clippings. We had come out of a very tough group, having lost our first two matches. In order to qualify, we'd had to win away to Montpellier and Toulouse. One of the best performances of the season by any club in Europe led to a four-try bonus point in Toulouse.

As we arrived back at the team hotel at 4 p.m., my parents were walking past. I gave them their tickets and we had a good long chat in the hotel bar.

'You're going to get a great reception when you come on,' Dad said, not for the first time. 'I just hope you get enough game time now. You should be starting.'

The usual father chat, adding to your self-belief; what parents do. It reminded me of all those days when Mum and Dad called in to the old Berkeley Court for their tickets before Ireland matches. And, as in the old days, they were staying with Dad's twin brother, George, in Blackrock.

I roomed with Kyle; he was snoring by nine o'clock, with the curtains open. I don't know how he does it. I rarely fall asleep before 11 p.m., at the earliest. I flicked through the channels, found *The Shawshank Redemption* and nodded off at about 11.30 or midnight.

We had breakfast at 9.30 and, with nothing scheduled until lunch at 12.15 – three hours before kick-off – Kyle and I went for a stroll. I had taken him to the Munster–Clermont game in Limerick a few months before. Coming from Oldham and a rugby league background with St Helen's, he was taken aback to see that Limerick is such an intense rugby bubble, and by the number of fans asking him to pose for photographs. That morning he was amazed that people walking around Dublin, in Leinster jerseys, approached me to say hello and to wish me well. 'It wouldn't happen with opposition supporters in rugby league,' he said, with a smile on his face.

Back at the hotel, most of us did a light power-weights session just before our meal, to have our bodies primed for kick-off. I was a little bit late going down for lunch because at 12.15 Dad rang me, as he does before every game, exactly three hours before kick-off.

'I hope things go well. I hope you get a decent enough run. Mum says hello and if you get a chance to see us after, great. If we don't see you, give me a shout. I'll have the phone on.'

It's been a great journey for them, too, and it's been pretty special to have them there with me along the way. They know it's coming to an end. I've spoken to them about the possibility of moving to Leinster, among other options. I want to prepare them for the worst-case scenario, that there actually might not be a contract of any kind after this season.

After lunch I had a shower and shaved my head: the usual routine. I was one of the first into the team room for some stretching. A few of the physios were packing for the bus when Fordy walked in.

He said: 'What are you thinking? Do you have anything for me?'

I answered: 'I know from playing these guys over the years that we need to start the game as the dominant force. We need to be the bullies. We need to control them up front, and the scrum is crucial.'

With Munster we usually felt we had an advantage over Leinster in the scrum. But today we were missing our two tight-head props – a real concern.

I said: 'We need to be physical. We cannot wait to react.'

He said: 'Yeah. That's good. I'll use that.'

We had a backs meeting for five minutes, while the forwards had theirs. Then we came together for a team meeting. Mike stood up and reminded us what we'd been through to reach this quarter-final. And then he said: 'We wanted Strings in the squad because of his career in Europe and what he's done for us since he arrived at the club. It's his hundredth cap today. For the final comments before we leave for the ground, I'd just like to ask him to share his experiences of playing against Leinster in the European Cup and whatever else he wants to say.'

This was news to me. Normally, if he wanted someone to speak he'd tip them off beforehand, but he hadn't said anything to me. I more or less repeated what I'd said to him a few moments earlier.

'This is a massive game for everybody. My experience of playing these guys is that they will be cocky. They'll feel they have some sort of divine right to win on this pitch today. We've got to be the bullies. We have to dominate them from the first whistle. This competition is unbelievably special to me for so many reasons. Something or someone motivates everyone in this room. Find that one thing which inspires you to perform and gets the best out of you.'

I became more emotional than I normally would. I was conscious that attention spans are limited, but afterwards Ross Batty, our reserve hooker, said: 'That was pretty special, thanks for that.'

On the bus journey to the ground, I always sit four seats from the front, on the left, by the window; always, be it with Munster, Ireland, Newcastle, Saracens or Bath. I looked to the empty seat beside me and I recalled that for the vast majority of my career John Hayes sat there.

He'd always take up a seat and a half.

'Hayes, there's a gap separating the seats for a reason. Move over.' He'd be pouring over on to my side.

We left the hotel at 1.30, and arrived at the Aviva at 1.45. The man with the white beard and glasses, whose name I can't remember, was at the door. He hadn't been there the day before. 'Great to see you,' he said, with a handshake. In the dressing room, I couldn't wipe the smile off my face. I was so excited.

Kyle was sitting down, sorting out his boots. He looked at me, smiling and shaking his head, because he knew how much I was looking forward to this.

'Come on!' I said. 'Are you not excited?'

It reminded me of being in the changing room with Ireland when Keith Wood was in the team. After his last few motivating words, followed by one final squeeze in the huddle with the intensely focused faces staring across at each other, I'd look up with a smirk. He'd always make eye contact and smile back. It was a little ritual we had.

Players deal with nerves in different ways. On the nights before-hand, and right up to kick-off, my nervous energy expresses itself as childlike excitement. At Bath they play loud music in the dressing room. Some players wear headphones in order to listen to their own music.

I went for a stroll around the pitch. The first person I met was Pro-fessor Arthur Tanner, the Leinster doctor; then the Leinster bag man, Johnny O'Hagan.

I said: 'Jesus, they're still wheeling out all the old lads, aren't they?'

Johnny said: 'Ah, you little bollocks.' We chatted for a couple of minutes.

As I was walking off, Guy Easterby, the Leinster manager, came on to the pitch. We had been the two scrum-halves in the Irish squad on many match days here at Lansdowne Road. We were always vying for the same position, but there was a partnership too – all that passing and kicking practice together.

There was no mention of my possible move to Leinster – it wasn't the time or place.

I went back in, got ready, and then returned for a fifteen-minute warm-up before we came together as a team. I spoke to players indi-vidually, beginning with our full-back Anthony Watson.

'You and the wingers need to work hard as a back three, as a pen-dulum, and make sure we're all working together. I need you talking.' Anthony can be quiet enough at times. 'They will look to play those corners, Madigan, Gopperth and Kearney; they'll look to pin us back.'

I spoke to our number 8, Leroy Houston, too. 'Look, more often than not, a lot of their back-rowers won't physically tackle you low; they'll look to push you down and get over the ball.' Leroy's great quality is keeping his legs going. He'll bump a guy and he won't stop. 'Just keep your leg drive going, do what you normally do. Bump that first guy and if they don't want to tackle you, then just keep running, keep driving through, and that will give us the momentum.'

I said bits and pieces to other lads. With George Ford, there's no need to say much. He's only twenty-two but is very experienced already. He sees space and he has a turn of pace as well. He's a really intelligent guy, and seems to have so much time on the ball.

Back to the changing room and then on to the bench. You start watching it as a supporter and then realize you could be on at a minute's notice. I was sitting beside Sam Burgess, who has little experience of rugby union; I gave him a running commentary. Our lack of discipline cost us hugely in the first half: five Ian Madigan penalties put them 15–5 ahead at the break.

George had scored our try by taking it to the line and cutting through himself. Early in the second half he created a try for Stuart Hooper by doing the same.

Just past the fifty-minute mark Leinster led 18–12 and I was itching to get on. Time for another warm-up.

Fordy always watches the first half from the stand, before coming down to the touchline for the second half. I wanted to remind him that I was around! I stood next to him and stretched the hamstrings. It worked.

'Strings, are you ready?'

'Yeah, I am.'

He didn't give me any instructions, as he normally would. There are many factors you have to take into consideration when coming off the bench, in a key decision-making position like mine. I would say that the scrum-half can control and influence what happens on the pitch more than any other player. If your team is leading, you might play a bit more conservatively, and play the corners to keep the opposition in their own half. On the other hand, you may feel that you have a chance to put the other team to the sword and finish off the game by increasing the tempo to look for another score. It's a judgement call, based on your analysis from the sideline. If you're losing, more often than not something needs to change. On my introduction with fifteen minutes to go, my mindset was to change the dynamics by speeding things up and by bringing a new energy to the game.

Our play improved and we created an opportunity to win. Sean O'Brien came through on me and played me without the ball for a penalty in front of the posts. George made it 18–15. If we could get one more penalty and take it to extra time we'd be well placed, because if it stayed level we'd win on try count.

As we were attacking in their 22 with the clock past eighty minutes, their hooker Richardt Strauss scooped the ball out of a ruck with his hand. We thought it was a penalty for us, but the referee, Jérôme Garcès, said the initial penalty was against us for coming in from the side. It was marginal. I was frustrated and angry but I guess I've never yet known a referee to change his mind.

After the final whistle and just before we formed a huddle on the pitch, Madigan made a beeline for me. He shook my hand and said: 'Hard luck, Strings, delighted to see you get on. Well deserved.'

I said thanks and congratulated him on his performance and the win. We'd only met properly the week before, when we'd done an hour-long joint interview for Setanta Sports. He's a nice lad.

Jamie Heaslip also shook my hand. 'Feck it, you came on there and you nearly turned it for them. You nearly stole it from us.'

And then an embrace with Luke Fitzgerald. I'd probably be closest to Luke of all the Leinster lads. 'Hard luck. Great to see you back out here.'

In the circle I became quite upset. It hit me then. *This could be my last European Cup game.* One hundred and out? I hadn't thought about it before because I was thinking, 'We'll have a semi-final, we'll have a final.' There'd be no semi-final now.

We walked the pitch to thank the Bath fans who had travelled over, and a few Leinster fans called out my name as well. I was nabbed for a couple of radio interviews with Newstalk and RTÉ.

Then the drug testing. This fella grabbed me and I wasn't even allowed a shower. After every match, four players are randomly selected to provide a urine sample, with each player assigned to a doping control officer (DCO). He began explaining the rules and I interrupted him, saying, 'Look, I'm fully aware of all the rules.' I just wanted to have a minute to myself, but this guy literally sat down next to me and wouldn't leave me alone. I'd stand up and he'd still be talking to me. When I took a sip of water, he said: 'You realize that your urine needs to be at a certain level because if you are over-hydrated we cannot . . .'

'I'm fully aware of all that. I've just come off the pitch; I just want a drink of water, please.'

He stood up when I stood up, and sat down when I sat down. I was playing musical chairs with him for a couple of minutes. He was just doing his job, I suppose, but he had no compassion.

I went into the testing room. Leroy was the other Bath player who'd been selected, along with Jordi Murphy and Jack McGrath from Leinster. We had to provide ninety millilitres before we could leave. There was no craic with the DCOs, no chat. For two hours I waited, just wanting to eat something and meet my family.

After about an hour and a half, Jordi stood up. 'Yeah, I'm ready, I'm ready.'

When he came back, I asked: 'Did you go?'

'Yea, three mils,' he said. He just had another eighty-seven milli-litres to go!

That's the nightmare scenario: you're better off waiting till you're feeling a hundred per cent ready. If you waste any at all, you could be there for a very long time.

Jack was done first, then Jordi. I wished them the best of luck for the rest of the season.

'Thanks,' Jordi said. 'We might be seeing you next year anyway.'

I laughed.

Finally, after a couple of hours, I have produced my ninety milli-litres. Leroy is still in the testing room with our doc: they'll probably miss the bus and have to get a taxi to the airport. Our dressing room has been tidied and emptied. Leroy got permission to have a shower before his test, so he has his bag with him. There's just my gear bag in the corner, and one banana on the table. I demolish it, then take a shower.

It is now about two hours and forty-five minutes after the full-time whistle. Everyone has left the stadium. I'm not flying back with the team; tonight I'll meet up with my brothers and their wives, and I'm staying on in Dublin for a family get-together tomorrow.

I look around the changing room. Not a sinner to be heard. All swept up, cleaned and ready for the next game.

Time waits for nobody.

1. A Competitive Little Effer

I was born on 13 December 1977 in Erinville Maternity Hospital, in Cork. Naturally, I don't remember much about it! The door of the Erinville was across the road from the gates of Presentation Brothers College, where I went to secondary school. From an upstairs class-room in 'Pres' I remember looking out the window at a sign for the Erinville – a daily reminder of where I came from!

When I was little we lived in a semi-detached house in Beechwood Park, Ballinlough, on the south side of Cork. There was a green around the corner, and just across the road was St Anthony's Boys National School. Before I was big enough to go there, I went to Mary McHale's nursery school, which was a converted garage to the side of her house in Douglas. Some of my earliest childhood memories are of Mrs McHale's: cycling on a tiny tricycle, sitting on bouncing balls and playing in the garden during our breaks. In my second year there I was joined by my younger brother George, but he hated it. He would become absolutely hysterical when Mum left us there.

George and I shared a small bedroom with bunk beds, and from our window we could see the gates of St Anthony's School. I took advantage of living so close to the school, especially on winter morn-ings. At bedtime, after Dad tucked us in and read us stories from an illustrated children's Bible and the usual Ladybird books, I'd put on my school uniform, in order to save time in the morning. Having to be in school by nine meant I could get up at ten to nine, swallow a quick bowl of Rice Krispies and still be on time. I had the upper bunk bed, with the clip-on ladder. In my mind no one else in the world was sleeping this high. I was on top of the world.

There were small gardens to the front and the back of our house, and in the big green there was plenty of space to kick a ball around. One summer, about eight or ten of us built a fort out of sticks and bales of freshly cut grass. It took weeks. Older brothers helped carry

the heavy bales. It was quite a piece of work, with rooms and tunnels –
a proper little house which could fit all of us. You entered by going
down on your knees and crawling inside and then you stood up in a
room with a roof of cut grass. For a couple of evenings we 'lived'
there. A couple of days later we returned to the green to discover
some other kids had destroyed our fort. This was the first major disappointment of my life. I was six or seven, and I was devastated.

My dad, John, has an identical twin, George, and a younger sister,
Felicity. My paternal grandfather died before I was born. He was a
manager with the Bank of Ireland, and the family moved around
regularly when Dad was a kid, setting up home in the bank houses
where my grandad worked. There is a photograph in the family home
of a Bank of Ireland in Ballinasloe, where they lived upstairs. For
years I didn't realize there was a kid looking out of a window above
the bank, and that this was my dad. I had just seen it as an old
black-and-white picture of a building.

Every Christmas my father's mother, Cynthia, would visit. She
had her spot in a chair in the corner of the living room, interrupting
movies with her snoring – the usual granny stuff. She had a lovely flat
in Dún Laoghaire, and when I was taken to Irish international rugby
games we stayed there. My first international was the Ireland–
England game in 1987, when I was nine. Ireland won 17–0, but it
wouldn't always be like that.

My grandmother had been quite a good tennis player and golfer –
she played off three – and Dad still proudly displays medals and cups
she won at home. She won the Leinster Scratch Cup in 1940 under
her maiden name, Cynthia Carroll.

My dad followed his father into banking. He wasn't out of school
long when there was a bank strike in Ireland, so he moved to London
and worked in bars for a while, and he was also a postman with the
Royal Mail, which necessitated signing the Official Secrets Act. He
always advised me not to go into banking. It was a hard slog and not
a job he would recommend for his kids, even though he progressed
pretty high up the Bank of Ireland chain. Apart from a year in New
Hampshire with a Bank of Ireland subsidiary, he was always based in

Cork city. He was, by all accounts, tough enough to deal with. When you worked in the bank it helped to have that attitude, and he worked his way up quite quickly. He would visit all the branches and departments in Munster, making sure their lending was being run properly. I remember speaking to one cashier in a Bank of Ireland branch and he told me that the sight of John Stringer coming through the door was never a comforting one. If everything wasn't up to scratch they knew they were going to incur his wrath.

My mum, Aileen, grew up in Rosscarbery in West Cork, and she had a very different upbringing from Dad. She was a country girl, the third of five, with two older sisters and two younger brothers. Her dad was a teacher in a national school in a village called Reenascreena, four miles from Rosscarbery. His name was Paddy Kelly but we knew him as 'Pop'. They lived in a big house that had an old pub on the left-hand side and a shop on the right-hand side. The main door had a bell that rang when you went in, and both the bar and the shop had wooden countertops. There were always the same old characters at the bar when we used to go there for the summer. They wouldn't say anything. They'd keep their heads down and sip their stout.

At some point my grandfather bought the local courthouse, which was directly across the road, and split it into three summer houses for his three daughters – Mum and her older sisters, Laura and Noreen.

'Pop' Kelly furnished the summer homes with furniture from an old British Antarctic Expeditionary ship, the *Discovery II*, which was being dismantled in Passage West: doors, staircases, tables, all solid mahogany. Being the eldest, I claimed a bedroom downstairs which had a brown door from the ship, engraved in black with the wording: 'Certified to accommodate the master'. I loved that door. Being the eldest had its advantages.

George and I were joined in March 1982 by a third brother, John, and in June '84 by a fourth, Dave. Our family spent virtually all of every summer until my mid-teens in Rosscarbery.

Mum's sisters would use their houses across the road as summer holiday homes, so even though her two brothers lived in the big family home, there was still plenty of room for the Stringers.

After dinner we were sometimes allowed to go behind the shop counter and pick one item for dessert. I usually opted for a Curly Wurly. Even though there looked to be more of it when wrapped, and the holes were always too big, it was chewy and lasted a long time. There were also Golf Balls and Humbugs and Clove Drops – all the old-school sweets.

Alternatively, Granny would sometimes make a dessert which I thought was the most amazing thing ever. She called it 'red wine and ice cream': HB vanilla ice cream with raspberry cordial poured over it. Like the slightly stale fig rolls in the biscuit tins after dinner, it was a luxury dessert I associated solely with that big house in Rosscarbery.

I must have been going there since I was four or five, because there's a picture of George and me posing in matching dungarees, with toy rifles, standing over a dead badger. It's quite a disturbing picture really, like something out of the American outback. I promise you we did not shoot that badger. It was lying there, dead, on the side of the road when my dad thought it would be a funny idea for us to pose alongside it with our toy rifles. We did not shoot badgers!

We swam and played on the beach mostly. There was a Pitch & Putt club next to the Warren beach, and then another beach called the Long Strand, about a mile long. Usually there was no one on that beach because it was quite unsafe for swimming; but Dad liked the privacy of the Long Strand, which backed on to sand dunes and huge mounds. We'd climb up to the top and then jump off on the descent into the sand. Of course I remember only sunny days.

In the evenings we would dive off the pier in Rosscarbery, or go to the GAA pitch, beside our house, where we'd play Gaelic football, soccer or rounders until it became dark and we were called in.

We'd look forward to those summers in Rosscarbery for months and with increasing excitement, and we hated having to leave there to go back to school. At the start of the summer, it felt like we would be there for ever. At the end of the summer, saying goodbye to our cousins and friends who lived there was the most upsetting thing ever.

★

Before we started playing rugby, I remember Mum bringing George and me up to Nemo Rangers GAA club on a Saturday morning. I was terrified. I knew nobody. I was six. We didn't have any football boots. We had matching runners with pictures of Snoopy all over them. Everybody else had laced-up boots with studs. I think I just turned and walked away. Looking back now, maybe that was best for all concerned!

My first day at primary school was equally nerve-racking. I remember the smell of the new grey woolly jumper. It was too big for me: the story of my life. 'Ah sure, you'll grow into it.' But I never did. The sleeves were turned up and I had to roll up the bottom bit around my waist too. As if my first day at school wasn't uncomfortable enough! If you could feel good about what you were wearing, you could feel good about yourself and everything else that followed. But if you don't feel self-confident when you get dressed, and you don't feel good about how you look, then you are off to a bad start.

We sat on tiny little chairs with wooden seats, wooden backs and yellow legs. There was one of those flip-over blackboards at the top of the classroom, and to the back was a stack of books on shelves. I loved arts and crafts, bringing out the big tubes of paint and glue.

On one of my first days in St Anthony's there was a lad with a leather satchel, and somehow I broke its strap. The boy started to cry. A terrible fear went through me. Throughout my whole first year in primary school I had it in my head that this guy's mother was after me and was going to get me. Every time there was a knock on the classroom door I thought it was her. Throughout that first year, I was convinced she would be waiting for me at the school gates one day to reprimand me for destroying his bag.

In senior infants we had a teacher called Miss McAuliffe. One day she left the classroom unattended and one of the lads dropped his pants and mooned the rest of the class. Another did it and pretty soon it was going around the classroom. Everyone had to do it. Of course, when it was my turn, Miss McAuliffe walked back through the door just as I dropped my pants. She had a scream on her that would ter-rify and certainly scared the life out of me. 'STRINGER!!! Get out of this classroom and go to the principal's office.'

'The principal's office.' When I think of it. Six years of age!

She dragged me by the arm to the principal's office. I was shaking and crying. She knocked on the door. The principal wasn't there.

'Right, back up to class and don't ever do that again.'

I don't think Mum and Dad ever found out about it.

I always lived in fear of getting into trouble at school. Some kids in school are not affected at all when given out to by teachers or kicked out of class. By contrast, I generally cried on the spot. I took care to stay out of trouble, although there was one other memorable incident. I had not done my homework, and I should have had a note signed by Mum to say that this wouldn't happen again. I must have been only seven or eight, and I tried to forge Mum's signature. I signed the letter 'Miss Stringer'. I didn't even join up the letters.

So to the next day.

'Did you get your mother to sign the note, Stringer?'

'I did, Miss.'

The teacher looked at it and said: 'Did your mother really sign this note, Stringer?'

'She did. Yes, Miss.'

' "Miss Stringer"?'

'Yes, Miss.'

The teacher had a metre-long stick permanently in her hand. It was a heavy yoke. A weapon of mass destruction in our eyes. She'd use the flat side of it for a relatively minor offence, but for the more serious ones the sharper edge would come down on your hands. You lived in fear of that stick. If a fella misbehaved, she would bring him to the front of the classroom and slap him with both hands simultaneously on each side of the face.

'You live across the road, don't you, Stringer?'

'I do. Yes, Miss.'

The teacher told me to go home and show Mum the note.

Mum freaked. 'What are you doing? You shouldn't be writing my name.'

She signed the bottom of the note and I went back across the road to school, and showed it to my teacher.

'Do NOT do that again.'

I didn't.

By the time I was eight, the eldest of four brothers, the Stringers had outgrown the house in Beechwood Park. One of Dad's friends from Dolphin RFC was selling his house on the Douglas Road, just a few hundred metres from where we lived, on the other side of the public playing fields: a three-storey, six-bedroom house called Leahurst.

My bedroom was on the top floor, which I thought amazing. You went up eighteen steps to the first floor, turned left around the corner, up another six steps to where the bathroom and Mum and Dad's room were, then another seven to a tiny landing, and then five more to the top floor, where there were another three bedrooms and a storage room. For the sets of stairs with even numbers you'd do them in twos, and then for the odd ones you'd try to go for a three. That was the quickest way to the top.

George and I initially shared a room with two beds in it, before we got our own bedrooms. Being closest in age, I suppose I was always closest in most senses to George. We did everything together. There were, naturally, rows. Plenty of them. Being given boxing gloves one Christmas, when we were about seven and five, possibly didn't help. But those boxing matches usually made me feel pretty good about myself, being that bit older, bigger and stronger. The mum of one of my schoolmates was an orthodontist and she made us gumshields: the real deal, white with proper filling. I can taste it now, that gel which goes into the white mould. The gumshields would only encourage us to hit harder and aim higher when we put on our gloves in George's room. It usually ended with one or both of us in tears. More often than not it was George. When John grew a little older I boxed against him as well and, given he was a good five years younger than me, that went even better.

The four of us played two-versus-two rugby games on the first floor in Leahurst, even though there was barely room for more than one person to walk along the landing. We played on our knees with a squidgy little rugby ball. The two try lines were bedroom doorways at opposite ends of the landing. We'd literally slam each other into the hot press door and into the walls.

John Hayes used to slag me about my upbringing. 'Not just one tennis club, but three tennis clubs,' he'd say, and then add: 'And fillet steaks for breakfast.'

We never had steak for breakfast, but we never lacked for anything either. We weren't spoilt. We didn't get everything we wanted, but we got everything we needed. There wasn't a huge amount of money coming in. My mum did some child-minding in the house when I was in nursery school and primary school.

It's true, though: we did have links to three tennis clubs. Mum was chairperson of the Ballinlough Tennis Club, so we played tennis after school, and we also joined the Sunday's Well and Douglas clubs.

Sunday's Well had Savanna courts, Douglas and Ballinlough were hard courts. Rushbrook, in Cobh, had a grass-court tournament. We'd take the train down from Kent Station. All your friends were on the train, with rackets, gear bags and lunches packed for the day ahead. Your name and match time would appear in the paper the day before, and you couldn't wait to see it.

Rushbrook Boys, Under-12s, Singles, P. Stringer v. Whoever, with the starting time.

You'd check in at Rushbrook, they'd give you your court number and your can of tennis balls, and off you'd go. The best of three sets. It is a lovely club. Great setting. Loads of grass courts and plenty of areas for people to sit down. You might have a bit of spending money for a burger and chips, and a Coke, to keep you going. Then you'd get the last train back from Rushbrook at seven in the evening. The next day, whether you were playing or not, you'd still go down to watch the tennis and hang out. It was a social event, the same as the Douglas Open or the Sunday's Well Open. If any of these tournaments were being played while we were in Rosscarbery, Mum would have driven us up and down, or if they were at the start of summer, just after school had finished, we might hold off going to Rosscarbery.

You could be unlucky and be drawn against one of the top seeds in the tournament. I wasn't great. I might get to the third or fourth round, before the quarter-finals. So there were quite a few players competing. George was good and would reach the quarter-finals or so in his age group. He made the Munster Under-age squad when there were about five players in the panel of Under-12s. He could beat me too, which must have been nice revenge for the pummelling I'd given him with the gloves on.

We also played doubles with Mum and Dad, and would rotate the teams. But no matter what combinations we picked, and whether I played with Mum or Dad or George, it generally didn't last the hour which the court was booked for. If I played with Mum and she put a ball into the net I'd become absolutely livid with her. I would roar at her, 'Can you not just get it over the net?' I was a competitive little effer even then. I'd lose the rag with whoever I played with, but mostly with myself when I hit shots long or into the net.

'Ah, I don't care. I don't care,' I'd yell, which didn't convince anybody.

The next day I'd play with Dad, and of course George and Mum would beat us. No matter the combination, it never worked. George could be quite stroppy too, flinging the racket into the net. We were a very competitive family. Even when we played board games in the evening in Rosscarbery, it was the same. Trivial Pursuit was not very aptly named in the Stringer household. No game was trivial. The answers were on the back of a card, and if you gave an answer which was close enough and by rights should have been acceptable, the person asking the question would say: 'No, that's not the answer on the back of the card.' Another row would ensue. I don't know why we bothered!

2.   Starting with a Size 4

At parent/teacher meetings over the years, teachers would always tell my mum and dad: 'We just need to get him reading'.

And Mum would say: 'I can't.'

The teacher would ask what I was into. From the age of seven or eight, the answer was always the same.

'Rugby. Rugby. Rugby.'

'Well then, could we get him to read rugby magazines?'

So I got a subscription to *Rugby World*. As the years passed, piles of copies grew in my bedroom. I even ordered back issues pre-dating my subscription. It did get me reading a bit.

Fiction just never interested me at all. It seemed to me that any Joe Soap walking down the street could invent a story, or imagine something, and put it down on paper. It wasn't real. And that didn't appeal to me. Why would I read someone else's fictitious or imaginary thoughts?

Reading still doesn't come easily to me. I pick up sports books and other real-life stories, but I often lose concentration. I prefer to learn or experience things visually.

Dad always had old rugby balls lying around the house – the laced-up leather ones. They were quite light when dry, but if there was even a hint of dew on the grass in the garden, never mind rain, they absorbed the water and became like a medicine ball.

No two of them were the same shape. There was one, a size 4, that was lovely. It had been a Christmas present in 1960 to Dad and his brother George from their parents. It felt right when you were kicking, passing or catching it. With some of the other ones, the leather was harder, coarser and heavier, and just didn't feel as nice. My first memories of rugby were of that size 4 and playing in our back garden, which had a boundary of fencing and greenery.

Dig deep into the family tree and there is some international rugby in the bloodline. A man by the name of Claude Carroll, who played for Bective Rangers, won one cap for Ireland in 1930 against France, playing lock. France won 5–0. He was a first cousin of my grandmother's. And in the centre that day was Paul Murray, who was my grandfather's best man and was also my uncle George's godfather.

Dad played for Dolphin. He was a small openside flanker and he played up to Junior 1, or seconds. Almost every weekend I was in Musgrave Park or wherever Dolphin were playing. The club had the use of one pitch down by Cork Airport, with a Portakabin as its changing room, and another pitch on the straight road which leads out from the County Hall. Not the most glamorous settings or surfaces. Thick, muddy pitches. I'd get the wellies on for those games on Saturday mornings with Dad, and stand on the sidelines.

We'd go into the changing room after the game and I can still smell the wintergreen and see the dirty headbands chucked on the ground, along with piles of jerseys and jockstraps. Not an easy memory to forget.

One guy I remember clearly was Kevin Corcoran, a second-row for the Minor Bs. To this day he works as a bouncer in a nightclub in Cork. I was only five or six, and the Dolphin players were my heroes, but he was the tallest. I just couldn't believe how tall he was. A man mountain.

Sometimes we'd go to Musgrave Park to watch the Dolphin seniors play, and then into the clubhouse. Mum and Dad would be there, and the place would be jammed for the evening, with people smoking and drinking. Dad would buy me a bottle of Score Cola, for 25p, and a packet of Planters dry roasted peanuts. My friends and I and loads of other kids would then go out on to the back pitch or on the main pitch, playing with a rugby ball in complete darkness. You couldn't see two feet in front of you but you'd throw yourself around the place and be covered in mud. I loved every second of it. I never wanted to leave. Mum and Dad had to almost drag me off the pitch.

Dad has collected international match programmes going back to when he was young. They are stacked high at home, like my copies of *Rugby World*. We'd go through them in the evenings, flicking through pages from programmes from the '40s and '50s.

The distinction between players who I know by name and those who I actually saw play have become blurred by those programmes. Dad told me about players like Tony O'Reilly, and so my knowledge of rugby extends back to way before my life even started.

My first recollections of playing with that size-4 rugby ball, from the age of five, are of me running around in a circle with Dad stationary. I ran anti-clockwise and passed off my right hand, then ran clockwise and passed off my left. After a while I might become dizzy and start to wonder, 'Why am I running around and he is standing still?' It didn't seem fair.

It's funny to realize, now, how specifically these childhood drills were orientated towards being a scrum-half. Given my size, I was never going to be tried in any other position. Dad had never been a scrum-half, and had never coached, yet he taught me how to pass the way I do. I remember him showing me how to use my hand over the ball, the energy coming from my shoulder and upper body more than my wrists and hands. Your hands are only there to guide the ball; all the power comes from the outside shoulder.

As I grew older I discovered that when I was passing right to left, the left hand wasn't contributing much to the power of the pass, and vice versa. I realized I didn't need the bottom hand much, so to improve my skill level and maintain an equal standard off both sides I would regularly practise one-handed passes.

'No backswing, no backswing,' Dad would shout. I had the idea of placing the ball against a barrier, to force me to pass the ball in one snappy movement, without backswing. Our house had a pebbledash wall, and I decided to use the wall for this purpose. It was in the ideal position to allow me to pass the ball across the garden to Dad, without the risk of breaking any windows. And if I used any backswing on the pass, the pebbledash would rip up my knuckles.

As a mentor, Dad was always there for me. In the summers at Rosscarbery, when I was twelve or so, we'd get up early and go for a jog on the Long Strand. It was about a mile long and we'd be continually trying to better our times each day.

He also taught me how to swim, describing how to coordinate my hands and feet for the breaststroke. When I was fourteen and fifteen

I used to go swimming two or three times a week, swimming 25-metre lengths of breaststroke non-stop for most of my hour's slot after school.

That's when I noticed my body changing. My arms and shoulders became much more developed. After twenty or twenty-five lengths, my arms would become tired; but I always found that when I reached thirty or thirty-five lengths I felt really good. And that's been the way throughout my career. The more I do in fitness sessions, the better I feel.

When I see other people tiring, I grow more comfortable and my breathing becomes stronger. If I don't do anything for a day or two, the next time I go to the gym or for a run I don't feel good. I need to do something every single day. It's an obsession. A healthy body makes for a healthy mind. If I feel good physically, I feel good mentally.

That need started with those runs and swims with Dad. The effort and time he invested in us has made us what we are, and me into who I am today. Doing those extras, trying to be one step ahead of everyone else and feeling you were doing something that others your age weren't doing, was always so satisfying.

Watching the 1987 World Cup in New Zealand was another source of inspiration. Dad and I set our alarms for three or four in the morning to watch those games. No matter who was playing, Tonga versus Fiji or whatever, we were in front of the TV for the kick-off. I studied the scrum-halves: Pierre Berbizier, David Kirk, Nick Farr-Jones.

Dad shared in my love for the game and was there whenever I needed his advice, but Mum deserves equal credit for helping me: she simply couldn't have done more. Tirelessly and without fail, she took me wherever I needed or wanted to go: for tennis, football, rugby, anything. All four of us played rugby, at scrum-half; and we dumped our dirty gear outside the washing machine – didn't even put it in. I used to get annoyed if my gear wasn't as pristine as the day we bought it. Mum tried everything, even boiling the clothes in enormous saucepans and stirring them with a wooden spoon. She tried bleaching them, but some would turn yellow and I'd become more annoyed with her.

It was ridiculous, really. To my shame, thinking back now, I realize I just assumed that was her job. I'd say she would have loved to have had a daughter.

Nursing was her calling. She has an unbelievably caring nature. I remember once looking through photos from when I was a baby. Some of them showed me sitting on the floor with three or four other babies around me. I asked Mum: 'Who are these people?' She explained that she looked after neighbours' kids when they were out working.

On the Douglas Road we were next door to a couple called Nancy and Walter Strong. When Walter became terminally ill, Mum moved in and slept on a single mattress some nights with them to help Nancy look after him, and to nurse him through the night. This went on for a few weeks. A year and a half later, contrary to the doctors' prognosis, Walter was still alive. Mum still went in to them quite regularly, sometimes bringing Dave with her, until Walter died. Sadly, as is often the case, Nancy became very ill herself and she died soon after.

Dad was the strict parent, and Mum the lenient one. If we were playing in the back garden and broke the window with a tennis ball, it was a case of 'Oh shit, he's coming home at six o'clock.' We'd be absolutely terrified.

I remember once asking Mum: 'Look, will you take the blame for this? I can't take another one.'

And she said: 'I am not taking the blame for this.'

Those passing drills with my dad in the back garden might have seemed monotonous to most kids, but when I first started in Cork Con a year later, at the age of six, with their Under-7s, I knew how to pass better than most kids. I suppose when I realized that, it made me more confident in myself and encouraged me to continue doing the drills with Dad.

It also established a pattern in my life. The year before I went to secondary school, I found out that German would be one of the subjects in Pres, so during sixth class in primary I went to German classes for a year. I had all the basics down to a 't', be it counting, where I lived, my family, what I did in my spare time – all the general conversation. When I went into German classes in first year, and we began learning how to count from one to ten, I thought, 'This is so easy.' Ever since, I've always liked to feel I was one step ahead of everybody else, in the team or the classroom.

Although Dad was a big Dolphin man and would go on to become club president in 1988, and there was an edge to their rivalry with Cork Con, they didn't have an Under-age set-up like Cork Con's at the time. He didn't see the Under-age set-up in Cork Con as being the same as the senior scene, with all the politics and alickadoos in charge there. Somehow, the Under-age level wasn't part of that Dolphin–Con rivalry.

The Under-age structure in Cork Con was very well organized, and we won plenty of tournaments from Under-8s all the way through to Under-12s. I started at Temple Hill on Saturday mornings, and I loved it immediately. That was probably when I first discovered that everyone else was bigger than me, but I never had any fear in what I was doing. I just loved being out on those pitches, running around. Going past a guy and scoring a try, those little moments with your buddies, were the first real thrills of my life. I guess they made me feel tall.

The Monday after my failed introduction to Gaelic football with Nemo Rangers, Mum bought me my first boots: Hi-Tecs with a yellow-and-blue striped tongue, and thin yellow-and-blue stripes down the sides. We bought them in Moss Finn's shop, Finn's Corner. That was the place to go for your boots, because Moss had played with Con, Munster and Ireland. You couldn't go anywhere else. They were really comfy boots. I'll never forget the padded tongue and padded inside.

My Under-8s coach was a guy called Dominic Conlon. He was my first coach after Dad, and he taught us all the basics. Another man, named Tim Herbert, was on hand to show us how to tackle. I can still hear that resounding echo in my head of 'Take him by the leg-gggggs!' in what was a very posh voice, certainly by comparison to every other accent I heard while growing up in Cork. I can still hear it now. I can still hear it sometimes when I go to make a tackle on a pitch.

Starting out at the age of six or seven, you'd be trying to pull down guys by their collars or shirts. But if you go low enough, one guy's ankles are the same as another guy's ankles. 'Take him by the legs' has stayed with me for over thirty years.

Another early rugby influence was a schoolteacher, Ger Stack, whom I came to know well in fourth class. He played rugby in High-field. We would come in on Mondays and chat about our games. This made me feel like I had one up on all the other kids. In fifth and sixth class there was some tip rugby, and it was enjoyable to run rings around rugby novices.

My two main friends at Cork Con were Tim Cahill, a number six who later played with me at Pres and on the Irish schools team, and Paul Barry, a centre who I would also play with at Pres and UCC. Ronan O'Gara was a year older than me, so we had one year together at Under-8s, another at Under-10s and one more at Under-12s. My first real memory of Rog is with the Under-10s, when his dad, Fergal, was our coach. Rog was the out-half, and that was probably the only year at school when I played a few times alongside him, to go with one year at Under-8s and one at Under-12s. People have a somewhat romantic notion of us playing together all the way from Under-8s to the final year at school, before partnering each other for Munster and Ireland. But one year older or one year younger can be a different world. You play with your own age group, and that's it.

David Wallace was also involved at one point. Funny, I've no real memory of Wally at Cork Con other than his appearance in a photo-graph of our squad in the all-white gear. He looked like a freak, towering about two feet taller than everyone else, with legs the size of tree trunks. It was something of a one-off, an Under-9 tourna-ment, which would have been unusual, as most of the tournaments were at Under-8s, -10s and -12s. But for some reason there was an Under-9 tournament, I think in Highfield; and Wally, who is a year and a half older than me, is in the picture. But I've no memory of him actually playing with us.

They were truly great days, winning trophies in Highfield, Thurles and other grounds around the province at Under-10s and Under-12s. We were always well looked after in Bruff, where we won the James Keating Memorial Cup. Rugby was also my introduction to travelling abroad. I was ten when our Cork Con Under-10 team went by ferry to a tournament in Harrogate in England. We stayed in hostels and competed in the tournament over a Saturday to Sunday.

We were the only Irish team in an otherwise all-English competition, and we won it. I still have the cutting from the Harrogate newspaper at home, revealing that I was voted the Player of the Tournament by the Ladies' Committee. There's a photo of me receiving my tie and plaque outside the Harrogate clubhouse at the trophy presentation.

We also travelled by ferry to a tournament in Wales and stayed with a family in Cardiff for a one-off game against Whitchurch High School. It was during the Easter break and we went over on the Wednesday. I was paired up with a guy called Nigel Murphy, so I stayed with him and his family. Whitchurch had been over to play Cork Con earlier in the season and, although Nigel didn't stay with us, we became mates and I requested that I stay with them.

When I went back to Cardiff in 2008 for the Heineken Cup final with Munster against Toulouse, we walked the pitch the day before the game. I was tapped on the shoulder, turned around and saw this guy looking at me. Immediately I recognized him.

'Hi, Nigel. How's it going?'

He looked at me in disbelief. 'How can you remember who I am? I remember you staying with me, but I still watch rugby and know who you are.'

But those memories from the age of ten and twelve, competing abroad with Cork Con, and staying with families, are very vivid.

Nigel was working on the pre-match events and fireworks at the stadium the next day. We exchanged numbers, stayed in touch and have met up a few times since, when I've been in Cardiff.

In 1988, when I was eleven and playing on the Cork Con Under-12s with Rog, we travelled to Roche-la-Molière in the Loire for another tournament, by ferry once more. It was a hell of a journey. Thirty kids, representing Cork Con at Under-11s and Under-12s, piled into a coach, along with about ten adults, including my dad.

We travelled by coach from Cork to Swansea, a ten-hour crossing, then drove to Dover, for the ferry to Calais, and then the 800km coach trip to Roche-la-Molière, stopping off in a hostel in Brittany en route. This was the furthest I'd ever travelled, but as the weather was poor, it didn't seem especially exotic. Again we were the sole representatives from Ireland. Our invitation had come through the IRFU, who passed it on to Cork Con.

There were thirty-two teams, from clubs in New Zealand, South Africa, Australia, England, Scotland, Wales, Italy, Romania, Russia, Latvia, Lithuania, Sweden, Belgium and Hong Kong, plus a few from France. We played two or three games a day over the three days of the tournament – ten-a-side, twenty-minute matches. We beat teams from Wales and Italy, and had a particularly good time with the Italians. They were housed in the same boarding school, and we played basketball with them.

The Russian team were absolutely enormous. No way were they all under twelve! Somehow we beat them, and a French team, and I'm pretty sure we played the Romanian team in the final. They wore yellow shirts and blue shorts, and were pretty big for an Under-12s side as well. The match finished level and went to extra time; and we scored the next try to win the game.

The Under-11s final followed, and George was captain of the Cork Con team. They also won. Rog captained our team, and there are photos at home of the two teams with the two trophies.

The French were brilliant hosts and put on a huge fireworks display on our last night there. On the journey home we stopped off in Wales for our annual games away to Whitchurch High School and Cantonian High School, and we won them. There were at least forty-five or fifty boys in the Con Under-12s set-up, and the rest of the squad arrived from Cork within about five minutes of those of us coming back from Roche-la-Molière. The best Easter ever!

My first game on the main pitch at Musgrave Park was in the curtain-raiser to the Munster–New Zealand game in 1989, a Cork Con v. Thurles Under-12s game. They erected a temporary stand on the far side of the ground. It was filling up nicely before Munster and the All Blacks warmed up. It was quite surreal. We played across the pitch on one half of the ground, with another game going on in the other half. Everyone who played was given a T-shirt, with a map of Ireland highlighting the four provinces on the front and 'New Zealand tour of Ireland, 1989' on the back, along with all the dates and fixtures of their tour. I still have both the match programme and the T-shirt.

Fred Casey, a coach in our Cork Con Under-age teams, is a guy I will always have huge respect for. His enthusiasm drove the whole Under-age structure in Cork Con as much as anything or anybody else, and he's still coaching there to this day. It was his vision and organization which brought us to those tournaments in England, Wales and France.

No other Irish team was doing this. Crosshaven were our main rivals, all the way through Under-8s, -10s and -12s. We generally met each other in finals, be it Thurles or Bruff or other local tournaments around Munster. They had Rory Collins and Ronan O'Donovan, who then went on to Christians before we all played on the Irish schools team together. They also went on to play for Cork Con's senior team as well. But no matter what way the tournaments were drawn, we'd both invariably reach the final. It was as if we were seeded.

My love for the game, and my development as a player, were entirely down to those first five or six years with Cork Con. Training was never boring with Freddy. He understood that to keep kids motivated, interested, entertained and in the moment, it's all about making things fun. Guys always wanted to come training, which at Under-12s was moved to Wednesday afternoons after school. No other age group trained on Wednesdays.

Freddy allowed us to come up with our own moves, with guys buying into them so that we would use them in matches and tournaments. This was just so exciting: 'That's my move and I own that.' I was an avid reader of a coaching manual by the former Welsh centre and coach, John Dawes. He captained the Welsh Grand Slam winners of 1971 and, in the same year, the British & Irish Lions squad, which remains the only Lions team to win a Test series in New Zealand; he then coached the Welsh golden generation of the '70s. So I would come to Cork Con training with loads of moves.

By contrast, when I went through secondary school and university, the coaches decided the moves and everything else. They did the talking. They didn't ask the players to come up with ideas. Or if they did, they already knew the answers they wanted.

I remember devising a move that had me passing to the out-half, who'd do a switch with the first centre, who would then do a switch with me coming back around. I remember teams looking on and wondering: 'Where's the ball gone?' I'd set up the wall moves that New Zealand used and send a guy through the middle. The coaches at Con gave us that freedom.

I've seen different styles of coaching over the years, and it's nearly come full circle now, to coaches putting it back on the players because ultimately we go on to the pitch for a match, we're the ones who are going to have to come up with ideas. We can't go to a coach during a game for him to give the answers.

That was why I enjoyed Cork Con so much. I wasn't being told what to do. If you feel like you're coming up with the ideas yourself, it's really empowering. I don't know if I'd have had that same type of liberating enjoyment had I begun playing in school, with the emphasis on winning cup ties and medals. In fact, probably not.

3. Size Doesn't Matter

At Under-8s, -10s and -12s, I was always the smallest player. I never felt discriminated against because of my size, and I was always picked on the first team by the coach. But my parents suffered plenty of advice and questioning on the sidelines.

'Are you sure you should be allowing him to play rugby? The size of him!'

'Are you not being a little irresponsible letting him play?'

Out on the pitch, from Under-8s up, I was oblivious to all of this. I just went out on the pitch and played.

No one ever said to my face, 'You're too small.' But in later years Mum told me some of the stories. She recalled one specific Under-13 game when Pres travelled to Dublin to play Blackrock College.

As I was captain of the team, I led them out, followed by one of the second-rows.

Some of the Blackrock mothers were on the sidelines. 'Ah look, they brought a mascot out on the pitch.'

'No, no,' Mum said to them, 'he's actually the captain of the team.'

That shut them up, but Mum constantly had other parents approaching her on the side of the pitch while I was playing, with comments like: 'He's too small' or 'He's going to get hurt' or 'How can you stand by and watch him out there?'

Some were very strongly opinionated about it, and weren't shy about questioning her responsibilities as a mother, or Dad's as a father. It must have been difficult for them.

At times they must have wondered: 'Are we doing the right thing? Obviously he loves playing. Do we stop him playing?'

Things reached a head in my first year at Pres. Opponents and teammates were developing, growing bigger, and I wasn't keeping up with them. I was still very small.

Mum had spoken to her cousin, whose son was of similar size, and

who had undertaken several tests. On foot of these, his parents
decided to take him to hospital, where he was hooked up to drips for
a procedure to administer growth hormones over a couple of days.

Apparently the results had been remarkable. Within a few months
he'd grown by several inches and had bulked up.

So one evening Mum and Dad sat me down at home. 'Look, we've
talked to your cousin and he's happier being bigger. How do you feel
with regard to your size?'

'I feel OK. I feel fine.'

'Well look, we think there's an operation that maybe you should
have done,' said Mum. 'Your cousin had this operation done, and
they had great results. We'd just like you to see this specialist first, to
check whether you're growing OK, and that everything is normal.'

We went to this specialist, who lived in Douglas. She had a surgery next to her house, and she measured me and weighed me and
tested me, before giving her analysis and opinion on what should be
done. She recommended to Mum and Dad that I should go into hospital to undergo the same procedure as my distant cousin.

I remember standing at the bottom of our stairs as Mum and Dad
read the letter which advised this procedure. 'We're going to look
into booking you into the hospital.'

I was absolutely devastated. I felt good in myself, in my size. I
didn't feel there was anything wrong with me. I was entirely happy
with the way I was and I didn't want to change anything. I didn't
understand why I had to do it, but Mum said: 'We think it will be
good for you in the long run. It will give you a kick-start and help
you compete with bigger boys.'

I said: 'I don't want to change anything. I just want to stay as I am.'

Standing in the hallway, I was bawling. As I chatted to Mum and
Dad I could see in their faces that this obviously was important to
them. 'Look, think about it,' they said. 'Just think about it.'

I ran upstairs to my bedroom on the top floor and threw myself on
the bed. Although it was only seven or eight o'clock, I didn't come
downstairs for the rest of the night. I pretty much cried through the
night. I didn't want to go to hospital. I didn't want to go through any
procedure. I didn't want drips attached to me. I didn't understand the

need for it or what it was, and the prospect scared me. The bottom line was, I didn't feel sick. I didn't feel there was anything wrong with me, and certainly not enough to merit a couple of nights in hospital.

When I came down the next morning, Mum and Dad had obviously talked, and had reassessed things. 'Look, if this is something that you don't want to do, then that's fine. We can look at it some other time if you don't want to do it now.'

'I don't ever want to do it,' I said. 'We won't be talking about this again. This is me and this is how I want to stay.'

I went to school exhausted, shattered even, but so relieved. I wanted to remain in control of my own body. I didn't want to have others making decisions about my body and my growth. If I had been sick, that would have been a different matter. But I wasn't. I think I floated through school that day, I was so delighted that I had persuaded my parents not to go ahead with this procedure, and I could resume my life. They meant well, and the barrage of criticism had backed them into a corner and made them question their own responsibilities as parents. But ultimately they listened to me more than to anyone else.

Not only could I have turned into a different person, it might have detracted from my game as a scrum-half. Or I could have outgrown scrum-half altogether and never been suited to another position, which would almost certainly have been the case.

No regrets. Who wants to be the same as everyone else, anyway? My size, and my stubbornness about not undergoing that procedure, make me prouder of my career. At the 2003 World Cup, I was the second-smallest player at the tournament. I wanted to be the smallest. There was one Japanese player listed as being shorter but heavier than me, and my listed weight was probably a few kilos higher than the reality, so who knows? But officially he was slightly smaller.

I am 5' 7", and probably weigh 72kg, and I have never really varied from that as an adult. When I was on the Irish schools tour to Australia in 1996, I weighed in at just under 9 stone (57kg). One of the Irish locks on that tour, Bob Casey, was not far off the size he was in his senior playing days (123kg/19st 4lb).

I am sure I am not alone in never having tasted alcohol, I've never taken a drag of a cigarette, and I've never taken an illegal substance to help make me bigger. To be honest, I've never heard of illegal drugs being taken by players in Ireland, although I have heard of it happening in one or two other countries. A few names have been mentioned, but I have genuinely never heard of it in Ireland. If a player is injured for a lengthy spell and comes back, say, six or nine months later, noticeably bigger, that can be a telltale sign that he's taken growth hormones or steroids. No one can ever accuse me of that!

My size is a major part of who I am, maybe it even defines me as a rugby player. I suppose little guys can stand out from the crowd too, and my size has appealed to the maternal instincts of grandmothers and mothers and has contributed to their affection for me. To this day, that is still the case. I received a letter once from a ninety-year-old woman, in which she wrote of how inspiring my career had been.

I think kids also identify with me, as a little guy competing among big guys. Maybe it gives them hope that they can play rugby too. Even Eliya, my wife Debbie's niece, who is only three, already has a different relationship with me compared with anyone else. Because I have no hair, she also thinks I am a big baby, a big version of her! For the first two and a half years of her life, she did not have a hair on her head. Ciara, her mum, would always say: 'Ah look, Eliya and Peter are the same; no hair.' And Eliya latched on to that and identifies with me when she watches me play matches.

Kids generally identify with the smaller guys in rugby. Shy kids, of around ten or eleven, come to me after games and say:

'Have you any tips for me?'

'I'm a really small scrum-half as well, and what advice would you give me?'

I suppose I'm also seen as being more approachable because I'm small. They maybe think: 'He's just a normal person, doing what I'd like to do. He's not a 6' 7" giant.' In their minds, it probably makes a career in rugby seem more attainable.

The game has changed completely since I started playing, thirty-odd years ago, and especially since I moved into senior rugby almost twenty years ago. It's much more of a collision-based sport, and players have got significantly bigger.

As my career has progressed, I have sometimes found myself discarded at the expense of bigger scrum-halves. There's been an increasing perception that teams need bigger scrum-halves to play behind bigger packs. But if you're good enough, you're big enough, and there's definitely a place for small players in the game – especially at scrum-half.

In a specialist position like scrum-half you have a certain job to do. Throughout my career, my role has always been to be there quickly, be a distributor, read a game well and put guys into space. I see myself as a facilitator rather than the one who finishes moves.

It suits my body type and it suits my personality.

If I had undergone that procedure, I would never have achieved what I have done in my rugby career. It would have made me three or four inches taller, and I would then have blended in with everyone else.

I'd have been a bigger man with a smaller career.

4. Schooldays

For a Cork Con boy, school was only ever going to be a choice between Pres and the Christian Brothers College, known as 'Christians'. The older brothers of my close friends had been to Pres, and Dad knew Declan Kidney, from Dolphin. Declan was teaching in Pres as well as coaching rugby, and so Dad always had Pres in mind for me and my brothers.

I preferred the Pres colours – the black-and-white hooped jersey as opposed to Christians' yellow-and-red. It was more striking. The entrance exam for Christians was held first, so I did that, and I received an acceptance letter from them. But in my mind the Christians exam was practice for the Pres entrance exam. When I received an acceptance letter from Pres, I duly accepted their invitation and declined Christians.

I've always loved training, from Saturday mornings with the Cork Con Under-8s to Wednesday afternoons with their Under-12s, and on through school. In Pres it was just the same, except with new training grounds and new mates, and a mad rush for the bus after school from the Mardyke to Wilton training grounds, as all age groups trained after school on a Wednesday. A number 8 or 5 bus would stop at the school and go past the grounds. If your teacher didn't let you out immediately, and a single-decker was coming towards the stop, there mightn't be room for you to get on board, and you'd have to wait for the next one. There was also the chance that older boys might have sprinted to the stop ahead of you. If it was a double-decker, you'd be OK.

I loved the early days in Pres. Joe Gray, who passed away recently, was the coach of the 13s. Those first few weeks of training included a few of my former Cork Con teammates, along with other guys who had never picked up a rugby ball. In those sessions, I found standards a little sloppier than I was used to with Cork Con Under-12s.

We also went from a half pitch and ten-a-side to a full pitch and fifteen-a-side.

Joe, a lovely man, was in his late fifties or early sixties then. He was small and stocky, with glasses, and he'd arrive in his tracksuit with the legs tucked into knee-high socks, and layers of clothes. He looked like the Michelin Man.

He knew a few of us had played in Cork Con, and it was good to feel you had one up on the others who had never played. Initially, many boys tried playing rugby, but most drifted away after a few sessions.

Again, the emphasis was on fun, and Joe had a good way about him: always smiling, always enthusiastic, and always encouraging. I was fortunate in that all of my coaches were like that, and if I go into coaching I want to bring that approach with me. There's nothing worse for young, impressionable kids than a negative adult barking criticism at them. It can turn them off the game completely. Thankfully, in those early years they were all upbeat and positive, be it my dad or all my coaches. No one had anything negative to say.

Like Freddy in Cork Con, Joe let us have ownership of the Under-13s, and if he needed to chip in with comments or suggestions, he did so. I was scrum-half and captain. Helpfully, we still played with a size 4 ball at Under-13s, because I was also the team's place-kicker. I had it all!

There were no major trophies at Pres in that first year, but it was the start of our cycle's six-year rivalry with Christians. In the second year, there was an Under-14 Cup called the McCarthy Cup, and Christians beat us in the final at Musgrave Park – my first match there over the full pitch.

In the summer of 1992, while Dad was based in New Hampshire, the rest of the family flew to the USA for our summer holiday. But I passed up the chance to finish the trip with a two-week family break to Florida. Instead, I flew home with a friend for a summer rugby camp in Clongowes. Rugby came first.

In third year I captained the Junior Cup team. The coach was Michael O'Sullivan, better known as 'Mickey Sull', a full-back for Cork Con who had been an unused sub in Munster's win over the All

Blacks in 1978, and who passed away in recent years. He wanted me to change my pass, to make it a dive pass, for some reason that I could never grasp. Throughout the season, he kept telling me to make the dive pass my main pass, but I refused to do it. He kept playing me anyway!

In that Junior Cup campaign we beat Rockwell and St Clement's on the way to the final, which was in Thomond Park. (I had played there once before, in one of those Under-12s mini-rugby tournaments, the Pat Lawlor Cup, which we had won, in 1990. It was named after the father of Mossie Lawlor, who would be a Munster teammate in years to come.) We lost the final 5–0 to St Munchin's. Marcus Horan was the loose-head prop for Munchin's and to this day he doesn't let me live it down. A Junior schools' medal over twenty years ago! Munchin's were tougher and rougher than any team we'd ever met. Two of our players needed plastic surgery on their ears after what was an incredibly physical game. We had never experienced anything like it.

Marcus was always on for taking a quick tap from a penalty, and towards the end of the game he was about to do so again when the referee, Jimmy Clancy from Limerick, grabbed him by the collar and said: 'Hold on, the game is nearly up. Kick it into touch.' Game over.

At the time I was gutted. That was the first devastating defeat of my rugby life. The bus brought us to the Deer Park Hotel in Charleville, where we were collected by our parents.

Mum kept trying to reassure me: 'It'll be all right . . . You can't win every game . . . You still have three more years in school.'

Mum had been at my granny's bedside that week, before going to my match, but I had no idea how sick Granny had been, or that they weren't giving her long to live. I had met my parents on the morning of the final and they hadn't said a word.

It was only when I saw Mum in Charleville after the game that she told me how sick Granny was. Mum received a call from her sister Noreen saying she had taken a turn for the worse and that Mum should come back to Rosscarbery. She drove back to West Cork that evening to be at her mum's side. Granny passed away on the Sunday.

Even a fifteen-year-old suffering the most disappointing defeat of his career to date had a sense of perspective. I knew Mum was trying to put on a brave face for me, but it must have been one of the saddest weeks of her life.

At Under-16s we had the Bowen Shield. It was conducted on a league basis, and we clinched the trophy by winning our final game, against St Munchin's.

By then, most of the lads were going into bars and having their first drinks. As ever, I was smaller than everyone else, and I didn't have a hope of getting into any bar. In truth, I didn't have the confidence to approach a doorman and claim I was eighteen when I still looked about twelve.

Staying at home on a Saturday night was an easier option, and I lost plenty of what at the time I regarded as friends. I went through a couple of years of relative isolation from everyone else on Saturday nights, and I was happy in my decision. I didn't feel I should go along just to do what everyone else was doing.

Travelling up to Dublin and going to Irish internationals had been influential in my decision never to drink. About an hour after a Five Nations game, after a few of us had played with a ball on the main pitch, I was walking along with Dad and my Uncle George, and I saw a drunk guy on his own, unconscious on the steps of the south terrace in the old Lansdowne Road stadium. He had no one looking after him, no one to care for him, and he wasn't in control of himself. Seeing that guy comatose on the steps, I told myself that I would never be in that situation. I wanted to be in control of myself and what I did at all times.

A team had come over from Canada during that season when we won the Bowen Shield, and their scrum-half, Eric Bogart, stayed with us. The evening after we played the Canadians, both teams went into town. I was petrified. I didn't want to suffer that awful awkwardness of being turned away.

I said to the lads, 'Look, I'm not going to get in. I just want to go home.'

But the Canadian guys wanted me to come along, so two of them took off their jackets – bomber jackets with their team logo on the chest – and told me to put them both on. 'Just pretend to be

Canadian, and one of us, on this rugby tour.' This was the very last thing I wanted to do. It made me cringe. But there was no one on the door and we walked in as a group. Two barmen were working behind the counter, and we sat at our table with my back to them. I sat there, still terrified, waiting for the tap on my shoulder, and to be asked: 'How old are you?' I was never any use at spoofing or making up stories about anything, and least of all about myself. I just did not want to be put in that position. If I had been tapped on the shoulder, I simply would have crumbled.

I lasted about ten minutes, one of the longest ten-minute stretches of my life, before saying: 'Lads, I gotta go.' I wrote out our home address for the Canadian guy who was staying with us, handed it to him, and told him to make his own way back by taxi or whatever. I just had to get out of there.

Those years, from sixteen to eighteen, were difficult. At house parties, guys were always drinking and putting me under pressure to drink. It continued in college, but over time I felt more comfortable with my decision to be different from virtually everyone else. I've always been like this, stubborn in my own decision-making and in not necessarily doing the norm.

I was on the bench in fifth year at Pres, when Eddie Hogan O'Connell, who was in sixth year, was the starting scrum-half. Declan Kidney picked Eddie ahead of me and, typical Deccie, he'd ask me: 'Do you know why I'm going to go with him?'

I'd hum and haw, and then he'd explain: 'He just does a bit more than you. He takes the ball on around the fringes.' Eddie was a bit bigger, naturally, and I was never going to be that kind of scrum-half.

'That's fair enough,' I'd answer. 'I play a different game.'

We had that conversation several times that year, and it was also a foretaste of the conversation I'd have with him much later in my Munster career. Pres won the Cup that year, 1994–5, but I sat on the bench for all three games, including the final against Crescent, without playing a minute in any of them. Conor Kilroy, who would play for Garryowen, was the kicker for Crescent but had an off day.

Playing alongside and against older guys was quite new. At that age, even a single year makes a big difference, and especially so for me. The year before, there had been talk of me being promoted from the Under-16s to the senior squad, but sanity prevailed!

But even just being part of the senior squad was enjoyable, as was playing with the 'firsts' throughout my six years at Pres. Rightly or wrongly, it seemed like you got more attention, from teachers as much as from other pupils, and maybe also had a slightly easier ride as a result.

That was certainly true of my final year, when I was starting for the senior team and Pres retained the Munster Schools Senior Cup. We beat Christians in the semi-final, 7–6, at Musgrave Park. It was a cracking atmosphere and a cracking game. Tim Cahill, our captain, scored our try. The final was against Ardscoil Rís in Thomond Park. We went 18–0 up at one point and finished up winning 18–7. But we had really won the Cup in the semi-final against our most bitter rivals.

During the season I made the Irish schools squad, but I sat on the bench for all three games as Ireland won the Triple Crown. Ciaran 'Skids' Scally, from Blackrock College in Dublin, was the starting scrum-half. After I finished with Pres, the Irish schools were scheduled to tour Australia. Sitting in front of the TV and watching teletext at home with my family, the squad came up on screen, and I was named in it: 'P. Stringer (PBC, Cork)'. That's how we found out!

I was to be part of a six-week tour of Australia. We went nine games unbeaten, beating Australia in the only Test, which was also the last game. I was picked in a few games, and played well in the game before the Test. I scored two tries against New South Wales Country Schools in Wagga Wagga, and thought I might be in with a shout. But Skids was first choice. We won the game with a last-minute penalty by Bryn Cunningham.

The following summer, 1997, I was named on another Irish tour to Australia, with an Irish Universities team, so I had seen most of Australia by the age of eighteen.

Rugby was taking up more and more of my time. I had done well in first and second year, and had a good Junior Cert. I think I got nine

Bs and an A, or something like that. But in the last three years in school, as I concentrated my energies more and more on rugby, my studies suffered a bit. I completed a reasonably good Leaving Cert, about 400 points, but was short of my first choice in college, Electrical Engineering, and my second choice, a general science course known as 'Chem/Maths/Phys'.

We received our results while we were in Australia. Mum went to the school, opened the envelope and rang me with the news. I was very disappointed: 400 was a fair bit short of the previous year's points threshold for my first two choices.

We then looked at Arts in UCC. Anything would have done: I just wanted to go to UCC, entirely for rugby. Mum rang a few days later to say that for some reason the threshold for Chem/Maths/Phys had dropped 100 points to 360, and I had enough points. Phew!

I was going to UCC. To play rugby!

5.   Going Pro

At school I came across guys who knew what they wanted to do with their lives.

'I want to be a doctor.'

'I want to be a dentist.'

'I want to be a scientist.'

'I want to be a vet.'

'I want to be a banker.'

'I want to be a teacher.'

Or whatever.

I could never picture myself on any of those career paths, or even in a job of any kind. All I knew was rugby and, looking back, it is impossible to guess what else I could have done.

I sat my Junior Cert in 1993. Rugby was still an amateur game at that point – not a career option. Filling out my application form before the Leaving Cert, outlining my choices after school, I couldn't picture myself doing anything in particular. I had no real burning ambition, and I didn't love any subject enough to want to study it full-time. I had no vision for what was going to happen after school, or indeed after college.

After the Irish schools tour in the summer of 1996, with professionalization having come in the year before, the IRFU created a rugby 'Foundation' for ten or twelve promising young players. I was interviewed in the Limerick Ryan Hotel by the IRFU's George Spotswood, and Brian O'Brien, who would later become Munster and Irish manager, and I made the cut. This came with a stipend of £3,000 a year, so straight away I had a little spending money and was effectively a semi-professional. I was able to train every day and go to the gym a couple of times a week. The Union would provide a coach for the four of us in UCC who were on that first contract; the aim was to show us how to do weight training. Until then we had been told that weight training would stunt our growth!

So I left school, to be slowly absorbed by a professional system that was just coming into existence. In hindsight, I was blessed with the way the timing worked out. Professionalization, and that first Foundation contract, came at exactly the stage when I would otherwise have needed to decide what I might have to consider doing instead of rugby.

A core group of guys came together to play rugby at UCC, including Paul Barry, Tim Cahill and Mick O'Driscoll, whom I had known and played alongside at Pres. Two of our rivals, Rory Collins and Ronan O'Donovan, whom I'd played against from Under-8s to Under-12s while they were at Crosshaven, and later at Christians, were now teammates. You never really get to know opposition players socially from school days, but at UCC we realized these were normal guys who just wanted to play rugby too. Years of bitterness can be quickly forgotten when you play and socialize together.

On one of my first days there I went to the Students' Union office to collect my white coat, my safety goggles and all the bits and pieces for the chemistry lab. An XXL lab coat was the only one remaining. I tried the thing on and was virtually tripping over the ends. I rolled up the sleeves three or four times. It looked ridiculous. It would have been too big for Mick O'Driscoll.

That was the first day I met Mick Riordan, who became and remains a good buddy. He remembers seeing me walking into that chemistry lab, and thinking, 'Who's got their little brother in for the day to show them around the place?' The whole class stopped to turn and look at me. I'd say I was a sight to behold all right.

Thereafter, I didn't attend too many lectures. UCC was all about the rugby, really. I had enjoyed the practical side of chemistry in secondary school, but studying Chem/Maths/Phys at degree level you needed to know twelve different subjects. After two years I opted out.

I received a sports scholarship worth £1,500 in my first year at UCC, and between this and the Foundation money and free accommodation at home, I had no need to find a job to put myself through college. The IRFU had created the Foundation for guys who had been on the Irish schools tour to Australia, and we were paid three grand a year.

I began training with the seniors, and I was the smallest by an even more noticeable degree than before. In first year at university you're playing with guys up to four or five years older than you.

And that was just my teammates. Going into senior rugby, you're playing against fully fledged adult club teams. My first game for UCC was a Cork Charity Cup game against Skibbereen at home in the Farm, out in Bishopstown. Brian Hickey was the coach, and he rang my dad to ask for permission to select me for the game. He was concerned about my size and wanted to feel sure that my parents were happy for me to play.

We won that game 52–10, but our first AIL Division Two game, soon after, didn't go so well. UCC had won promotion from Division Three the season before, when Rog was the main man before he joined Cork Con. Most of our squad were still in the US on their J1 visas and we were beaten 78–3 away to Old Crescent; Stephen Tuohy ran us ragged!

But college rugby was ideal in helping me make the step up to adult rugby. I broke into the senior team quite quickly and played eighty minutes every game. We had away-day trips to Derry, Greystones, Skerries, and so forth, where we always came up against players and teams who were much older than us.

We were given licence to play a very fluid, running brand of rugby, which suited me down to the ground. It was like a continuation of school. I was constantly tapping penalties, playing with pace and intensity, trying to move the other team around the pitch. We may not have won every week, but I'd say other teams dreaded playing us. 'Here come the students again.' Our opponents invariably tried to slow everything down.

All the alickadoos who looked after UCC rugby very much bought into the social aspect of the club. In the Mardyke clubhouse after home games, the likes of Cillian Twomey, Dick Kennefick and Len Harty would generously look after the players for the night. They knew students didn't have much money at the time, so we were given a kitty to cover expenses. It was a brilliant social scene. Every-one stuck together. Everyone went out together, and you'd see each other every single day of the week in and around UCC. We were very tightly knit and I couldn't imagine there would be any club side quite like a university team.

Mick Riordan played flanker, Dave Lane was my number 8 for years, and John Fitzgerald – an athletic, ginger-haired Irish schools and Irish Under-21 player about three years ahead of me – was in the second row. He was involved with Munster in the early days, and his nickname was TFI – Tipped for Ireland. He never quite made Ireland, but he was brilliant at schools and for UCC. He just lacked the natural bulk and physicality to make the next level at that position.

Mick O'Driscoll was alongside him, with Jerry Flannery and Mike Ross in the front row. Our out-half was Brian O'Mahony, who had played for the Irish schools. Aidan O'Shea captained the team from centre. Colin Healy, the full-back, had been a couple of years ahead of me at Pres, and Frankie Sheahan and John Kelly were also involved. Looking back, we had a hell of a team.

I thought very highly of Brian Hickey and another coach, Peter Melia, an English guy who was backs coach in my first year and became head coach the following season. Peter completely bought into college-type rugby and encouraged us to play off quick taps and quick line-outs. We did backs training on Tuesday and Thursday nights: seven backs against seven backs, on the full pitch. It was exhausting, but great for fitness levels and skills, and also very enjoyable.

It wasn't simply mindless running with a ball; they were competitive games that defined the whole ethos of university rugby. Like my Cork Con under-age coaches, Peter made it fun. We practised the way we wanted to play. He came on to the training pitch with a smile and encouraged us to come up with moves and play in an unconventional way. He'd say: 'Go wild, lads.'

We competed well in that first season in the second division and finished in about mid-table. We also played some cracking Munster Senior Cup games. One was a semi-final against Shannon in the 1996–7 season. They were then the dominant club force in the country, with

Mick Galwey, John Hayes, Alan Quinlan, Eddie Halvey, Anthony Foley and all the rest. By that stage, I hadn't yet trained with Munster.

Before the game, Peter Melia said to us: 'Now go do that voodoo that you do so well.' They had a fairly full team out, but we gave them a really good run for their money on a warm spring day in Musgrave Park. In our second season we came up against the Cookies, Young Munster, again in the semi-finals at Musgrave Park; pushing them all the way until Peter Clohessy and his forwards said enough was enough.

In that second season, 1997–8, in the second division, after a typically slow start for a college team as guys drifted back to university and rugby, we went unbeaten from December to April. But a few draws meant we finished fourth, when we were almost in danger of being promoted!

Dr Len Harty, the team doctor, was also one of the main organizers and founders of the Students' European Rugby Championships, which was held in November and December 1998 season. There were more than twenty teams from universities around Europe, including Oxford, Loughborough, Toulouse (who had won it the first two seasons), Edinburgh, Birmingham, Cardiff, Swansea, Grenoble, Paris, Queen's, Trinity and UCD.

Oxford and Loughborough were in our group, and the Mardyke was crammed for those games: maybe four to five thousand people on Friday nights. Niall Hogan was scrum-half for Oxford, and to come up against an Irish international in front of thousands of your fellow students was a major deal. We won 17–13 in a game where I claimed the only line-out of my career. Oxford were slow coming to the line and two of the forwards hoisted me up for a quick throw to the front. That was the kind of thing we did off the cuff. 'Go wild, boys. Go wild.'

We played Grenoble in the cup final in Donnybrook on a Saturday morning in January. We were trailing 10–0, and Grenoble were mauling over our line, when I managed to knock the ball out of the hands of one of their forwards. We went on to win 14–10.

Later that day the squad was brought on to the Lansdowne Road pitch at half-time to be presented with the trophy during the European Cup final between Ulster and Colomiers. That was a memorable day, watching Ulster become the first Irish side to win the trophy, with nearly 50,000 of their supporters taking over Lansdowne Road.

But we were the first Irish team to win a European trophy, beating Ulster by about three hours!

6. Learning How to Bark

Growing up in the '80s and '90s, before professionalization, the club game ruled. The current full-time provincial structures didn't exist, and Munster was regarded simply as a representative side. I remember watching them lose by 60–19 away to Toulouse in the second season of the Heineken Cup, and the following season I went to Thomond Park to see them beat Harlequins. But even then there was some debate as to whether the clubs or the provinces should represent Ireland in that competition, and at the time nobody knew whether or not Munster would be a full-time team. So when I was at university, I wanted to play for Munster but I didn't really see it as the full-time option it developed into.

In the pre-season of 1998–9, Declan Kidney – who was now coaching Munster – called Mick O'Driscoll and Donncha O'Callaghan and me into training in the University of Limerick. I was suddenly out of my comfort zone. For the first time in my life I was training with guys completely out of my own age group; and these were no ordinary players. These were the ones you had looked up to over the years: Gaillimh (Mick Galwey) and Claw (Peter Clohessy), Killian Keane and Cian Mahony, Dominic Crotty, Axel (Anthony Foley), Quinny (Alan Quinlan), Eddie Halvey and so on.

For a twenty-year-old kid, entering an environment full of these huge names was intimidating. I'm shy at the best of times, but in those first few sessions with Munster on the back pitch in UL there wasn't a peep out of me. I tried to latch on to Donners and Micko as best I could. I just didn't want to be isolated among those big names. It was daunting and I felt very awkward.

There were three other scrum-halves in the squad, all older than me: Brian O'Meara, Tom Tierney and Stephen McIvor. Brian and Stephen had both played for Ireland, and Tom would soon do so. In training we'd rotate: I'd step in at line-out or scrum plays, and quietly stick to the basics.

Gaillimh pulled me aside and said, 'Look, to get guys' respect, you have to boss them around the place.' Over the years I've learned how true that is. If, as a scrum-half, you're quiet and you let things go and don't tell forwards what to do, they won't have any respect for you as a player or as a person. Gaillimh also said to me: 'If something isn't right you've got to tell us, and that includes me.' He added: 'Look, the only way you're going to get the respect of these guys is by telling them what you want, how you want the ball and, if things aren't good enough, demand the best. They'll have more respect for you and ultimately that will be better for you; if you're going to be in a team like this, you've got to be vocal and dominate them and tell them what you want. That's going to stand to you in the long run.'

A scrum-half must be bossy. He is the link between the forwards and the backs. But it took me a few sessions to feel comfortable asserting myself: a 5' 7", twenty-year-old UCC boy ordering international play-ers around. Because I was so small, the older guys definitely doubted both my physical ability and my ability on the pitch. They hadn't seen much of me playing over the years. Most of them wouldn't have heard of me. I had to prove myself. It was a case of boss them or die.

Claw was usually the least inclined to take any instructions, par-ticularly from a little UCC scrum-half, but if I felt he wasn't doing something right, then I had to tell him. He'd either take it on board or he wouldn't, but at least I felt I'd done my job. It helped that Axel and Gaillimh would often reiterate points I made.

It was a truly outstanding pack – and it wasn't long before Marcus Horan, Jerry Flannery and Paul O'Connell came along as well. These guys would form the core of the Irish pack for years to come.

There was a good mix, too, of players who put their heads down and worked, and others who had a bit of niggle about them too, like Claw. In one of my earliest Munster games I fell over a ruck and someone stood on my head. I needed six stitches and Claw told me: 'It serves you right for falling over the top.' But, later on, the culprit was taken off with a split head. Claw had returned the favour. I always knew that my back was covered. I had Quinny, Halvey and Claw to look after me and I learned from them over the years. They generally gave Rog and me a great platform to work off.

Rog and I weren't great friends off the pitch, but on the pitch, as the years went by, we developed a great understanding. I admit this sounds a bit clichéd because I've said it so many times, but instinctively I knew where he would be. He was comfortable coming on to the ball and taking it flat, comfortable with the way I pass and move. As soon as I put my hand down to the ball I'd be in motion to pass it. It wasn't a case of picking up that ball, looking to where the out-half was, and then throwing it; I had to have a pretty good idea of where he was in advance. Over time that became second nature between us, and if my pass wasn't right, if it was slightly too high or slightly too low, he wasn't shy about letting me know. And that's fair enough. That's the way it should be. It was a continuation from me dominating the forwards and demanding the best from them, and it was one of the keys to our success.

At times Rog and I had rows on the pitch. If I felt he'd had a go at me unnecessarily over a pass, I'd say: 'Look, it's just one pass.' But I understood that it could be just that one pass which made the difference. So I went into the next training session aware that if I didn't deliver my pass on the money each time, I was going to have someone in my ear. I was the same with the forwards. If they didn't deliver me quick ball and place it properly – or if they were lazy with their feet and nudged the ball even fractionally – then they would know about it. Everyone was fully conscious of their job and every little detail within it, because they knew their teammates would be the first people to expose them.

My first game for Munster, on 3 October 1998, was against Ulster. On that first day in Musgrave Park, I came off the bench for Brian O'Meara. When Declan told me to warm up I could not believe I was getting a chance to run out for Munster, particularly at Musgrave Park. I had played there a few times, and here I was, playing for the province in front of my own supporters. As I was just about to run on to the pitch, Declan grabbed me by the arm and said: 'Go out there and give me a reason not to drop you.'

I didn't know which way to think about that. I tried to put it to the back of my mind, but clearly I didn't as I've never forgotten those words. Soon after, we had a scrum about twenty metres in from the touchline in front of the main stand, and maybe ten metres inside their half, playing towards the Dolphin Pavilion. Their winger was up on the short side, and off the back of the scrum I kicked diagonally over my left shoulder and over the top of the scrum, in behind him. I have never done anything like it since, but I just saw the space and thought, 'Why not?' I didn't tell anyone I was doing it. Our out-half that day, Barry Everett, had called the ball for the backs, but I just instinctively kicked it. It probably could have been a bit longer, but the ball bounced awkwardly and their winger, Sheldon Coulter, missed it at the first attempt. When he eventually picked it up, he was tackled by Anthony Horgan. A few recycles later, Gaillimh scored a try.

Munster had beaten Padova and Neath at home in the Heineken Cup. The following week we were back in Europe, away to Perpignan, and Declan started me. Picking me ahead of Brian O'Meara, Tom Tierney and Stephen McIvor was a ballsy call.

I had come into the squad looking at these guys and thinking they were way bigger, older and more experienced. In training I had watched Brian O'Meara practise his box kicking, which was always a strength of his game. All through school and university, the only skill that I'd practised, and had been asked to use, had been passing, and maybe quick tap and goes. I had no kicking game whatsoever.

Now I was going into a more structured game in which scrum-halves had to be able to kick, and kick accurately. We practised box kicks every day.

The atmosphere at the Stade Aimé Giral in Perpignan was unlike anything I had ever known. The French crowd were jumping around the place and chanting incessantly, and we didn't give them too many reasons to stop. We did score three tries, but they scored six. I don't have great memories of my Heineken Cup debut and my first club game in France.

Munster had never won in France and we never looked like doing so that day. Rhys Ellison, our New Zealand centre, was our main ball-carrier, but he was injured. He was a tough guy and such a nice man as well. I met him on a few tours to New Zealand. He would usually come to our games. He was fearless and would put his head

1. With my mum and my brothers (*top to bottom*) George, Dave and John.

2. Receiving my Player of the Tournament award at a tournament in Harrogate in 1988. Cork Con was the only non-English side competing.

3. Honing my skills in the garden with my brother George.

4. When Munster played the All Blacks in Cork in 1989, the curtain-raiser was an Under-12s match between Cork Con and Thurles: my debut on the main pitch at Musgrave Park. (*Maurice O'Mahony/Cork Examiner*)

5. In the 1993 Munster Schools Junior Cup final, Pres travelled to Thomond Park to face St Munchin's. They were the toughest side we'd ever played against, and they beat us 5–0. (*Des Barry/Cork Examiner*)

6. With Brian O'Mahony, Ronan O'Donovan, Tim Cahill and Rory Collins, just before leaving on our Irish schoolboys tour of Australia in 1996.

7. Playing for University College Cork in 1998. (*Brendan Healy/Inpho*)

8. After trailing François Pienaar and Saracens 21–9 at Vicarage Road in a Heineken Cup group match in November 1999, we came back to win 35–34. That was the day we really started to believe we could win the Cup. (*Andrew Paton/Inpho*)

9. Along with (*left to right*) Shane Horgan, Simon Easterby, Ronan O'Gara and John Hayes, I was one of five new caps who faced Scotland in the 2000 Six Nations. (*Matt Browne/Sportsfile*)

10. On my international debut, we scored forty-four points against Scotland, and it felt like the beginning of a new era. (*Patrick Bolger/Inpho*)

11. Mick Galwey with Rog and me during the anthems before the Italy match in 2000. (*Patrick Bolger/Inpho*)

12. Although I was now first-choice scrum-half for Ireland, I played for Shannon in the off-week before our Six Nations match against France in March 2000. It wouldn't happen today! (*Patrick Bolger/Inpho*)

13. On the shoulders of giants: celebrating with former Munster and Ireland flanker Ken O'Connell after we beat Toulouse in the 2000 Heineken Cup semi-final in Bordeaux.

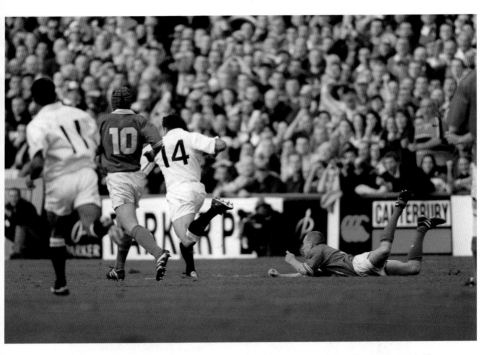

14. My favourite memory of the day we beat England in 2001, to deny them a Grand Slam, is my tap tackle on Dan Luger, which prevented a try. (*Patrick Bolger/Inpho*)

15. 'Here's my boy': with President McAleese before playing Scotland in the 2002 Six Nations. (*Brendan Moran/Sportsfile*)

16. With Mick Galwey after losing narrowly to Leicester in the 2002 Heineken Cup final. (*Brendan Moran/Sportsfile*)

17. Swapping shirts with All Black scrum-half Byron Kelleher in the Lansdowne Road dressing room after our match in 2001. (*Billy Stickland/Inpho*)

where most of us wouldn't put our feet. We really missed him that day.

We were also absolutely hammered in the scrum. I think John Hayes was taken off after about twenty minutes, and was booed off by the home supporters. Donncha O'Callaghan had also made his Munster debut against Ulster the previous week, and he was brought on as a sub for his Heineken Cup debut in Perpignan. He missed a few tackles. He fell off a few of their bigger forwards and was taken off soon after he had been brought on, so Donners will probably also remember that as being one of his worst early memories for Munster.

By the time we met Perpignan in the return match, we had drawn away to Neath and beaten Leinster at Donnybrook in the interpros. The game was moved from Thomond Park because the pitch there had been swamped with rain, and Musgrave Park wasn't a whole lot better. The pack were up for revenge and the ball hardly went beyond Rog. We won a thriller, 13–5.

That was the day I fell over the wrong side of the ruck, as Claw put it. The back of my head was split open after about twenty minutes and I wasn't brought back on. I came to the sidelines in Musgrave Park. Len Harty, our UCC team doctor, was also the Munster doctor. Len stitched me on the sideline under an umbrella in the pissing rain and strapped me up.

We went in at half-time and I said I was fine to return, but Deccie wouldn't put me back on and I thought: 'Shit, he's not going to put me back on now. That means Tom is going to be back in the team.' We had won but I was miserable, lost in my own self-doubts.

Afterwards, the cut in my head started swelling up with blood. The stitches were too tight, so Len had to drain my head with a needle at the after-match dinner. He emptied the syringe into a wine glass. I'll never forget it, people having their dinner around us and Len filling up a wine glass with blood from the back of my head.

I was still mainly focused on trying to second-guess Deccie. 'What's he thinking? Did he not bring me back on because he wanted to give Tom a go and he feels that Tom is better going forward than I am?'

I mentioned this to one or two people and someone said: 'Oh no,

I'm sure he just didn't want to risk you.' But all night there was no consoling me.

Deccie did pick me away to Padova the next week and, because of the wound, that was the only game in my career in which I wore a scrum cap. I went into town during the week but I couldn't find one that fitted me. In the end I had to buy a kid's scrum cap from Moss Finn's shop on the corner of Washington Street.

There was a five-week gap to the quarter-final, away to Colomiers, without any warm-up game, as there was no Celtic League in those days and the interpros were finished. So we went in cold to an away quarter-final, looking for Munster's first win in France.

Stade Selery wasn't a big stadium at all, but with about 8,000 there was a good atmosphere. The pack stayed down for an early scrum, expecting a big shove from them, but instead their number 8 broke quickly and made big yardage before they scored. They had jumped out of the blocks early and, as with any French team, if they get their tails up and the crowd gets going, you are in for a long day. And we were. It was another one of those days to forget. We were never in the game and never looked like winning.

If you are to have any chance away to a French side, you have to perform well in the first twenty minutes, and so quieten the crowd or turn them against their own team, start making them doubt themselves. Then they'll make more and more errors, and try too hard to rectify things.

But although it didn't feel like it that night, we were learning.

7.   Beginnings

The setting was a theatre hall, with steep tiered seating, in one of the old sports buildings in the University of Limerick. The entire Munster playing squad and management were in attendance – at least forty of us. Dave Mahedy, the Sports Director at UL, who had worked with Shannon and other rugby clubs as well as St Patrick's Athletic FC and Limerick's hurlers, was facilitating what was called a 'purposing meeting'. This was August 1999, before some of the Munster lads hooked up with Ireland for the World Cup that autumn – although most of us had been overlooked.

Keith Wood hadn't been able to attend our first week of pre-season in Kilkee, but he was there for our second week in UL. Woody had last played for Munster in 1996 and, after a bad injury, had joined Harlequins for three seasons before coming back to Munster for a year's 'loan', as it was a World Cup season. During his time away he had also been one of the stars of the 1997 Lions, who won the Test series in South Africa.

Dave told us that the purpose of the meeting was to set attainable goals and targets for the season ahead. He wanted our views. 'Lads,' he said, 'there's no wrong answers here.'

To begin with, there was a pregnant pause. Finally Woody spoke up.

'Obviously, we have to believe we can win the Heineken Cup,' he said. The room didn't quite break into open laughter, but there were a few sniggers. At Harlequins the target at the start of every season was to win everything. But this attitude wasn't very Irish, and certainly not very Munster.

Woody must have sensed the general attitude, but he pressed on: 'If you want to win it, then you've got to put it down.'

I don't know whether any other person in the room fully believed at that stage that we could win the Heineken Cup. Of course, Ulster had won it the previous season – but the English clubs had boycotted the tournament. They were back now, and the bookies didn't fancy our chances. Munster were 66–1 to win the Cup at the start of the tournament.

Three seasons earlier, Munster had conceded sixty points in Toulouse. We had never won in France. The previous year, in the quarter-final away to Colomiers, we were well and truly beaten.

But the world was changing. I moved to Shannon that season, having left UCC, but by then the provinces had taken over to such an extent that I didn't play more then ten AIL games for Shannon over the coming years. The seriousness and professionalism on display in that Munster 'purposing meeting' told its own story.

And when Woody spoke, guys listened. You had to respect what he said. If almost anybody else had said it, the sniggers would have turned to laughter. However, along with our more modest targets, winning the Heineken Cup was now written down as our season's ultimate goal.

Ireland warmed up for the World Cup with games against the provinces and Argentina. A Munster team with Marcus Horan, Frankie Sheahan, John Hayes, Mick Galwey, Alan Quinlan, David Wallace and Anthony Foley – none of whom had made the national squad – beat Ireland at Musgrave Park. Rog and I played half-back and, while there had been some talk that Rog was unlucky not to make the World Cup cut, I didn't have any complaints after just one season with Munster.

Munster's season went into cold storage until after the World Cup. Woody, Claw, Mikey Mullins, Quinny (who'd been called up as a replacement), Tom Tierney and Brian O'Meara returned after a disappointing tournament and that infamous defeat to Argentina in Lens. No one mentioned it. It wasn't part of Munster's season. We made a clean sweep of the interpros, winning all six games; the win in Belfast was our first in twenty years.

Two short-term goals had been achieved, and now came the big one. Yet nobody saw us as potential winners, perhaps including ourselves. After we beat Pontypridd at home, next up was Saracens at

Vicarage Road. They were a serious team. In the back row alone they had François Pienaar, a World Cup-winning captain, Richard Hill and Tony Diprose.

Within Munster, we now believed that at home we could beat anybody. For whatever reasons – and I still don't know why – in sport it is never quite the same when you're away. In order to establish ourselves as serious contenders – not least in our own minds – we would need a major victory away from home.

That was, famously, the week that Declan had music blaring on the tannoy at training in Thomond Park. He also wore a fez at one of our team meetings, to imitate Saracens' fans. It was all done to prepare us for the razzmatazz of games at Vicarage Road, which included the use of a remote-controlled car to bring on the kicking tee.

We trailed 21–9 at half-time, but scored four second-half tries. When Jeremy Staunton went in beside the posts from Rog's long left-to-right pass, we were within a point. Rog's conversion gave us a 35–34 win. That was definitely the day when we started to believe. That's where it started.

We began to realize we had a bloody good team. We'd Woody, Wally and Mikey Mullins to carry the ball. John Langford, our first big 'signing' from overseas, had arrived from the Brumbies to play alongside Gaillimh in the second row. John's arrival caused quite a fuss. He had won four caps for the Wallabies. Until then the squad had been made up entirely of players who had been born and bred in the province, or had joined a club (like Jason Holland), or were Irish-qualified (like Mikey Mullins and Rob Henderson).

John was thirty-one, but to see what this guy could do in training was an eye-opener. To this day, you speak to Donncha O'Callaghan and the rest of the forwards, and they'll talk about how much they learned from Langford. He had a different mindset. Players coming from the southern hemisphere, who had played in Super Rugby, had an aura about them. He was athletic – superb in the line-out – and good around the pitch. But it wasn't just his game. He was as fit as anyone in that squad. I'll never forget one fitness session in UL, which included a three-kilometre run on the track. His stride, his leanness and his fitness set a high example and brought another dimension to our training. He was such a gentleman as well. A humble country guy from Wagga Wagga, he put his head down and did the work. It would be easy for players from the southern hemisphere to come here and take it handy. But he wanted us to step up to the next level and he inspired everybody, including me, with that attitude. Never injured, he played thirty out of our thirty-one matches in his two seasons with Munster.

The win at Vicarage Road was big news in the Irish media, and that week there were reports of 4,000 people queuing outside Thomond Park for tickets for the home game against Saracens. The following Saturday we were back in the Stade Selery to play Colomiers again. It was a six-day turnaround, but no one was complaining. In fact, we couldn't wait to play, and there were only two changes – Mikey Mullins was back and Marcus Horan was in for Claw. Jason 'Dutchie' Holland, a New Zealander who had come over to play club rugby in Midleton and would become a Munster coach, scored two tries, with Marcus and Woody scoring the others. We gained revenge, winning 31–15. We'd had our first win away in England and our first in France inside seven days.

We completed the double over Colomiers a week later in Musgrave Park, and we faced Saracens at home in January, just one win away from reaching the quarter-finals, with a game to spare. The capacity at Thomond Park was supposed to be 10,000, which was the attendance given on the day, but I'd say there were close to 20,000 in there. It was just unbelievable. I'll never forget when Gaillimh scored from a maul in the first half. I jumped up to celebrate and Dave Wallace's two front teeth went into the top of my head! I had to be taken off and stitched up. Rog had to go off to be stitched up too, as did John Hayes; so all three of us finished up wearing white bandages. By the end it really did look like trench warfare.

Once again we were behind at half-time, 17–8, and trailing 30–24 entering injury time. I've watched Woody's try a few times since, and Rog's conversion. Saracens charged early, so he had the chance to re-take the kick, and it went in off the post. As a young Munster player going into those Saracens matches I wouldn't have been alone in thinking that, coming from the Premiership, they were performing in a better league. But now, having beaten them at home and away, we knew we were on their level. They were benchmark wins, for us and for our supporters too. Until Vicarage Road, our support was mostly family and friends. After that, the supporter base started growing dramatically.

We'd won twelve from twelve that season, but maybe we became too confident: the following week we lost 38–36 away to Pontypridd, who were bottom of the group. A win would have made us the number 1 seed for the quarter-finals. Still, we were seeded for a home quarter, against Stade Français.

Things were happening quickly now. I was called to Ireland training in January 2000, at the ALSAA complex beside Dublin Airport. Jumbo jets flew overhead, every ten minutes or so, passing about ten metres above our heads. I've rarely felt so grateful to be the smallest! There was a hell of a lot of people there, maybe fifty or sixty including players and coaches. Whenever a plane roared past, the coaches had to stop talking until the din subsided. Being involved in the Ireland set-up, with all the guys from the other provinces and players based in England, truly was a dream come true.

When the squad was trimmed to thirty for the week of the opening game against England, Tom Tierney and I were the scrum-halves. I was named as a replacement for Twickenham, and for once I wasn't disappointed to be on the bench. I suppose I was feeling pretty good about how the last season and a half had gone with Munster, and that my chance might come.

I watched our complete annihilation (50–18) from the stands. 'You were better off not getting on,' I was told. But that's not the way you think about the possibility of your first cap. You just want to be on the pitch. You're thinking, 'This might be my only opportunity. They may change the whole squad after this game.'

I felt I could have done something, could have made a difference. I knew we'd been absolutely hockeyed but I always feel I can do something to change a game, and it was no different that day. Hell, it was an opportunity to play for my country for the first time. I definitely never thought, 'I'm better off being on the bench for this one.'

When we returned to camp in Co. Wicklow the following Sunday, I tried to read Warren Gatland's mind at training, in meetings and around the Glenview Hotel. OK, if he makes eye contact with you and asks you a question, does that mean he's looking for your opinion because he's going to pick you?

Gatty made it very clear that all bets were off and places were up for grabs. We had a full-on contact session with 'live' scrummaging in Dr Hickey Park in Greystones on the Monday. It was a case of 'last man standing'. I looked at it as a chance to stake a claim.

On Tuesday morning, 15 February, we convened in the Glenview and Donal Lenihan read out the team: '15: Girvan Dempsey; 14: Shane Horgan; 13: Brian O'Driscoll; 12: Mikey Mullins; 11: Denis Hickie; 10: Ronan O'Gara; 9: Peter Stringer . . .'

Everything after that was just background noise. I'd been named in an Irish team for the first time. I wasn't alone, as Rog, Hayes, Shaggy (Shane Horgan) and Simon Easterby would also make their debuts. It's traditional for new caps to be congratulated by everybody in the squad, so there was plenty of hand-shaking at the end of that meeting.

The first person I rang was Dad.

'I'm starting next Saturday against Scotland.'

He was as thrilled as I was. 'Brilliant news. Congratulations. You deserve it.'

Dad told me to continue doing what I was doing, to think of it as just another game. I heard the same thing from Gatty, Donal, Gaillimh and Woody.

Another tradition is that new caps are presented to the media, and the attention when we went back to the Glenview was unlike anything I'd ever known. The cameras clicked as the five of us sat together, and again when we posed outside. It was all very new to me, and quite daunting, although it lightened the load to have four others in the same position!

Tuesday night was relaxing, as was our day off on Wednesday, and Thursday's training was about refreshing our calls and moves. After dinner in the hotel, as was also the custom on Thursdays, we went to the cinema. I quickly came to love the rhythm of Test weeks: the intensity of Monday and Tuesday, the relative wind-down of Wednesday, the fine-tuning of Thursday, the transfer to the city that night, sampling more of the atmosphere on Friday, then peaking on Saturdays. I loved the change of scenery that came with the move to the Berkeley Court Hotel, and the buzz of being in town. Suddenly everyone is talking about the game. You can see the billboards and the flags, and on Friday you can hear the opposition supporters. On that Friday, I went back to the Berkeley Court to meet my parents in the foyer and, for the first time, hand them two tickets to a Lansdowne Road Test.

Match day. Supporters have begun to assemble in the lobby and bar. When we come down the stairs, they form a human tunnel, through the doors and on to the coach. It raises the hairs on the back of my neck. Even though you can see the stadium from the hotel entrance, just down Lansdowne Road to the right, the coach takes a left out of the hotel, then a right on to Northumberland Road, right again at Haddington Road, another right on to Shelbourne Road and then left into the West Stand car park. We pass the Shelbourne House pub, where the fans drinking outside cheer when they spot the Irish team.

Once off the coach, we walk past the programme sellers, some food stands and into the old entrance to the players' tunnel and the dressing rooms. It's a very special feeling, very hard to describe. You feel very privileged. You're representing Ireland, you're entering our arena, Lansdowne Road, where I first watched Ireland play, thirteen years ago. We come around the corner, down the brown steps, down the corridor to the changing rooms, through the door. The number 9 jersey is hanging to the left. I put my bag down and read the embroidered words under the crest: 'Ireland v. Scotland, February 2000'. My jersey to keep!

I try to go through my warm-up routine, and passing and kicking practice, as if it were any other game, but the atmosphere is building in the ground and I'm more nervous than usual. In the dressing room we put on our training tops, as we still have to meet the president, Mary McAleese. I just want the game to start. Even though I can't sing, I belt out both of the anthems: 'Amhrán na bhFiann' and

'Ireland's Call'. Some lads have their reasons for singing one or the other. I regard one as our national anthem, the other as our rugby anthem. I try to become fully immersed in the ritual of the anthems. It's positive energy.

It's true what they say about your debut going by in a blur. I don't remember much about the first half-hour, to be honest. A couple of dodgy passes probably didn't help Rog. It was a new team, with five new caps. We all needed time to settle.

By the end, the noise was unlike anything I'd ever experienced. Having gone 10–0 down, we cut loose and scored 44 unanswered points, before they got a couple of late consolation tries. David Humphreys came on for Rog, and was on fire. So too was Denis, and of course Drico.

After the World Cup and Lens, and after we'd been thumped by England at Twickenham, and after twelve years without a win over Scotland, a huge wave of relief spilled on to the pitch. In the thirteen years I'd been going to Lansdowne Road, this seemed new. They loved the way we played, loved the tries we scored. The atmosphere around Irish rugby changed from that day.

I met my parents and my brother George at a small reception hosted by the IRFU committee in the West Stand. The post-match dinner was at the Berkeley Court, and being a non-drinker I escaped the worst of the excesses! I can't say the same for my fellow new caps.

Our training session on the Thursday before the Italian game was shocking. We dropped the ball so many times, no one could have kept count. We were all over the place, so much so that the coaches had to intervene to restore some structure. Come match day, though, everything clicked. We beat Italy 60–13 at Lansdowne Road. That was also the day Gaillimh pulled me and Rog in under each shoulder during the anthems. Most people think that happened before our debut against Scotland two weeks earlier. But my dad has a copy of the picture with the caption underneath: 'Goodfellas'. And the date. Billy Stickland's agency Inpho has the same date on their website: 4/3/2000. The day Ireland beat Italy.

In Paris we stayed in a hotel next to the Palace of Versailles.

Nothing but the best for the lads. As memorable as the gardens was the police escort into Paris. Les gendarmes don't take any shit when they're on motorbikes. If you leave at a certain time they ensure you arrive at the stadium on time.

France had won the previous fifteen meetings between the nations, and Ireland hadn't won in Paris since 1972 – five years before I was born! I had watched France–Ireland games on TV, and there was a familiar pattern. For the first twenty or twenty-five minutes Ireland would usually play reasonably well and then capitulate. France then invariably ran riot. Two years before, I'd been in Stade de France for the first time, having played for the Irish Universities the day before. It was Gatty's first game as Ireland coach, and against all odds Ireland had nearly won. Ireland led until seven minutes from time, but then fell behind 18–16. Victor Costello made a late break but couldn't get his pass away for a match-winning try.

That gave us hope, and after our couple of wins we went there without fear. We had a core of Munster players who had won away in Colomiers, and this was a new Irish team, most of whom had never before played in Paris. I know it sounds crazy, but we felt invincible. The mind is a funny thing.

The Stade de France was as comfortable as a hotel. The pitch was perfect. The sun was shining. 'La Marseillaise' was fun to hum along to. What was there to be frightened of?

Drico's hat-trick was nearly all down to him. He made the break that led to his first try. After Claw had taken it on, Mal O'Kelly popped Drico a lovely pass and he sauntered in under the posts. Then, from a scrum, Rob Henderson cut them open and passed inside to Drico for his second. Denis cut them open for the third, before I was scragged and my pass went to ground. Everyone stopped except Drico, who scooped up the ball and scampered through. Emile N'tamack looked like a spectator as Brian ran past him. Humphs' conversion made it a one-point game; then he nailed a brilliant penalty two minutes from time.

Denis had already kept us in the game with his first-half tackle from behind on their hooker Marc dal Maso, who was sprinting towards the line. Denis came from a long way back and hit dal Maso from completely the wrong angle. He had to throw his head in front of him, otherwise dal Maso's momentum would have carried him over the line. Denis took one for the team there.

I was the man to kick the ball off the pitch for the final whistle. I dropped to my knees, closed my eyes and put two hands in the air. I shed a tear in that moment. Mikey Mullins hadn't been used off the bench but he was the first to hug me while I was on the ground. We did a lap of honour and there seemed to be only Irish supporters in pockets all around the Stade de France. Gaillimh virtually picked me up on to his shoulders.

In the dressing room and at the reception, Syd Millar and Noel Murphy – both legends of the game – were as emotional and thrilled as if it had been their old playing days. We moved into the hotel where the IRFU were staying near the Champs-Elysées that night. Judging by the way lads looked the next morning, and the stories that were told, some had a later night than I did.

Three wins in a row was unheard of for Ireland. And it went straight to our heads. Maybe there'd been an element of fear going to the Stade de France that was missing at home to Wales in our last game. That was one of the most annoying and frustrating defeats I've ever experienced. We hardly played. It wasn't as if Wales were an outstanding team, but they were good enough to beat us. Axel was within inches of winning the game at the end, but we lost 23–19. It was no way to end such a good season, nor to end Donal Lenihan's time as manager, as he was turning his attention to the Lions. Still, the turnaround within a few weeks had been incredible.

In the run-up to Munster's European quarter-final against Stade Français, Brian O'Brien, our team manager and a shrewd rugby man from Shannon, went over to Paris to watch Stade, and he identified the need to rattle their gifted but twitchy out-half, Diego Dominguez. Woody was entrusted with the task.

Declan picked Eddie Halvey ahead of Quinny, and Jason Holland had to miss the game because of a family bereavement, so Killian Keane came back in. Little was made of this being Munster's first European knock-out game at Thomond Park. We chose to play into the wind, and we were 12–0 up inside the first ten minutes with tries by Anthony 'Hoggy' Horgan and Dominic Crotty. We then preyed on their ill-discipline and built on our lead, Rog kicking five penalties in the second half. We won comfortably, 27–10, to earn a semi-final away to Toulouse in Bordeaux.

It was in Bordeaux that the Red Army was born. All of the Stade Lescure was bathed in hot sunshine, and by seas of Toulouse black and Munster red. We warmed up in the in-goal area in front of their fans, to loud booing and whistling. That was clever. Not even those passionate fans could sustain that level of hostility for all of the warm-up, and nothing that followed in the match could be as loud or intimidating.

It was baking hot, ideal for a French team, but we backed our fitness levels by playing a high-tempo offloading game. Hayes finished off the first of our three tries after a big break by Woody and an offload by Dominic Crotty. Having carried in an earlier phase, Hayes stayed on the ground for about ten seconds, managing to rest on one knee, before getting up just as Crotty broke the line to receive the pass and flop over the line. For years afterwards that try was shown on videos at squad meetings, and all of us counted the seconds Hayes was on the ground, taking a rest. The count got faster and louder, until we got it up to thirty or forty seconds.

And then he'd reply: 'I was in the right place at the right time, and that's all that matters.'

The slagging was daily and constant, at his and everybody else's expense, but only because deep down we'd massive respect for one another. You had to have a thick skin. If you weren't getting slagged, there would have been something wrong with you.

Woody injured his calf in that move and was replaced at half-time by Frankie Sheahan. Seeing Woody coming back from Harlequins can't have been easy for Frankie. Straight away, Frankie must have known he'd be playing less. But he came on, nailed all his throws; and he always prided himself on his scrummaging.

At half-time, there was a long walk past the home dressing room to the away one. Their door was still locked and they were stretched out on the ground. We had to step over and around them. They were feeling the heat as much as we were!

We survived ten minutes of intense pressure while Mikey Mullins was in the sin bin for a deliberate knock-on. Then, from a scrum on our own 22, Rog hit Mikey with a long pass and he worked a switch with Dominic. John Kelly and Anthony Horgan both had big carries, and it ended with Rog scoring under the posts. Munster have a reputation for playing a forward-orientated game, but I doubt if we've ever scored a better try in Europe. Jason Holland, back in the team, scored an intercept try and, although they eventually scored their one try near the end, we won 31–26.

Northampton awaited in the final at Twickenham, three weeks away. That semi-final was our only match in the six weeks since the quarter-final. On the other hand, Northampton had come through tough knock-out games against Wasps and Llanelli, and had re-arranged league games in midweek. They came into the final, having played seven games in the same six-week period.

I'll never forget the team room in our hotel, the night before the final. One wall was covered in fax messages of support. We came into that room from dinner and there literally wasn't a blank space on that wall. Amongst the faxes was a poem from Cork, along with good luck messages from Limerick, Tipperary and the rest of the province. And there were plenty more from Munster ex-pats living in Dublin, England, America, Australia and elsewhere. In some cases, they hadn't been home for years. They took so much pride in having watched Munster that season. For some it made living away from home a little easier. We began to realize what reaching a final had meant to so many people, and how much winning the final would mean.

We read them all and then sat down for our team meeting.

Almost everybody spoke. Dave Corkery was sitting next to me and Corks is an emotional guy at the best of times. He was sobbing. The talk was about the next day and its importance to everyone in this circle: what we'd been through and what our families had been through. We'd come such a long way in such a short time. Perhaps the pressure we felt that night lingered into the following day.

I couldn't watch the video of the final for years, because the disappointment of going up the steps at Twickenham to collect our losers' medals was still too raw. I'll never forget being in that huddle on the pitch after the game. Not one Munster supporter left the stadium early. As they sang 'The Fields of Athenry', Declan stood in the middle and spoke: 'Remember how far we've come, and we'll be back next year. I'm massively proud to coach you, massively proud to be part of this Munster set-up.'

I eventually watched the game, and it wasn't a classic. There was no structure to it. Northampton were on top for most of it. Wally scored a great try; when tackled going over the line, he still managed to ground the ball. Rog had no luck that day, missing all four of his shots at goal; the last two were very well struck and missed very narrowly, including one that would have given us the lead, a minute from time. The final score was 9–8.

Reflecting on that meeting the night before, I took the lesson that it was important to be a bit less emotional before kick-off. You want to save it. You want to keep something in the tank. You need to have a good night's sleep. You cannot become too worked up too far out from the game itself.

It was one of the most painful lessons of my career. Maybe the most painful.

8.   Second Season Syndrome

The 1999–2000 season had been a remarkable one for me: a run to the Heineken Cup final with Munster, and three excellent wins as Ireland's starting scrum-half in my first Six Nations. The second half of 2000 was, by comparison, a little bit anticlimactic.

The day after the Heineken Cup final, I joined the Ireland squad for my first Test tour abroad: a three-match tour of the Americas.

First up, in Buenos Aires, we played the Pumas in the Ferro Carril Oeste, home to a Primera B side. The ground was like one of those old, rickety roller-coaster stadiums that you'd see in the States. The stands seemed almost vertical and looked as if they could easily topple over. At the captain's run on the Friday we thought, 'Surely this will not be full to capacity?' But it was – about 25,000, jumping up and down, and singing.

This fixture was meant to be our revenge for Lens, but with that win, and their first World Cup quarter-final, the Pumas had arrived. We began well but we left points behind and were over-run by the end. Some of us were still feeling the effects of the previous week, and a long-haul flight six days before the match probably wasn't the best preparation for a Test against a seriously good side.

The atmosphere was like that of an Argentinian football match: loud, passionate and abusive. Bishy, Justin Bishop, played really well and scored two of our four tries to their three, but not one was converted. I've never heard such whistling and booing for a kicker, and it seemed to affect Humphs.

The next day we travelled from Buenos Aires to Boston for a game against the USA Eagles in Manchester, New Hampshire. As ever, when there weren't enough business-class seats for the squad, being the smallest I was relegated to economy. But Paul Wallace had been late for the squad meeting that morning, and his punishment was a seat in economy. Woody held court and decided I was to be bumped up to Paul's seat in business class.

On our down day, Wednesday, some of us went to a shopping mall. We were supposed to be back in Manchester for a 5 p.m. squad photo shoot. My first tour photograph. But we lost track of time and couldn't hail a cab for love nor money. I'll never forget the sight of Trevor Brennan trying to thumb a lift on that highway. Drivers weren't inclined to stop. Trevor finally flagged down a farmer's pickup truck with caged chickens in the back, and he, Mal O'Kelly and I hopped on board. The truck screeched into the car park, where everyone else was in their 'number ones' – official Ireland suits and ties – and ready for the photo. We must have cut quite a picture ourselves.

When your team wins 83–3, as we did against the Eagles, you'd hope to be given a run, but I was the only sub not to be used. Guy Easterby played well, scoring two of our thirteen tries, as did his brother Simon and Geordie Murphy on his debut, while Mikey Mullins scored three. I sat in the stand, thinking, 'Feckin' hell, let me on the pitch.'

A week later the tour and the season ended with a 27-all draw against Canada at Fletcher's Fields, in the suburbs of Toronto. It really was just a field with a temporary stand on one side, and the match felt like an off-season club game. Canada are a fired-up, physical bunch of lads to play at the best of times, but it didn't feel like a Test international at all, and we gave a performance to match. Certainly I did. That was probably one of my worst games in the green jersey. I played inside Humphs, and nothing clicked. I just didn't play well. I was taken off early in the second half, disappointed with the tour in general.

I would never be considered big – even in Japan – but I did score my first international try against them in the opening 2001 November international. Admittedly, it was one of eleven tries in a 78–9 win. I have a vision of running in from maybe thirty metres, but that could be my imagination! I've never seen it, and I would love to. It came off a loose ball, or a turnover, and I had a clear run-in. Maybe it was forty metres. It didn't matter. Nor did the opposition. It's an unbeliev-able feeling to score for the first time for your country, all the more so at Lansdowne Road.

It was slightly different, a week later. South Africa beat us 28–18, with Joost Van der Westhuizen among their try scorers. He was def-initely one of the best scrum-halves I ever played against; completely different from me, both in size and in his game. He was a 'ninth for-ward', very difficult to play against. He wasn't a particularly good passer – he usually took a couple of steps – but his strength was carry-ing around the fringes. He held the ball in one hand, with his arm stretched out, and used his other to fend. When tackling him you couldn't get anywhere near the ball. He had that ability to step and use his long reach to offload or break tackles, and to bring his for-wards into the game. What a tragedy that he is now suffering from motor neurone disease.

Woody had returned to Harlequins, but otherwise Munster had the same squad. For our first Heineken Cup match, at home to Newport, the only changes from the team that started the final were Frankie Sheahan for Woody and Quinny for Eddie Halvey.

We no longer saw ourselves as one of the minnows of European rugby. We were finalists who had fallen short by a point. We also dis-covered that we'd become a prized scalp: every team would raise their game against us. They were so fired up, and a few caught us off guard in the first twenty minutes or so. But we believed in ourselves now as well, and it showed in our results.

The rivalry in the interpros was edgy: they were like Irish trials. The national team invariably reflects the dominant province at a given time. Ulster had been the main men in the '90s when I started playing, and Leinster had their spells. Gaillimh and Claw always said the interpros were the bread and butter. You wanted to be the best team in Ireland, and after winning six from six the previous season, we won five out of five going into the Heineken Cup.

The interest and support within Munster were at a different level, too. It seemed as if the rugby team had indeed taken over the whole province. The official attendance for the Newport game was 9,200. For the opener against Pontypridd the previous season it had been 6,500 and for the Neath game the year before, 1,500.

Newport was a home banker, but the following week in Castres, with Jeremy Davidson their captain and Gregor Townsend kicking everything, was a different story. They flew out of the blocks, scoring a pitch-length try off the first scrum, and we were 20–9 down at half-time.

But after the Saracens matches the previous season, no matter how deep the hole we were in, we now expected to dig ourselves out of it.

We prided ourselves on our fitness and work rate. Self-discipline ruled in pre-season and throughout the season. If any extra fitness work needed to be done, players drove it themselves. This gave us confidence to up the pace when necessary, against French sides especially. In the second half against Castres I was tapping penalties, we were taking quick line-outs, and we hurt them out wide. After a try by Dominic Crotty, we hit them with two late tries in a row. Hoggy scored off Rog's long, flat pass, and straight from the restart Wally made a big break out wide, and Dutchie and Crotty carried it on for Rog to score. We won it 32–29.

Next up were consecutive matches with Bath. We won comfortably at home, but I remember the defeat at the Rec a week later more clearly. The defeats generally do stand out more than the wins. It lashed rain. The Rec was a mudbath. So much for ideal Munster conditions! We were actually more of a good-weather team.

The away changing room at the Rec is ridiculously claustrophobic. Bring small rucksacks with just the bare essentials was the advice. We were on top of each other.

Maybe at the time we held English sides in higher regard than they deserved, even after beating Saracens twice the season before. I don't know if that was a factor, but they had a huge pack – Dan Lyle and Ben Clarke in the back row, Steve Borthwick in the second row – and we never established a foothold in the game.

In January, our penultimate pool game was on a cold, foggy Friday night in front of a packed Rodney Parade. Newport had Gary Teichmann, the Springboks captain for their record seventeen Test

wins in a row, and Shane Howarth at out-half. They also had the
Canadian prop Rod Snow, the Fijian lock Simon Raiwalui, Jason
Jones-Hughes, Matt Mostyn on the wing and good Welsh players
like Ian Gough.

The home crowd were not shy about expressing their opinion of
us. It was a pretty intimidating place. Darren Edwards, later one of
my coaches at Bath, was my opposite number. He remembers that
night vividly. He told me that Newport regarded Munster as their
prized scalp, more so than Bath or Castres. They led 21–10 at
half-time. But Mikey Mullins came off the bench, made a great break
and scored under the posts to put us in the lead.

Mikey could use his footwork, beat a guy, and also offload. Our
backline always needed that one game-breaker to get us over the gain
line; to help us play off quick ball. Back then, we were at our most
dangerous off unstructured play and quick ball. But if we were
dragged into a dogfight, we often struggled. Over our years of success, we always had someone in that role first played by Mikey:
Trevor Halstead, Rua Tipoki, Lifeimi Mafi, Jean de Villiers . . .

In the end we won 39–24, and Rog was our match-winner, landing seven place kicks and two drop goals, and scoring a try. We had
huge travelling support and, as with all our big wins on the road, by
the end you could hear only them. To this day, many of them remember that win in Newport as one of our stand-out away games.

The following week we beat Castres at Musgrave Park to secure a
home quarter-final – and because the quarter-finals were being played
before the Six Nations that year, we entertained Biarritz just eight
days later, on a cold, crisp January afternoon. They had a serious
team. Serge Betsen, Olivier Roumat and Philippe Bernat-Salles were
there. And so was Frano Botica, a former All Blacks out-half who
had become a legend in Rugby League before coming back to Union
late in his career. I'd been a big fan of Rugby League since I was fourteen or fifteen and I could not believe I was going to play against this
guy. He was thirty-seven then.

Although Biarritz outscored us by four tries to three, we won 38–
29, with Axel scoring all our tries. After the game Brian McGoey, a
scrum-half who had played alongside Axel with Shannon and who

managed Domino's Pizza in Limerick, announced that the scorer of three tries for Munster in a Heineken Cup match would be entitled to pizzas for life. As publicity stunts go it wasn't the worst, but I'd say he's probably regretting it to this day, knowing the quantity of pizza that Axel can eat.

Quinny was awarded Man of the Match; we reckoned this was because he had the same headgear as Axel. When Quinny came into the dressing room, Axel said to him: 'How the hell did you get it? They definitely thought you were me.'

But when he realized he'd won pizzas for life he didn't seem to mind too much!

Ireland started the 2001 Six Nations in Rome, winning 41–22. We led by just four points at half-time, but a hat-trick by Rob Henderson killed them off. That was the day Alessandro Troncon was red-carded for taking a swing at me.

It was funny. I'd always have craic with Gaillimh. I'd slag him, he'd slag me, and he was always up for a bit of fun, but he'd also say: 'Look, kid, as a pack we've got your back, do you know what I mean? Whatever happens we'll be fucking there, don't you worry. Have no fear of that.'

When I first came into the Munster side and then the Irish side, the core group of Munster forwards always protected Rog and me: Claw, Hayes, Gaillimh, Axel, Quinny, Halvey and Wally.

So, in the last five minutes of the Italy game, the ball shot out of a ruck and I was on the wrong side. Troncon was trying to get to the ball and I tugged his jersey as I came back to my side. He turned around, swung his arm and hit my jaw with the back of his closed fist. He gave me a fair old whack. The ref, Jonathan Kaplan, saw it and sent him off. I was down for a little while and could have carried on, but I was taken off as there were less than five minutes remaining. The physios and doctors walked me off with concerned expressions, but when I reached the dug-out, Gaillimh, Quinny and Axel, who had already been replaced, were in absolute hysterics.

I said: 'What are you fucking laughing at?'

Gaillimh said: 'For fuck's sake, kid, I know I told you that we'd look after you, but there's not much we can do when we are sitting in the dugout ourselves! If you're going to do something like that, do it while we're on the pitch.'

They were caught on camera, in stitches, and this was replayed regularly at the video analysis for the next couple of weeks. 'Glass jaw' and 'Rubber legs' were my nicknames for some time afterwards.

That night I was rooming with Hendo, who was having a cigarette – as he did. Two cleaning ladies knocked on the door to provide the turn-down service.

On seeing me, they exclaimed: '*Il bambino! Il bambino!*'

They had seen the game on television, and me being flattened by yer man. They were very concerned about me, asking me if I was OK, and hugging me. Another example of that motherly attention I have attracted due to my size.

A fortnight later we played France. We hadn't beaten them at home since 1983, but we'd taken confidence from the win in Paris the previous year. They had Philippe Carbonneau at scrum-half, a horrible fella to play against. He was a chunky little guy and a pain in the ass, to be honest; a typically dogged French scrum-half.

They had a better team than the one we'd beaten in Paris, but Rog kicked five penalties to make it 22–3 before they came back at us. The key moment was a try by Drico early in the second half. Rob Henderson made the initial break – Hendo was on fire that season – and Wally provided the link. Drico ran along the left touchline under the East Stand as Xavier Garbajosa came across and put in a good hit. Drico fended him off with his right hand and tried to ground the ball with his left. It went to the TMO. In a situation like that, a player ordinarily tries not to react negatively because he knows the camera is on him. But when a couple of lads asked Drico if he'd scored, he shook his head: 'No, I don't think so.' All the French players walked out from the in-goal area for a 22-metre restart. Drico looked as surprised as anyone that the try was given.

We were training on the Tuesday before the Welsh game when we got word that, because of the outbreak of foot-and-mouth disease, the game had been called off. No one had any idea when it would be rescheduled.

It was like being in school and being told that you suddenly had a half-day. There was a call for a night out in town, but before that Wally was stripped and dragged around the car park of the Glenview Hotel. Yep, just like being back in school. I drove Gaillimh's car into town and there was an almighty piss-up. It was one of the few times I've seen John Hayes drink.

As a designated driver, I took a few of the lads back from Copper Face Jack's to the Glenview. It was a big car! Willie Bennett, our physio, was in the boot, and we had to leave it slightly open to give him some air. There were at least four stops for one or two of the lads to catch some air, too.

The restrictions arising from the foot-and-mouth outbreak applied mainly to travel between Britain and Ireland, so all the other matches went ahead as scheduled, while our games against Wales, Scotland and England were rearranged for September and October.

As Munster's Heineken Cup semi-final away to Stade Français wasn't until 21 April, we all went back to our clubs. I played a few games for Shannon but hurt my ankle against Blackrock – one of the few times I've been injured in my career – and it was touch-and-go whether I'd be fit for the semi-final. I made it, just about, but didn't train much and played in some pain.

We'd signed Dion O'Cuinneagain, who had captained Ireland, on loan from Ulster as cover, and a few back-row injuries meant he was on the bench. As usual with Munster, the semi-final was in France, in Lille; and we played on a horrible, waterlogged pitch.

I remember a winding road towards the ground, a huge car park with marquees erected for the day, and again the travelling support sent shivers down your back. We were rusty – we hadn't played a competitive game in eleven weeks – so we were never going to throw the ball around. It was a back-to-basics, territory-based game.

My one abiding memory is of the John O'Neill try that was wrongly over-ruled. I remember it clearly. Wingers tend to creep up and I always keep an eye out for that space behind them. I put in one of those rolling kicks to the right-hand corner. Johnno was a madman at the best of times and would chase anything. No better man to get on the end of it and score what is regarded now as a perfectly legitimate try. Chris White was the referee, but the freeze frame shows that Steve Lander, the touch judge, had a clearer view and should have given it. That was the winning and losing of the game. That was playing in another Heineken Cup final, or not.

Walking around the pitch after the match, we were absolutely devastated. We'd lost the final by a point the previous year, so to miss out on another final due to a refereeing decision made it even more bitter. But despite the disappointment, the supporters stayed in the ground, and kept singing and chanting. There was a sense of something huge building within Munster now. Now, winning the Heineken Cup became the Holy Grail. We simply had to win it. It became a mission for us.

My season wasn't quite done. Those of us who didn't make the Lions had to pitch up in Bucharest for a one-off game against Romania on 2 June.

Every touring team has a local Union man as their appointed liaison officer. The Romanian liaison travelled with us and stayed with us, and told us stories of winters in Bucharest, where some families lived in the sewers, for the warmth of the underground pipes.

I'd never been to a place with such poverty but, of course, there was wealth too.

On our down day we opted for a visit to the palace, and our liaison officer told us of Ceausescu's fall; and of how helicopters arrived to take the dictator and his wife.

The function rooms in this palace at the top of a hill were, honestly, the size of rugby pitches. It made you wonder how much money Ceausescu had siphoned off for himself, while ruling a country and a city where so many of his people lived in abject poverty.

We beat Romania 37–3. It was played in the Dinamo Stadium, and the attendance was given as 1,900.

Ceausescu's palace was infinitely more memorable than the match.

9.   Second Best Again

On the Tuesday before our rearranged game away to Scotland, we congregated in the team room of the Glenview. Some of the lads were playing pool. Gatty came in, tapped me on the shoulder and called me aside.

He simply said: 'We're going to go with Guy.' Guy Easterby was six years older than me, but we'd made our international debuts around the same time. I was in shock, primarily because I didn't see it coming. And as I never asked, I never really understood the reasoning.

Munster's season had begun in mid-August, to make room for the three rescheduled Six Nations games, and I thought my form was good. Ireland had won two out of two the previous spring with me at scrum-half. But for injuries, the team was largely unchanged. Since breaking into the team I'd been an ever-present player except for that USA game. But all of a sudden, I wasn't picked.

Sitting on the bench was bitterly disappointing. It was also a disastrous game for us. Scotland were sharper from the first minute. Nothing went right. We couldn't hold on to the ball. We were 17–3 behind when I came on, and it went to 32–3 before Girvan Dempsey scored with the last play of the game.

That autumn involved an unfamiliar shuttling between province and country. Back at Munster, after beating Castres at home, we won away to Harlequins. Woody was playing for them, which added fuel to the occasion for Frankie and the rest of the pack. English grounds had been graveyards for us, but that was one of our best performances. We had laid down a marker.

Back to the Ireland camp, for the game away to Wales. No tap on the shoulder this time: my name was among the starting XV read out on the Tuesday morning by Brian O'Brien, who had taken over from Donal Lenihan. Eric Miller, Wally, Humphs and Kevin Maggs were

also recalled and, of course, Gaillimh. You can't keep a good man
down. He reckons he and Geordie Murphy are vying for the record
as Ireland's most-dropped player. But that means they're contenders
for the most recalls as well.

My name is inextricably linked with Rog's, for Munster and Ireland, but neither Gatty nor Eddie O'Sullivan was afraid to pick me
and Humphs together. Of my eighty-one Test starts, fifty-five were
with Rog, twenty-two were with Humphs, two with Ian Keatley
and one each with Paddy Wallace and Johnny Sexton.

I loved playing alongside Humphs. As with Rog, I could fire the
ball out in front of him, and I'd know he'd run on to it. Humphs was
quick and skilful, and he liked that attacking style of play, running to
the line, showing on the inside and going himself. He didn't like to sit
back in the pocket. He also had the ability to release the outside backs
with his passing game, and slot kicks under pressure.

I had great time for Humphs around the camp. Like me, he never
sought attention – he was quiet and relaxed, and comfortable staying
in the background. But he was always in good form and up for a
laugh and, like Rog, an intelligent fella to have around the squad; a
good talker on the training pitch and in matches.

A backlash was needed after our abysmal showing in Murrayfield,
and we won 36–6. It wasn't a great performance, but we took our
chances; Humphs kicked everything and Wales were as rusty as we'd
been in Edinburgh.

England arrived in Dublin a week later, seeking the Grand Slam.
They had been tearing up the record books, scoring twenty-eight
tries and 215 points in their previous four games, beating Wales 44–
15, Italy 80–23, Scotland 43–3 and France 48–19.

Even if we beat them, we had no chance of taking the title on
points difference. Anyway, on form there could be only one winner.
Thus it was perfectly set up: we were underdogs at home, playing to
deny England a Grand Slam. Wales had done the same in 1999 and
Scotland in 2000. It was up to us to make it a Celtic hat-trick. We also
had the advantage of having played two Six Nations matches already
that autumn, whereas England hadn't played in six months.

I'd already developed a niggly rivalry with the England scrum-half,

Matt Dawson. Never really chatted to him off the pitch or after games. I perceived him as arrogant. More generally, there was a feeling, with a few of the English players, that they always looked down on you. You'd hear them using derogatory terms like 'Paddy' on the pitch. That changed in later years – and recently I had a good chat with Matt – but back then, it gave us extra motivation.

Woody scored our first-half try off a line-out when charging round the tail to take Axel's pop ball. A nice bit of obstruction by Eric Miller on Richard Hill helped clear the path. That had been identified during the week as part of the move. Using Woody as a strike runner, and especially off the tail of the line-out, was one of our go-to plays.

My favourite memory of the day is my tap tackle on Dan Luger in the fifty-fifth minute. I've watched the video a few times and chatted to Woody about it. We were leading 14–9. They were on halfway and had held on to the ball for a number of phases. But Woody came out of the line and misread the pass to Luger, leaving a hole for Luger to run through. Luger set off, went around me easily and then beat Girvan. He had phenomenal pace and was crossing the 22 towards our try line. Drico reckons he was already thinking of his celebration, with the conversion to put them in front. But Girvan had slowed him down, allowing me to catch up a bit. I had only a split second. He was eating up the ground, and the longer I left it the less chance I had. I dived full length and hit his right foot with my right hand. Thankfully, he stumbled enough for Denis to arrive and complete the tackle. We recycled the ball and I cleared it to touch for a breather. The roar that followed was nearly as good as the final whistle. Rog came on to kick two penalties before a late Austin Healey try had us on the rack again at the end.

The win was bittersweet, because England were still champions. Their players looked suitably glum receiving the trophy. Did we let a Grand Slam slip in Murrayfield, a month earlier? Perhaps – but the England match might have unfolded differently if we'd been going for a Grand Slam as well. We played shit against Scotland, hadn't even played that well against Wales, so we could afford to come out firing. The crowd loved it, and so did we.

The following Friday we played in the Heineken Cup against Bridgend, in the Brewery Field. By now I'd learned that anything called a Field is unfit for rugby. Horrible pitch and a gloomy night, not helped by the floodlights.

Paul O'Connell was breaking into the team around that time. He had been a replacement in the wins over Castres and Quins, but my abiding memory of him is that last half-hour in Bridgend as a replacement. He'd just turned twenty-two and it was clear he was here to stay. You could sense the sheer emotion he brought to the game. He cleaned up in the line-out, got stuck in, was everywhere. Sometimes you just see a player and think: 'He's got it. He's going to be special.' We won 16–12, and Paulie started when we beat Bridgend at home the following week.

Back to Ireland again, for the November internationals. First up, we beat Samoa, who had Inga Tuigamala and Brian Lima in midfield. Hard to forget those two units! Lima would have a short stint with Munster, three seasons later. He was some hitter.

I'd been a fan of Tuigamala when he played Rugby League with Wigan. Seeing their team sheet, I knew that if they had a 10–12 switch, Tuigamala would be my man. Only about six stone between us! Before the game, I concentrated more than I normally do on warming up my shoulders.

From one of the early scrums, they did a 10–12 switch. I thought: 'Here he comes.' I went as low as possible. Anything higher than his ankles and I'd no hope of stopping him. I managed to be a bit of a speed bump!

We had the All Blacks six days later. In training on the Tuesday, I was running with the ball when Simon Easterby tackled me and his knee landed on my heel bone. In considerable pain I was sent to see Steve Eustace in the Mater Hospital for an MRI.

After the scan, Steve and the team doctor, Mick Griffin, held up the results and Mick said: 'You've cracked your heel bone.'

I said: 'What does that mean?'

They said it meant I was out of the All Blacks match, and I said: 'Yeah, sure, look, we'll see how it goes for the rest of the week.'

Steve said: 'No, you've cracked your heel bone.'

Mick was examining the scan as well. 'You can't play with that.'

I said: 'Look, I'm walking around now and it's not too bad. We'll see how it pans out.' I was trying to convince myself that I'd be fine. Wednesday was our day off, and I iced my foot constantly. But both the bruising and the pain were becoming worse. I sat out the Thursday and Friday training, and the coaches and medical team gave me until the Saturday morning of the game.

I did a fitness test with our physio, Ailbe McCormack. I'd say I slept for about two hours the night before, as I had a bucket of ice and a bath full of hot water for the hot-and-cold treatment. Before the fitness test I had my foot in a hot bath for about an hour. Ailbe drove the short distance to Lansdowne Road.

'Just go for a lap on the main pitch,' he said.

I remember thinking that my foot was absolutely fucked. I came out of the changing room, went left towards the north terrace end and thought to myself: 'There is no way I can do this lap.' I considered making the call at that point: 'I can't do it. It's too sore.'

But after about twenty metres Ailbe said: 'Just stretch there, actually. Take a quick stretch, before you jog any more.'

I reconsidered, and said to myself: 'No, I'm going for it.'

The day before, I had spoken with Claw, who told me he'd never played against New Zealand. That started me thinking: 'If I go through my career and don't get a chance to play against these guys, I'll be absolutely gutted. I need to play this game. I need to play this game.'

I managed to warm up again and somehow got through the fitness test. But as I walked back to the dressing room, again I considered admitting: 'Look, I can't play. It's too sore.'

Back at the Berkeley Court, Dr Mick Malloy came in to examine me. 'I've seen the scan results,' he said. 'You've a hairline crack going down the inside of your right foot.' He told me to hop on my heel bone. I think he really wanted to call it there and then, and rule me out. But for some reason, that hopping action didn't hurt. This seemed to be enough to convince Mick that the crack wasn't that bad.

I didn't have any injections or painkillers, and I was worried during the warm-up. But it's amazing what adrenalin can do. I didn't feel any pain in my foot, I was able to get to breakdowns as quickly as normal, and when I look back on the video I can't see any evidence that the injury hindered me in any way.

The atmosphere, even for the warm-up, was as good as anything I remember. Playing New Zealand is the ultimate one-off test. It was a dull, dark winter's day, but it was such an open game. We started quickly, and Humphs had a show-and-go to break their line, shaped to pass wide and instead put Maggsy under the posts. The place went wild, and we kept going for it. The pace of the game was relentless.

They had a big, strong, physical pack and we wanted to keep the ball away from their forwards. And their backs too, come to think of it; especially Jonah Lomu. We played with huge width, so the half-backs had to pass long to shift the ball to Drico, Denis and Shaggy in the wider channels as quickly as possible.

There was one key moment when we surprised them with a quick tap inside our own 22 and we kicked downfield. Lomu fumbled, Denis tackled him, we recycled the ball and Axel would have scored off my pass but for some 'lazy running' by Norm Maxwell.

We conceded a try just before half-time. I was defending next to a ruck on our goal line, but when a guy like Chris Jack, who's 6' 7", reaches out over me there's little I can do. It was a soft score, but we still led 16–7 at half-time, and a try by Denis early in the second put us 21–7 ahead. That jolted them into life, though. Andrew Mehrtens, Tana Umaga and the rest of them decided it was time to play. In the next thirty minutes they scored five tries and thirty-three points. Humphs had kicked a second drop goal but, despite another try by Eric, we lost 40–29.

It was an incredible game to play and must have been a cracking one to watch. We had thrown everything at them, but they wore us out in the second half. Richie McCaw was named Man of the Match on his international debut. He made steals before some of our guys even hit the ground. He received a standing ovation at the post-match dinner when presented with his first cap. It's fair to say his career has stood the test of time.

When I woke up next morning in the hotel and went into town to grab a coffee and some lunch, I realized I couldn't walk. I couldn't put any pressure on the heel at all. I had to return to the hotel for a set of crutches.

Twelve days later, Gatty was sacked and replaced by his assistant coach, Eddie O'Sullivan. I was shocked, to be honest. Results hadn't been that bad. In fact, they'd been good: eleven wins, a draw and five defeats in the seventeen matches since a bunch of us broke into the team. We'd beaten Scotland for the first time since 1988. We'd beaten France for the first time in Paris since 1972 and for the first time in Dublin since 1983. We'd beaten England. And then, on the back of a hell of a performance against New Zealand, the coach was sacked. It seemed strange.

There'd been criticism of Gatty in the media, and apparently there was friction between him and Eddie, but if some players were in the know, I wasn't one of them. When you're a new kid on the block you keep your head down.

I got on well with Gatty, although at the start I found him quite difficult to approach, and maybe he found me the same. That Christmas he sent me a letter, admitting that initially he hadn't understood the hype about me, and that only when he started working with me did he realize what I could bring to a team and what I had as a player. Reading that letter was very touching because he wasn't a guy that I spent a pile of time with. I didn't have that connection with him. Everyone is different. Some are more able than others to express their feelings. His way was to write it in a letter to me. That meant a lot.

Life moves on. Rugby is a business. I got on well with Eddie, too.

Chatting with him in pre-season or at a function was one thing. In a match week he became a different character. The pressure showed. He wasn't very approachable in a match week, even around the hotel. There was pre-season Eddie, and there was Six Nations Eddie, but I liked Eddie as a coach.

He always came up with different game plans. Eddie was the only coach I've come across who would completely change the way you'd play, based on the opposition. For example, against Wales, who were slow getting around the corner, we would set a midfield target with forwards coming around the corner, or forward runners off me. When we beat England at Twickenham in 2004, we played a completely restructured, wide-wide game. He was also good at introducing new moves, and I enjoyed that.

The Munster squad assembled under the stand in the team room at Thomond Park in November 2001, twelve days after the All Blacks match. Declan Kidney and Niall O'Donovan stood in front of us, said they'd had an offer to join the Irish coaching staff under Eddie O'Sullivan, and that they were accepting it. They were to continue with Munster until the end of the season, but they'd be joining up with Ireland for the Six Nations, and moving full-time to the Ireland set-up after the end of the season.

I remember feeling disappointed, because things had been going well at Munster. We had the sense that we all were at the start of a journey, and we didn't want anything to change.

Because of my cracked heel bone, I missed the quarter-final in the first season of the Celtic League; somehow I played in the semi-final win over Ulster at Lansdowne Road, then I missed the final there against Leinster. That was a hard one to watch from the stands. Not far away from the touchline, one of their backroom staff came on to the pitch with water and nudged Donncha O'Callaghan. That sparked a scuffle and the simmering tension remained.

Leinster's support caught even Leinster by surprise, so much so that extra turnstiles were opened to admit the late rush. The attendance was given as a nice round 30,000. Munster had won four and drawn one of the previous five meetings, and Leinster were pretty fired up. Eric Miller was sent off for kicking Axel on the ground and we led 12–6 at half-time through tries by Axel and John O'Neill. But they swung from the hip and scored tries by Gordon D'Arcy and Shane Horgan, and they deserved to win. The rivalry had gone up a notch, and watching from the stands didn't make the taste of defeat any less bitter.

I also missed the last two Heineken Cup group matches. The defeat away to Castres condemned us to a quarter-final in Paris against Stade Français, two weeks later.

We had a mini-camp in the Inchydoney Hotel in Clonakilty, and I convinced myself that my heel was fine. I've always done that with injuries. Over the years I probably could have done with a couple of small operations, especially on my shoulder, but I always felt that with some rehab and hard work it would be fine; forget the pain, get through it and it will heal itself.

The Stade Jean-Bouin was a strange old ground for a club with the profile of Stade Français. On a bitterly cold day, a wind down the centre of the pitch made it feel like the Sportsground in Galway.

No one gave us a chance that day. They'd roared through their group, we'd qualified as one of the best runners-up, and they'd beaten us in the semi-finals the year before. But Axel, Hendo and Hoggy all had big games, and our pack bullied them. Hoggy scored a great try down the middle, but in the second half we had to defend a 16–3 half-time lead into the wind with our lives.

Paulie had a massive game, or an 'unreal game', as he would say himself.

He has always been humble, and in those days he was quieter than he is now. In his post-match interview, as Man of the Match, everything was 'unreal'. It was the only word in his vocabulary.

'Strings was unreal.'

'Hendo was unreal.'

'The lads were unreal.'

'The game was unreal.'

The following Monday I played the video in the team room. Paulie hadn't seen it. I still have it on my phone and I sometimes send it on to him, just to remind him where he came from.

But you can see his passion in that post-match interview. It was as if being involved in the Munster set-up had been his life-long dream, and he wasn't going to let go. He was that ambitious and driven from the start. The way he trained, the way he applied himself, his enthusiasm from minute one of his first training session – nothing was ever going to stop him. That was his attitude. Even though he was young and new to the scene, he quickly became one of the characters within the squad who set an example, and others followed. To see such an incredible player and incredibly good guy develop over the years, physically and mentally, to become such a leader, was phenomenal. A very special player, and man.

A week later, he made his debut for Ireland.

That first Six Nations game was at home to Wales, who were awful for the first hour or so. They had a couple of injuries early on and anything they tried to do they messed up. After a scrappy start, we played well. Paulie, on his debut, scored a try in the corner under the East Stand in front of the south terracing. I've a great photo of him after he scored. He'd burrowed his way through two or three guys, got up and fist-pumped the air. The picture captures the emotion in his face. Paulie was, and remains, someone who becomes very emotional on these occasions.

He was concussed soon after. We had a line-out call and Paulie stepped out of the line. I repeated the call, but when I looked at him I knew it wasn't registering. We walked towards each other. He was tapping his head and I repeated the call to him, but he clearly couldn't absorb it. I looked to the sideline and shepherded him to the medical staff, who'd been keeping an eye on him. He walked off, clearly in trouble.

Keith Gleeson also made his debut that day, off the bench, and he also scored, after a brilliant piece of individual skill from Drico. First he grubbered through, then kicked it on left-footed, then kneed it on, gathered and, when tackled, scooped the ball back left-handed to a queue of four Irish players. I think it might have been Keith's first touch. Gift-wrapped with ribbons on top.

In most games, it's hard to notice how others play because you are so involved in your own job. But, doing our video analysis of that game, I was taken aback by John Hayes' workload: scrummaging, lifting, carrying ball, hitting rucks, tackling. That was one day when I realized how unbelievably good John Hayes was around the field and what he did for that Irish team.

Along with Declan and Niall O'Donovan, Mike Ford came in as our first defence coach. This was a completely new concept. Fordy came from a Rugby League background, where defence is key and players 'number up'. He brought a structure, and an understanding of individual roles, firstly off set-piece and, more importantly, for our roles in and around the tackle area and at the breakdown.

The first guy in the defensive line next to the ruck was 'pillar'; next was 'A', then 'B' and so on. The pillars on either side of the ruck would each raise a hand and shout his position, so that teammates knew. 'A' was responsible for the scrum-half, 'B' for the first receiver and so on across the defensive line. All of this was new to us. Previously, there had been no structure to the way we set up the defensive line at a ruck, which meant that no one could be held accountable if a gap appeared.

Now, there was a whole structure of defensive accountability. In our post-match analysis, each player got a 'missed tackle report' and an 'impact tackle report'. Next to your name were also 'system errors' – if you didn't fill your pillar as quickly as you should, or if you filled the wrong side.

The campaign swung between good and bad, with little in between. At Twickenham, two weeks after the Wales win, we leaked six tries and were thrashed 45–11. We chased shadows for eighty minutes; were never in it, never had the ball. They seemed to score at will. Jonny Wilkinson converted all six: left corner, right corner. That was my first game against England in Twickenham, and it was the same kind of hiding I'd watched from the stands as a replacement, a week before my debut two years earlier.

A fortnight on we beat Scotland 43–22, another scoreline almost identical to two years before. The Scots began with huge intensity, piling guys into rucks, and led 9–3. But we liked that type of high-tempo game, and during that campaign and over the years, we always backed ourselves in the last ten or fifteen minutes of the first half. We scored three tries before half-time. First Drico steamed on to a Humphs cut-out pass, then he put Shaggy over, before picking up a loose Scottish pass on the run for a length-of-the-pitch try. They had to chase the game, throwing it around from everywhere, and we capitalized.

Off wide, flat passes from me and Rog, Drico beat their first centre, Andrew Henderson, to complete his hat-trick. A simple 9-10, with

Maggsy drifting outside Drico. You wouldn't really see a set-piece try like that nowadays. We played to our backline, the basic principle being to get the ball into Drico's hands as quickly as was humanly possible.

Rags, John Kelly, came in for his debut at home to Italy, Shaggy moving to centre. We beat Italy 32–17 and Rags scored two tries. I'd played with him since our UCC days, and he was one of the most consistent players Munster ever had, in defence and attack. His work rate was huge. He was so fit, had a turn of pace, could play inside centre, outside centre or wing, and was intelligent, on and off the pitch. It was great to see him finally getting some recognition.

Their prop, Salvatore Perugini, was sin-binned for having a go at me. The Italians clearly liked me! I was a bit niggly at the ruck, grabbing hold of a fella's scrum cap on the ground, and Perugini pushed his head at me. Rob Dixon, a referee I could not stand over the years, yellow-carded him. Scottish referees in general have been appalling. I don't remember a good one, to be honest, and he definitely was the worst of the pile. He hadn't a clue about the game.

A fortnight later we were back in Paris, trying to deny France a Grand Slam. We didn't. They won 44–5. Another horrendous day. They played a real wide-wide game and everything clicked for them. Early on, they moved us wide from one touchline to the other and our entire team seemed to migrate towards the far breakdown, like something out of an Under-10s match. A bit of a system error there! My positioning, as usual, was behind the ruck, a sweeping defender. I looked across and it seemed we had about four defending against ten. Two or three long passes later, they sauntered in.

Lining up for another kick-off, as the sun shines on a sunny April day in Paris, when the band strikes up and France are completing a Grand Slam, is not easy. You want to think of it as 0–0 and restart with a fresh mood, but in the back of your mind you think, 'Shit, we're thirty points down,' or whatever. Of all the places to be behind, Paris is as bad as it gets when Les Bleus are confident and playing with flair. You want that final whistle to come. As much as you want to keep competing, sometimes you know the game is up. Which can make the endgame an eternity.

When you come off the pitch after a loss like that, you come into the changing room, get dressed and on to the bus to the hotel; you want the Monday morning to come around rapidly.

I'm one of those players who will go through every fine detail if I'm allowed to stew on it; analysing it; over-analysing it. 'What went wrong? What could I/we have done differently?' It can completely consume you. The quicker I can look to the following Saturday the better. 'Who are we playing?' Concentrate on that game. Your preparations.

Luckily, we had some big games coming up with Munster.

After warming up with a 6-all thriller against Leinster, three weeks later we were back in France, in Béziers, for the Heineken Cup semi-final. And the opposition were our old friends from Castres, for our fifth clash in two seasons. There was bad blood between us by now.

Paris had been Claw's last Test, and during the week of the semi-final we heard about an accident on his 'ranch'. He'd put some petrol on a fire, which burned his hand. It sounded more serious than it actually was, and although it was a worry for all of us and he didn't train that week, he turned up on match day.

Claw was a product of the Cookies, Young Munster, and of the amateur era, and he never really changed too much, least of all in the way he trained. He just carried that through from his Cookie days. He was so relaxed. He'd have his cigarettes in the changing room after a game. I don't think I ever saw him in the gym doing fitness work. Yet he always got around the pitch and always showed up for me. He'd want the ball and he'd always carry hard, and was actually pretty skilful. For one of Geordie's tries against Wales, as he was being tackled Claw flicked the ball for Geordie to score under the posts. He had nice little touches.

When I first saw him play, I thought he couldn't move; he looked like a potato on matchsticks. In fact, he was pretty quick. A barrel of a man with a huge heart.

Claw dominated the build-up to that semi, and the aftermath. It was such a roasting hot day that our changing room had iced baths for us to use before or after the warm-up. Rags scored our try, Rog kicked seven from seven and we won 25–17. Job done.

Claw was yellow-carded after an incident with their back-rower Ismaila Lassissi, which left Claw with bite marks on his arm. A disciplinary hearing followed, with Lassissi claiming Claw said something racist. The charge was thrown out. Claw's last game would be the final against Leicester, the reigning champions.

To fill in the four-week gap, a fortnight before the final Ulster granted Munster a warm-up game in Ravenhill. They kicked us around the pitch and, had the shoe been on the other foot, we'd have done the same.

Cardiff is made for big match days. The Millennium Stadium is the heartbeat of the city. Supporters arrive early and fill all the surrounding streets. It's the stadium you want to play in, and there's no better atmosphere when the roof is closed.

Had we not come back to do it again in 2006, with that same bus journey but with a different outcome, when there was even more Munster support, that day in 2002 would have remained so painful for ever more. As much as it pains me to say it, Leicester were the better team on the day. Geordie Murphy, who was on fire for Leicester and whose skills fitted into that team perfectly, scored their first try and Austin Healey the second. Martin Johnson destroyed our line-out. We became more threatening when Mikey Mullins was brought on for the final thirteen minutes. Declan had started Dutchie Holland and Rob Henderson in midfield. They're both very good players, but they're both inside centres. With the way Leicester defended, we needed to move the ball around a little more. Had Mikey started outside one of the others, it would have given our attack more variety.

With two minutes to go, trailing 15–9, we had a scrum under their posts. As I was about to feed the scrum, as I've always done, their flanker Neil Back scooped the ball out of my hands to their side of the scrum and Healey cleared it to touch.

Back then, touch judges weren't miked up to referees, and the referee, Joel Jutge, was on the other side of the scrum. Nowadays, an opposing flanker probably wouldn't risk it, or if he did, it would be a yellow card and a penalty to us, with the option of another scrum against fourteen men.

I turned to the touch judge, but play went on. Whether the touch judge saw it or not, I don't know. He could have raised his flag, but he didn't. I waved my hands in the air. I pleaded with Joel Jutge, but he didn't seem to look across at his touch judge. I followed him to the touchline, but he wasn't for listening.

'I don't see it.'

'Rubbish,' was all I could say.

'Please, I don't see,' he repeated.

It had never happened to me before. Subsequently someone tried it once more, I can't remember when, but I've held on to the ball that bit tighter ever since!

The Hand of Back became a huge deal. It had cost us a chance to win the game.

But looking back on it now, who's to say we would have scored a try, not having done so for the previous seventy-eight minutes? We hadn't created enough during the game. We had plenty of possession but we couldn't break them down. They defended well and took their chances.

Neil Back has since said that it's made me a better player, and the only bad thing that came out of it from his point of view was that he had to polish two Heineken Cup winners' medals instead of one. I have never met him or spoken to him, but I received a letter from him a few seasons later. It was very blasé. He was putting together a few pieces for his biography and wanted me to make a contribution: 'I would love to get your thoughts on your experiences in the Heineken Cup final in 2002 when we played against you in Cardiff and would appreciate it if you would get in touch with me.'

I thought: 'Is this guy for real?' The letter made no reference to the incident. He certainly wasn't remotely apologetic about it, and isn't to this day. His attitude, and plenty of others would agree, is that players try things in rucks, scrums, line-outs or whatever; some succeed and some don't. Anyway, I never replied to the letter. So there's no contribution from me in Neil Back's autobiography.

Losing that final was all the worse for it being a last game for Claw, and Gaillimh's last as captain. Claw went quietly, slipping out by the tradesman's exit, which is how he would have wanted it. No fuss. In his own way I think he was shy. He didn't like the attention on him. But the endgame wouldn't have been how he wanted it.

We had now lost two Heineken Cup finals in agonizing fashion in the space of three seasons. Who knows what might have gone differently, in later seasons, if we'd won it in 2000 or 2002? Maybe we wouldn't have had that same obsessive drive. As champions, I'm sure our mindset would have been different. Instead, we remained, to a degree, the underdog, and we always thrived on that.

We landed in Shannon Airport that night and, like two years before, even though the plane was late landing at 2 or 3 a.m., a huge crowd was waiting patiently to welcome us back. We could hear the singing as we gathered our bags from the carousel. When we came through on to the balcony at Arrivals, we could see thousands of supporters, cheering and chanting, then breaking into 'The Fields of Athenry'.

They were still with us, but we had failed them. Again. I thought: 'We don't deserve this.' Feeling you've let people down – be it family, friends or supporters – is horrible. But then the way they stuck by us was also a motivation, to win this bloody Cup for them as well as ourselves.

Dunedin. Freezing, wet, dark Dunedin. One of the problems with facing the All Blacks in New Zealand in June is that you leave the nice end-of-season Heineken Cup weather for the depths of their winter. Darkness closes in by teatime, and you don't see much of the country. It's been the same every time I've been there.

My wife, Debbie, travelled around New Zealand in her year off, in their summertime, and she has told me it's the most beautiful country she's ever visited. She'd go back and live there in a heartbeat. But rugby is a winter sport, and it was certainly a winter's night for that first Test in Carisbrook, aka the House of Pain. The Irish living in New Zealand and Australia turned up in force. We spent plenty of the first quarter in their 22, but we only had a drop goal by Drico to show for it. Andrew Mehrtens levelled and then set up Jonah Lomu for a try before half-time.

Our only chance came at the start of the second half. Drico kicked cross-field to Geordie, who caught it beside the corner flag but couldn't quite ground it for the try.

The score stayed at 10–6 until Leon McDonald scored a try, three minutes from time. Lomu latched on to a kick by Justin Marshall and beat a couple of guys. I grabbed an ankle. It wasn't much of him but it was something. Watching it in video analysis, the commentators said Lomu had lost his footing and fallen over. They didn't give me any credit whatsoever for the tackle. I got some slagging over that!

The first Test of our tour is also usually their first Test of the year – our best chance, realistically, to win in New Zealand. It gets tougher thereafter, and the 40–8 scoreline tells the story of the second Test at Eden Park. New Zealand had a game under their belts and were a completely different outfit. They ran us ragged. We struggled to get hold of the ball, much less keep it.

I played the full eighty minutes, which was surprising, given the scoreline. Everybody in our changing room was down in the dumps, but Guy Easterby had his head in his hands, and was really upset. He'd also sat on the bench for eighty minutes in the first Test, and against New Zealand the previous November in Dublin. He never did get to play a minute against the All Blacks.

It must have been crushing for him, particularly as we were well and truly beaten. I know that if I'd been in that position, I'd be looking at the coach, waiting for him to give me the nod. The game was gone. There was nothing to lose.

But there was also nothing I could say. Along with the coaches, I was probably the last person he wanted to chat to.

Our flights out and back were through Los Angeles, so about fifteen of us hopped off in LA and stayed in Venice Beach for a week. We had a few nights out, and went to Hollywood and Sunset Boulevard. We needed it.

10.   A Miracle and a Mauling

Picture the scene: typical back-to-school weather, a beautiful sunny week, training in the University of Limerick as preparation for a Test match in the first week of September. And one of the smallest players ever to play international rugby would be jumping in the line-out.

As punishment for failing to reach the World Cup quarter-finals in 1999, Ireland had to play qualifiers, away to Russia and at home to Georgia, in order to secure our place in the 2003 tournament. To warm up for those games, we played Romania in Thomond Park, and during training the coaches devised a defensive line-out with me being lifted at '2'. Although it worked out quite well, I thought it was a joke. The key was keeping my feet together. A lot of guys, when being lifted for the first time, bend their legs and lose their balance. For some reason, I was able to stay dead straight and the lads could lift me from the ankles. Every inch counted!

I still didn't think it would be an option come game time. But beside the east terracing, just inside their half, Romania had a line-out and the defensive set-up was called. I was to step in at '2'.

Opposing me was their second-row, Cristian Petre – 6' 5" and eighteen and a half stone, against little oul me, 5' 7" and 11st 4lb. Their hooker threw in the ball, I was hoisted up side by side with Petre. He only just beat me to it. Really. As he caught the ball, I grabbed him around the neck in a headlock to bring us both crashing to the ground. Penalty to Romania. The move was never repeated.

We won 39–8 and set off to Siberia for the Russia match. It was a hell of a trip: first flying to Moscow, then another five-hour flight and finally a long transfer to Krasnoyarsk by coach. We'd been prepared for the worst in Krasnoyarsk. The IRFU's logistics man, Martin Murphy, had returned from a reconnaissance mission, warning us: 'There is no running water. The beds are tiny. The food is awful. The phones don't work. It's freezing cold. The place is danger-ous.' Basically, we'd been prepared for absolute hell on earth.

Perhaps it was a deliberate ploy. In reality, the hotel was basic, but fine: the water ran, the beds were big, the food was OK, the phones – or some of them, anyway – worked, the weather was sunny and warm, and the people were very friendly.

Martin is a lovely lad, very popular with the players, but for years – right up to when I was last involved in 2011 – whenever he boarded a team bus or was among the squad, we'd serenade him to the 'Winter Wonderland' tune that football fans often use.

> There's only one Martin Murphy,
> One Martin Murphy,
> Walking along,
> Getting it wrong,
> Walking in the Murphy wonderland.

He must have been driven demented by that chant for a decade. Even-tually he left the IRFU to become Stadium Director at the Aviva Stadium. I'd say that song might have had something to do with it.

As for the ground, there was a big stand on one side, and nothing much on the other sides. The pitch looked like the surface of the moon – clumps of grass here, holes there. We won 35–3, and the long haul back didn't do Woody's neck problem any favours. Shane Byrne was hooker in our win over Georgia at Lansdowne Road. We'd qualified for the World Cup.

By this stage most of the Munster internationals had played only one game under our new head coach, Alan Gaffney, an Aussie who had been backs coach under Matt Williams at Leinster. Alan's assistant was Brian Hickey, who I knew well from UCC. Alan was a highly intelligent coach who understood backs play inside out. Coming from New South Wales, where the coaching was very cutting-edge, he was incredibly detailed and introduced the kind of technical moves we'd never done before. You could see he clearly had a sharp rugby brain. Although he was a bit older than the coaches we'd previously had, he was easy to talk to and I got on very well with him.

The only negative vibe we heard about him was when we

internationals were on Irish duty and Alan had to prepare for matches without us. The other lads said it was like a different regime: that the same mistakes were not treated similarly. They didn't enjoy the set-up when we weren't around.

He was probably more suited to being an assistant coach, or a backs coach, than he was to being the top man. I don't think he dealt that well with the pressure. I felt sorry for him in some respects. When he first arrived at Munster, he was very placid and generally in great form, but over the months and the ensuing three years he become more uptight and quite cranky at times. But he was good for our back play, definitely, and quick ball from the 9-10 channel for those moves out wide fitted his vision.

A week after the World Cup qualifiers, Munster beat Neath away in the Celtic League, but then Gloucester thrashed us 35–16 at Kingsholm in our first Heineken Cup pool match. They were unbeaten and riding high in the Premiership, and led 35–9 into injury time. I scored a late try by diving over a ruck close to the posts, managing to ground the ball as Andy Gomarsall tackled me. At the time, that try seemed no more than a consolation, but as events transpired it turned out to be fairly significant.

We had a tough pool, and a week later our European campaign was already on the line. Lose to a good Perpignan side and we were gone. It was a tight game, but we pulled through 30–21 at Musgrave Park. At home, no matter who the opponents, we knew we could win. For me anyway, Musgrave Park was as much of a fortress as Thomond Park, even if the capacity was 5,000 less. It still generated a good atmosphere and the pitch was better. On a dry day, it's as good as you'd find anywhere. The same couldn't be said of Thomond then, although it is much improved nowadays.

A week later, against Caerphilly, I picked up the first of what I think have been only three yellow cards in my career. It was probably for stamping. When I look back on videos, what was acceptable back then is gone from the game now. As a scrum-half, if there were any hands slowing down that ball, or any leg lying on it, you had licence to use your studs. I've seen video clips of me back then, shoeing players, and it looks reckless. But the forwards were doing it as well. It was the norm. The game was more frantic then: get the ball back as quickly as possible. Look back on old clips of an All Blacks pack rucking over the ball, and it's like a stampede. Anyone on the wrong side of the ball was fair game. And they knew it, too.

The laws gradually changed to take raking out of the game, and at first it was hard to adjust. I had to think twice. But my mindset has completely changed. It's the same with foul play and discipline in general. There are more camera angles, and stricter disciplinary procedures. If you do anything on the pitch now, it will be seen and scrutinized, and if you're on the wrong side of the law there'll be a ban.

Australia, then the world champions, were first up in our November tests – Drico's first as captain. Even at the age of twenty-three, he was the man for the job. When he spoke at training or in the dressing room, players respected him. He had an intuitive understanding of the game. He was the figurehead of Irish rugby and our best player. He was a natural for it. Besides, there were plenty of other leaders in the squad to share responsibilities.

Ireland hadn't beaten one of the southern hemisphere big three since the series win in Australia in 1979, in twenty-five attempts, and eleven of those attempts had been against Australia.

I can never recall worse conditions in Lansdowne Road: a downpour on a soggy pitch, and already dark for the 2.30 p.m. kick-off. It was like one of those days after school, throwing yourself about in the mud and the rain, sliding around the place and wanting to get up and do it again. It was great fun.

Not Australian weather, and not a day for running the ball. Off turnovers, I put in little over-the-shoulder kicks which rolled on into space. Rog kicked brilliantly, six out of six penalties, and once we were ahead we tackled everything that moved and limited the penalties. In those conditions, attacking ball is slower. A defending team has more time to fill the pitch and push up in a line.

We won 18–9. Not the prettiest but, at the time, it was a major scalp.

A week later we beat Fiji 64–17 but, with Argentina six days away, Rog and I remained on the bench for the eighty minutes.

The following Saturday was a typical arm wrestle with the Pumas. A little like the Italians, you bank on them having a little ill-discipline. Then you acquire a lead and make it difficult for them to force things. If Argentina gain a lead, they're masters at strangling you and keeping the scoreboard ticking with penalties and drop goals. But chasing a game, and being creative, didn't suit them. We got our noses in front and won 16–7.

I played against Argentina five times, and Agustin Pichot was their scrum-half four of those times. He was quite niggly and temperamental: if you touched him, he completely over-reacted. A bit like the Italians, the Argentinians seemed to become particularly annoyed with someone so small showing any aggression. Once, when I tackled Pichot and we ran to the next ruck, he gave me a smack on the head and shouted something at me. I was thinking: 'I just tackled you. It's part of the game.'

The only time I ever spoke with him was five years later, after I'd been dropped for the final pool game in the 2007 World Cup in Parc des Princes. I came on to the pitch at the end from the stands. He was in his playing gear, I was in my suit. He came up to me and the first thing he said was: 'Eddie O'Sullivan. Stupid.' He could not understand why I hadn't been playing. He kept saying: 'Eddie O'Sullivan. Stupid.' We had a bit of a chat, and he seemed an OK guy.

I have more of Pichot's jerseys than most. We had swapped after the game in 2000 in Buenos Aires and again after this 2002 game. Sometimes your opposite number didn't want to swap; he'd promised it to another player, to family or a friend, or simply wanted to keep it.

Sometimes I looked to swap on the pitch, or in one of the changing rooms. On other occasions our masseur, Willie Bennett, would gather a few jerseys to take to the opposition changing room, and return with a few of theirs. For most games you'd get a starting jersey embroidered with your opponents' name and the date, and at half-time another one would be hanging up with just your number on the back. I've signed and given away lots of the latter to charities, kids and friends, whereas I've swapped more of the former with my opposite number. I still have the jersey from my debut, framed, at home, as well as Bryan Redpath's, thanks to Woody. He gave me his to swap with Bryan.

Back at Munster, we had a new captain. Jim Williams had joined at the start of that season and was immediately made skipper. The whole squad and supporters took to him right away because of the gent that he is. Gentleman Jim, or 'Seamus', as one of the fans nick-named him when he played for Cork Con one day. Like Langford, he came from the Brumbies, and he brought the same sort of profession-alism, and a fresh energy to the set-up. Playing at number 8, Jim was unbelievable over the ball at the breakdown – impossible to move. He had a huge, barrel-like chest, and the skinniest calves and ankles in the world, like a ballet dancer's. This gave him strength and footwork when he carried. He was one of the best signings Munster ever made. You wanted to play for him. He's someone I try to stay in touch with.

We moved on from back-to-back December wins over Viadana to a memorable League semi-final against Ulster.

That was one of the best Thomond Park nights. Playing against Ulster always got us and the crowd going. There'd been an edge to the rivalry, going back to Ulster's dominance in the '90s and the AIL club rivalry as well. There was an early bust-up when their prop, Justin Fitzpatrick, punched Frankie Sheahan; Donncha O'Callaghan arrived to help, but Justin kept punching. Donners and Frankie were yellow-carded and Justin was red-carded.

Everything clicked against their fourteen men. We scored some nice tries. Hayes scored one in the corner, going through two defend-ers, from about five metres out. The way the ball stuck to his hand was like Inspector Gadget with his arm extended. I made a fifty-metre break to set up a try by Rags – which I've had to watch over and over again, just to be sure! We won 42–10.

A week later we were at the sharp end of a 23–8 beating in Perpi-gnan. We were down, and seemingly out of the Heineken Cup. For the first time in four years, we began to wonder if we had slipped off the pace in Europe. The prospect of not making the knock-out stages was devastating.

Merely beating Gloucester would be hard enough, but in order to progress we needed to win by four tries and twenty-seven points, or by five tries. No one was talking about that. In fact, we weren't aware of the precise maths. As far as the players were concerned, we needed a four-try margin – and that seemed unlikely enough. I don't think anybody was actually aware that we'd need a five-try margin if the points differential was less than twenty-seven.

At the start of the week, Monday training was flat, and Tuesday's began the same way, until the coaches pulled us in. Some of the Gloucester players, it seemed, had been saying how much they were looking forward to visiting Thomond Park. Axel was one of those who'd heard these comments on TV the previous Sunday. We needed something to provoke us, and this was it.

Gloucester had reason to be confident. They were runaway leaders of the Premiership, losing just two of their first fourteen matches, and would end the season fifteen points clear. They were also top of our group.

Maybe Axel or the coaches jazzed up Gloucester's comments a little, but in those training huddles, that became the focus: Gloucester were expecting to be the first team to beat us in Thomond Park. Our mindset became: 'Who do they think they are, this English team coming to Thomond Park and with that attitude – expecting to win? Nobody has that right, coming here. They've got to earn it.'

And on the day, they didn't earn it. I think they expected to win from the moment their plane landed at Shannon Airport on the Friday.

Looking back at clips of the game over the years, I believe the key to achieving the miracle, as it came to be known, was not setting a miracle as our pre-match target. We never panicked. We never felt we had to do things straight away. We built scoreboard pressure.

We identified their full-back Henry Paul, who had come from Rugby League, as not the most experienced, or bravest, under the high ball. To see him running around aimlessly under Rog's first up-and-under put doubts in their minds and led to the first three points, and from then on the crowd roared every time we targeted Paul again.

We had two tries by half-time. Off a scrum with a big blind side, their number 6 was a little slow off the mark and I looked at the shoulders of their left-winger, Thinus Delport, to see if he would come in on me or stay out on Rags. He did neither, and Rags went in by the corner. In first-half injury time, Dutchie Holland grubbered through for Mossie Lawlor to score, leaving us 16–6 up at the break.

Mossie – who has only recently retired from playing with UL Bohs – never let us down. He was really skilful, he could play across the backline, had a great work ethic, and was very passionate about rugby; every day he arrived for training he was colour coordinated and pristine. His mum even ironed his socks!

In the second half we were unrelenting: running hard, clearing out, mauling, scrummaging, running hard again, clearing out again. We never let up, and the crowd never shut up.

It's said, and I say it, that every team will have their purple match, but they never had one. When they had the ball, we hunted them down. We smothered them. We suffocated them.

We kicked a few penalties to touch, before Rog opted to make it 19–6. Dutchie created our third try with a cross-kick to Mick O'Driscoll. Dutchie had no pace, but creatively he was as good as I've played alongside. He passed off both hands and had vision. Being a former out-half, he broke the mould of our 12s, who were usually more direct, and those two kicks that day were typical of his skill set. Rog's conversion, from near the right touchline, would end up being fairly important too.

Going into the final quarter, we thought we just needed one more try. Of course, we had to leave it until the eightieth minute. From a penalty on halfway, Joel Jutge informed us we had 'thirty seconds and maybe two minutes'. Rog found touch and the call was to set up a maul in the middle of the pitch with Dutchie turning and Mikey joining him.

The move was called 'back pitch' because Deccie had come up with it on the back pitch in Cork Con the previous season. It was a bizarre move and we usually didn't get it right, even in training. The centre has to run to the gain line, stop before contact, turn and not be brought to ground before the other players arrive.

This one was perfectly set up, though, and the pack drove it towards the posts. The ball scooted out. Jeremy Staunton nearly scored. It scooted out again, I passed to Rog and he gave it to Rags, who scored, thankfully, not too far from the posts. We had our four-try margin. Leading by twenty-five points, I didn't know it now hinged on the conversion.

As Rog was taking the kick, I looked over to the east terrace on our right. A single red flare had been set off. Rog kicked the conversion, from fifteen metres in, and off the restart I passed for him to kick it into touch. At the final whistle Rags went mental and the crowd invaded the pitch like something out of the '50s or '60s.

Some fans were randomly going crazy on their own. Others were hoisting us up on their shoulders. Donners and Jim Williams were jumping up and down like madmen.

It's one of my best experiences ever on a rugby pitch. It's for days like that that you play the game. The fifteen who started had been relentless for eighty minutes, and were still standing after eighty minutes. No replacements were used. That will probably never happen again.

It was old-school. It wasn't about a structured defence, or a structured attack, but about no one wanting to let the next guy down. We assembled in the main stand to sing 'The Fields' with the crowd. An unforgettable day.

We had a week off to recover, before playing Neath in the Celtic League final at the Millennium Stadium. I was yellow-carded, again for stamping. I ran into a ruck from about fifteen metres away without breaking stride, and put my boot into the back of Shane Williams, who had fallen over on the wrong side. James Storey, a centre who would subsequently join us briefly, reacted by giving me a slap, and he was yellow-carded also. I definitely deserved mine. It was a mistake made in the heat of the moment.

We won 37–17. We had a trophy. Not the trophy we wanted, but a trophy nonetheless, which was important after losing three finals in the previous three seasons.

The Millennium felt half empty rather than half full, and by the time we did our lap of honour the Neath supporters were already filling Cardiff's bars or were on the road home. It might have felt more meaningful if the stadium had been full.

Yet, on many levels that final helped us. It was part of the team's progression. Baby steps.

We began the 2003 Six Nations by breaking another hoodoo – beating Scotland in Murrayfield for the first time since 1985. They had plenty of the game but we scored three tries, Humphs contributed twenty-six points and Drico tormented them again. We followed that up with another win in Rome, where I burrowed over for the first try from about a metre. My third Test try. They all count.

A new format, squeezing the Six Nations into seven weeks, meant those away games were back-to-back. A fortnight later, France came to Dublin. It was one of those blustery days which made the old Lansdowne Road particularly difficult to play in.

Humphs, who was winning his fiftieth cap, dealt with the wind way better than his opposite number, François Gelez. They kicked four penalties each, but Gelez had more misses.

The only other score came in the first minute. Off the first scrum, Drico and Geordie Murphy stood directly behind me and then ran infield to the left, but Dimitri Yachvili slapped my arm as I passed. The ball landed on the ground to Geordie's right, but he picked it up and kicked a drop goal in one movement. Nearly everything he did that season, Geordie did with class.

We were becoming more and more confident in Fordy's defensive system. Kevin Maggs and Drico were hugely important to this. I had great time for Maggsy. You could always depend on him, in attack and defence. He was the definition of a battering ram. If you were ever in any trouble, Maggsy would say: 'Give me the ball. I'll take it up.' He didn't want the half-backs carrying into contact. He'd put his hand up, tuck the ball under his arm, head down, and run, no matter what was in front of him. In defence, he flew into contact just as fearlessly. No regard for his head or body. Maggsy was a dedicated, committed player on the pitch. Off it, he was always relaxed, up for some fun – a good-humoured guy who kept teammates smiling.

Humphs put us 12–3 up by half-time, but they came back to 15–12, and after Humphs hit the post they broke out as only they can. When Vincent Clerc chipped ahead, I had to turn as the last man, run back, slide on to the ball, gather it on the bounce and get buried. Luckily, Maggsy then won the ball back. I always liked Maggsy.

At the end, I hoofed the ball into the West Stand – with my left foot. I've rarely been so relieved.

There'd already been plenty of talk outside the camp, not in it, of the Grand Slam; now it went overboard. That's not good for the Irish psyche. Perhaps it affected us. England were three wins from three. We were three wins from three. In the meantime, we had to play Wales, who were three defeats from three. Ireland hadn't lost in Cardiff for twenty years. The Welsh were meant to be a speed bump. But two weeks later we really rode our luck.

I've never known such a manic endgame. We led 22–21 when the eighty minutes were up. Two minutes into injury time, Stephen Jones kicked a drop goal. Surely, now, the Slam was gone. But then Mal O'Kelly chased down Rog's restart, I passed to Rog, who'd just come on for Humphs, and his drop goal on the run cleared the crossbar. We hadn't constructed it. It was just off the cuff. The Slam was on again!

But Wales won a line-out, and Jones went for another drop goal. It skewed wide. Wales won another line-out and, six minutes into injury time, Jones lined up a drop goal from the 22, straight in front of the posts. But Denis Hickie charged it down!

This time I think I did find row Z with my left foot.

The shoot-out for the Slam with England was now a hot ticket. There was always the opportunity for players to sell their allocation of tickets on, and in that week you could have made a killing. But getting my family to the game was my priority.

That was the day when the English lined up on the wrong side of the red carpet for the anthems and the greeting by the president. Personally, I never had any huge issue with Martin Johnson and his team not budging. What amazed me was that an English set-up that prided itself on its professionalism and organization apparently hadn't read the protocol.

Our game plan played into England's hands. They read us like a book. They quickly identified that we were playing a wide-wide game and filled the pitch very well.

We found ourselves quite isolated at the breakdown, an area where they were very strong. We probably should have mixed it up a bit, taking it on around the corner, using the forwards and bringing them into the game.

The final score, 42–6, looks like a hammering, yet it was only 13–6 until well into the second half. The more errors we made, the more they lapped it up. They were the world champions in waiting. A really solid team, full of good players who'd been together for several years.

We'd been building nicely too, but that match was a wake-up call. It showed that we needed to be more adaptable, that when Plan A wasn't working, we needed a Plan B.

Two weeks later, Munster went to Leicester for a Heineken Cup quarter-final. Not only had we the memory of a fortnight before, but also of the Hand of Back from the previous May. Leicester were also back-to-back European champions.

With Munster, we always had more of a direct game than Ireland played in those years, using our pack to get over the gain line. We thrived on out-working the opposition. I remember speaking to David Humphreys in Irish camp that year about this, that it was the key to Munster. In the changing room before a game, I would approach each of our front-five forwards individually. 'Work rate. Work rate. The work rate of our front five will win us this game.' Once our front five out-worked their opposite numbers, we knew we'd win the game.

Humphs agreed one hundred per cent. Games were won by those front-five players. And no other Irish province had a tight five that could match ours. We'd had quite a turnover: Marcus Horan for Claw, Frankie for Woody, Donncha for John Langford and Paulie for Gaillimh, with Mick O'Driscoll there as well. And Hayes was the rock.

Leicester hadn't lost at home in Europe for four years but, believing in our tight five, we had the mentality for that game. My try sealed the win, and the key was a stable scrum in the middle of the pitch. As soon as that scrum went down and I fed the ball, Frankie's strike went straight to Axel's feet. The scrum didn't wobble. My pass to Rog couldn't have been better. He came on to it and hit a tackle side-on, and popped to Hendo. The timing was perfect. Hendo shimmied to take the tackle on the outside and offloaded to Mikey. He stepped, fended Geordie Murphy and popped inside to Quinny, who rode a tackle and freed his hands. Hoggy and I were waiting for the offload, and he was not getting in front of me. The in-goal area was quite small. In order to make the conversion a bit easier, I had to break and turn sharply right to dot it down. In that moment we knew we'd won. I don't normally show emotion when I score, but I kinda slapped their centre, Freddie Tuilagi, on the back after I touched down. When I watch the video I ask myself: 'What was I thinking?' I then jumped into Paulie's arms.

I'll never forget how the Red Army invaded Welford Road. When Rog kicked the ball dead behind the Leicester posts, it looked like the away end in a football match – pure red. Munster supporters in England had wangled tickets by signing up to the Leicester supporters' club. And the red was visible on all four sides. The pitch invasion was like the Gloucester game again, but this was Welford Road.

I well remember my dad telling me of a Leicester supporter coming over to him on the pitch after the match and, on shaking his hand, said: 'Are you Peter Stringer's father?'

On being told he was, the supporter said: 'Justice has been done today.'

I've no idea who lifted me up off the ground in the mayhem, but I was hand in hand with Gaillimh, as if body-surfing a concert crowd. It was mayhem. After the previous season's final, beating them convincingly on their patch was one of *the* best days.

The reward was another away semi-final against a French club. Jammed to its 36,000 capacity, the Toulouse football stadium rocked like, well, a football stadium. Munster fans travelled in huge numbers again, and Toulouse have great support. There wasn't a neutral in the ground.

There's nothing wrong in losing by a point away to Toulouse, but we'd led for virtually the whole game. Rog kicked two drop goals and two penalties to put us 12–6 up for most of the second half, before they upped it in the last ten minutes.

Freddy Michalak worked a switch with Xavier Garbajosa, who I somehow managed to tackle. He spilled the ball over the line. I thought then that we might have done enough. But five minutes from time Michalak, who had moved from scrum-half to out-half, scored on the short side, and Jean-Baptiste Elissalde converted.

Even then we had time to win it. Rog had two drop-goal attempts. The first was from halfway, if central, and it had the legs but drifted left.

With a minute to go, we drove a line-out up to their 10-metre line. The maul became a little disjointed and so I grabbed the ball and passed to Rog. This time his drop goal went right and wide.

After the game, in the changing room and on the bus to the airport, I kept replaying it. I kept thinking I should have let the maul drive further. I was happy with the rest of the game, but I blame myself for the defeat because of that decision in those last seconds, I gave it to Rog too early. We could have gone on for maybe another five yards. That could have made the difference.

To be honest, it still kills me.

At the end of every season, the whole squad meets up for a couple of sessions. The Cork guys go to Limerick for a day, and then the Limerick guys come to Cork. Apparently drink numbs the pain, so I always struggle with those days and nights. The entire squad meet up at two or three in the afternoon, and become happier with each pint. Donners, who also doesn't drink, found it difficult as well, and we gravitated towards each other. He also had a tendency to over-analyse his game. Chatting about it helped.

You don't want to be isolated from everybody else, so instead of joining the others in the afternoon, we might pop in at around eight or nine. It was the right thing to do, to show my face, to celebrate what we'd been through: the Miracle Match, winning at Welford Road and winning the Celtic League. But I couldn't forget that I was partly to blame for the defeat in Toulouse. I preferred to be at home, although, looking back, that probably magnified my dark mood.

It was a long four weeks to the end-of-season Test against Australia in Perth. We trained in the Manuka Oval, where the Irish schools had beaten Australia in 1996, but it wasn't a good omen. The result – we were thrashed 45–16 – and my performance didn't lift that mood. I was bitterly disappointed with how I'd played. George Gregan handed off my rather weak tackle to score under the posts.

In one sense, it was good to be excused from the Tonga and Samoa games. With fourteen others, I was in good company. But everyone else who went there said it was an unforgettable experience: hopping on the back of trucks to go training under a baking sun; open-air hotels on the beautiful South Pacific islands. And those Tests could have been another two caps!

11.   No Plan B

In the summer of 2003, prepping for the World Cup, we spent a week at the Olympic Sports Centre in Spala, Poland.

At least it was just one week. Gatty had taken us there for three weeks in the 2001 pre-season – the longest three weeks of my life. Management had cut it back to two weeks in 2002.

Even the one week wasn't much fun. Spala is in the middle of nowhere and we were on the complex the whole time. Up at seven in the morning; not finishing until seven in the evening. Training was the only thing to do. The rooms were warm, with tiny, camp-like beds. The only TV channel was Eurosport – in German. There was no internet at the time, so no computers or iPads to divert us. The only escapes were Kracow and Warsaw, on the two Saturday nights; both were about an hour and a half away. For an afternoon off in 2001, a visit to Auschwitz was optional. Most went, but it was such a harrowing experience that it worsened moods even without the three-hour bus journey.

An average day at Spala began with monitoring. A weigh-in, then a CMJ (counter-movement jump) on a square-metre pad, connected to a hand-held device that measured the height of your jump. Three jumps tested the fatigue in your legs, and this information would be used to tailor a player's schedule for the day.

After breakfast, players were divided into groups which took turns at various types of training: one group would start with weights, others with skills or speed work on the pitch. Each session would last forty-five minutes to an hour, before the first blast of cryotherapy.

The idea behind cryotherapy is that it improves your inflammatory response after training, which speeds up your recovery. I did notice a difference physically: you could get twice as much work done as in a day at home. The effects of cryotherapy may have been as much psychological as physical, but you bought into it. Before entering the chamber, you'd put on a headband, gloves, a paper facial mask, woolly socks, shorts and wooden clogs. You'd queue up, have your name taken and your blood pressure checked. Then, in groups of five, you'd enter the first of two chambers, where it was a chilly -60°C. You'd stay there for thirty seconds before going through an internal door to an even colder chamber, where it was -130°C, for two or three minutes.

A third room awaited, at normal temperature, with rowing machines, bikes and a stretching area. After ten to fifteen minutes of light cardio work and stretching to raise the heart rate and blood flow, we'd have lunch in the cafeteria.

The food was very basic. In years to come, we'd bring our own chefs to hotels, but in Spala we ate what we were served. There was a strawberry-coloured soup which no one tried. Everything else looked the same: whether it was pork, chicken or fish, it was all covered in breadcrumbs. But, given the amount of training we were doing, we had to tuck in.

A siesta was recommended before the afternoon session. The bed-rooms were tiny, warm and alive with mosquitoes. But you needed that sleep for recovery and for what lay ahead. After skills work, we had a full rugby session, finished off with 30–45 minutes of condi-tioning games – fitness-type matches. With such a heavy emphasis on gym and speed work, having a ball in your hands was the highlight of the day.

Then came the day's second cryotherapy session, followed by din-ner at around 6 p.m. Some chill-out time would normally follow, but Spala wasn't conducive to that. The downside of going to bed early was that the sooner you woke up, the sooner the routine would start again. Some evenings we'd sit around and chat, but often guys were too wrecked. By 8.00 or 8.30 p.m., you'd be virtually ready for sleep, with the alarm set for 7 a.m. Up and at it again.

You were there for one reason, and one reason only. Yet, in a strange way, I enjoyed it. It was our job. Tough as it was, you could throw yourself completely into training and your physical condition-ing. There were certainly few distractions. If you could survive Spala, you were probably stronger mentally as well.

We shared the complex with an array of mostly European athletes from different sports. I became friendly with Wilson Kipketer, a Kenyan-born 800-metre world record holder who ran for Denmark. He was there for a number of weeks with just his coach, which must have been quite intense.

After the 2003 trip to Spala, we beat Wales at Lansdowne Road in our first World Cup warm-up match, in mid-August. A week later a few of us, including Rog and me, were rested, and we watched the win over Italy in Thomond Park from the terraces at the Ballynanty end of the ground, for some reason. Humphs was playing and I think it was Frankie who tried to get the crowd chanting Humphs' name.

The subsequent win over Scotland in Murrayfield was over-shadowed by the broken leg Geordie suffered, a day before the World Cup squad was announced.

I remember being very close to Geordie when it happened, just outside our 22. It was horrendous. Whoever tackled him went low, and Geordie's leg bent in a way that wasn't natural. Although in extreme pain, he was also clearly in shock, because he didn't show any emotion. The medics gave him oxygen as players were dragged away.

For such a good footballer in his prime, that was cruel. It was also a blow for the team, to lose a match winner of his calibre. Geordie was at the top of his game then. He would have loved the top-of-the-ground pitches in Australia and I've no doubt he would have been one of the stars of the World Cup.

When the squad was announced, David Wallace's omission was the big shock. Wally was also my regular room-mate, but on that trip I roomed mainly with John Kelly, whose company I also very much enjoyed.

That World Cup in Australia was probably the most enjoyable rugby tour I've known. For the initial two weeks, we were based in Terrigal, on the coast, just north of Sydney, as our opening pool game was in nearby Gosford. Terrigal is a lovely beach town, very chilled out. We trained well and, as our hotel faced on to the beach, our recovery sessions were in the sea. That fortnight in Terrigal was the perfect start.

We got a comfortable enough win against Romania, 45–17, with five tries and a bonus point. Eight days later we played Namibia in Stadium Australia. Torrential rain all day, and during the game, but the pitch held up well, and we scored ten tries in winning 64–17.

Then we moved on to Adelaide to play Argentina. A repeat of Lens, with the same stakes – at least for the Pumas. Two teams from the group would qualify for the quarter-finals, and Argentina had lost to Australia in their opening match: if they lost to us, they were out. If we lost, we'd have to beat the defending champions on their own patch if we were to progress. If we beat Argentina, we were guaranteed a quarter-final.

There wasn't much to do in Adelaide, the City of Churches, and the Oval was like a step back in time. You could picture the cricketers in their white flannels. A charming, old-world ground in the shadow of St Peter's Cathedral, which was beside the cricket scoreboard on the hill.

There wasn't too much charm about the match.

This was our third meeting with Argentina since Lens – all of them tough, close and physical. They complained about having their four pool matches scheduled in a sixteen-day period, whereas ours were all at least a week apart. More fuel to the rivalry.

It was a strange old game. Very error-strewn. As taut as a guitar string. They were a complete nuisance, as usual, especially at the breakdown. They defended as if their lives depended on it. Their props, Mauricio Reggiardo and Martin Scelzo, were later cited and suspended for eye-gouging.

They also had more ball, and more of the game. We struggled to play through phases. Quinny scored the game's only try. Woody was defending at the back of a line-out and they overthrew to him. He chipped through, re-gathered, dummied, pirouetted – a great bit of skill – and offloaded to Quinny, who took Ignacio Corleto's tackle but, in reaching out for the line, dislocated his shoulder. I was behind him, roaring for an offload. I remember seeing the pain on his face. Everyone wanted to congratulate him, but he was grimacing and clutching his arm. To lose Quinny at that stage of the competition was devastating. In the changing room afterwards, he was in so much pain and was visibly upset. A scan would confirm a dislocation, but he already knew his World Cup was over. He'd have known from the moment he scored. There was no consoling him. In situations like that you don't want to crowd a guy too much. Quinny can become quite emotional.

He took one for his country that day, and wasn't able to play again for another seven months. In years to come he could make a joke of it, repeatedly saying he was 'the saviour of Irish rugby'.

Humphs kicked us 10–3 ahead, but they chipped away and took the lead before Rog put us 16–12 in front. Rog also played the corners and gave our game more width. We'd been crashing Maggsy up the middle, but Rog settled things down, played it in their half, and brought Drico into the game. Even so, they came back to within a point and we were grateful to see Drico tackle Corleto into touch at the end.

The atmosphere had been electric. The capacity was only 30,000 but it was like a home match, and we were in the quarter-finals.

We met Australia in the Telstra Dome a week later, with the prize a quarter-final against Scotland in Sydney. The losers would get France in Melbourne.

The game kicked off at 8.35 p.m., which meant you woke up about twelve hours before kick-off – not ideal. It was another wet day, but the Telstra Dome roof was closed.

The buzz in Melbourne was special. The Melbourne Cup and the Compromise Rules football series between Australia and Ireland were scheduled for that week as well. The Irish invaded from everywhere in their thousands.

We were based in the Crowne Plaza, and our team room was on the lower ground floor. We had to take one of the escalators up to the main lobby. We emerged from our team meeting to see hundreds of fans gathered in the reception area.

Picture the scene.

Only one of the four escalators was working. The other three were lined with Irish supporters, as was the balcony overlooking the lobby area. All wore green, waving scarves and flags, while singing 'The

Fields of Athenry' and 'Olé olé olé'. Our escalator moved very slowly. It sent shivers down my spine. I've been part of Irish squads who've been given some memorable hotel send-offs, but nothing quite like that. Hundreds more were also outside to roar us on to the team bus.

Come kick-off, the support was 50/50. For an away match, I've never heard noise like it.

Against Argentina we won a game we maybe should have lost. Against Australia, we lost a game we maybe should have won. We had more possession but again lacked that cutting edge. Injury struck once more when Denis Hickie snapped his Achilles tendon. He didn't play again for a year. I remember him telling me after the game that it felt as if someone had hit him from behind, so much so that he actually looked around. Apparently, that's what it's like when you snap your Achilles. Like you've been shot in the back of the leg.

We were 14–6 down with half an hour to go when Drico finished brilliantly. The ball shot out of a ruck and I hit Rags with a high pass, but he managed to offload to Drico for a one-handed dot-down in the corner. Rog converted from the touchline. A one-point game.

We threw the ball around. Eddie gave us licence to use our backline and we had a back row who were really good in the loose. But the Wallabies defended very cleverly. They looked like they were coming up quite hard, but then would turn their shoulders out and push you towards the touchline, which happened on a few occasions.

Five minutes to go. Off line-out ball, Drico threw a skip pass to Shaggy. Against Australia it always looks as if you have space in those outside channels. Whenever we played Australia, we'd have video analysis watching other teams attack them. Our coaches would pause the videos and say: 'Look, this is where the space is, out wide in those channels.' The thing was, when you played it on, two or three seconds later, they'd shepherded opponents towards the touchline where suddenly there was no space. You might get a couple of yards over the gain line, but you'd run out of pitch. They'd create a false impression that there was space out wide – just to lure you into their trap.

Come into the parlour, said the spider to the fly.

That's what happened with that late play: Shaggy was tackled into touch. We wouldn't get another chance.

This probably contributed to us playing such a narrow game in the quarter-final against France.

Melbourne remained a home from home for another week. The place was buzzing. We went to the Crown Casino most evenings, to play a little roulette, or have a bit of craic. One night I got asked for ID at the door. Frankie Sheahan wasn't in the match-day squad and he had a night out with a few others, which inevitably ended with a trip to the casino. The stories at breakfast the next morning were of how he'd won Aus$9,600 playing poker. In fact he'd won Aus$96,000; but he was keeping that quiet. A royal straight flush – the jackpot.

Despite the loss, we were still in the quarter-finals. We'd have preferred to play Scotland, for sure, but we were confident in the way we were playing and how we'd prepared that week.

Same hotel, same send-off, same trip, same ground. It could not have been set up any better. I was buzzing.

There were some empty seats in the Telstra Dome – there were way fewer French than there had been Aussies. But there were as many Irish as for the Australia game, if not more.

The French blew us away in the first forty minutes. At 27–0, at half-time, it was game over and World Cup over.

We'd studied France, and noted that they were very narrow in their defence. Instead of going wide straight away, we settled on a game plan whereby we'd begin by attacking narrowly. Say we had a line-out, we'd crash Maggsy up the middle, and return to where the line-out had been, and then hit our first receiver; then back the other way. It was zig-zag. We'd do that for maybe four phases; then we would unleash our backs, in the hope that we'd round them easily.

As it transpired, after we'd hit up the middle, then come back the other side, and back to the middle, when it was time to go wide we had no backs left. We had used them to recycle rucks.

In training, it had been nice and easy. A match situation is different. We didn't just play between the two 15-metre lines; we were even narrower than that. It just didn't work, but we kept doing it. We didn't identify the problem on the pitch. We had no Plan B.

They didn't have to work too hard for their points. They scored off a line-out when it looked like they were going in one direction, and then Michalak cross-kicked back to where the line-out had taken place. Imanol Harinordoquy and a few other forwards were waiting, for Olivier Magne to score. Then we conceded a turnover and gifted them a try as they ran the length of the pitch to score.

And, as always happens with French teams, give them a lead and their confidence soars.

Eddie often changed the way we played, based on our opposition. We probably focused too much on them, and should have backed ourselves and the game that suited us. We weren't used to this way of playing, nor were we comfortable with it. Only in the last thirty minutes or so, at 37–0 down and with nothing to lose, did guys' natural instincts come into play. We threw the ball around and scored three tries, but by then the French knew they were in the semi-finals.

It was Woody's last ever game. I remember him in tears in the huddle and walking around the pitch. His standards had been so consistently high and he'd had an unbelievable game against Argentina. He'd been everywhere, like another back-rower. For a man who had given so much to his country, to finish in such a disappointing way was heartbreaking for us and for him.

I was one of many who opted to stay in Manly for a week. There were pockets of us all around Sydney. You could easily escape the remainder of the World Cup in Australia. The last thing I wanted was a plane home, to face everyone and deal with the disappointment.

The game against Australia was the one that got away. We'd have played Scotland in the quarter-finals in Sydney. And who knows what might have happened, had we reached the semi-finals?

After that week's break we were back on the horse with Munster, back with familiar faces and a positive environment. While it was difficult to rediscover our continuity, we beat Cardiff at home in the league, and we ground out a tough win away to Bourgoin in our first Heineken Cup match.

We backed that up with a 51–0 win at home to Treviso, and then beat Connacht 3–0 in Dubarry Park on a Friday night. A cracker. We were a long, long way from Australia now. I'll never forget one moment inside our 22 into the wind. Marcus was the first receiver

and I hit him. Rather than carrying the ball, like any forward ordinarily would, Marcus opted to kick. The ball was blown back over his
head and the dead-ball line.

Due to the World Cup, we had four Heineken Cup games in a row
in January. Again, another defeat away to Gloucester, by 22–11, was
avenged with a bonus point win at home, by 35–14, a week later. It
was probably as good a performance, but could never compare to the
Miracle Match.

Marcus scored two of our four tries – one from a tap and go. He
had served a long apprenticeship behind Claw and he epitomized our
tight five's hunger for work. He also brought a different dimension to
our game, looking to take quick taps, throw dummies and score tries.
He was quick, had a swerve and skills. He had the instincts of a back
and the body of a prop. He had a feistiness as well – the last one to back
away from a row. That's what you want from a Munster front-rower.

He was one of my best friends. Like Donners, I played with him at
Under-21s. Like Quinny, he had trouble keeping himself under control but, also like Quinny, to be at his best he had to play on the edge.

Marcus is also very intelligent, especially for a front-rower!

We had two more bonus-point wins, away to Treviso and at home
to Bourgoin. I scored one of our four tries against Bourgoin. Not
much to do; just saw an opportunity to dive over a few Bourgoin
bodies lying on the ground from the previous ruck.

We'd earned a home quarter-final against Stade Français. Something to look forward to in April as we returned to Irish camp for the
Six Nations.

Our opening game was against France again, in Paris. We made sure
we started well this time. We had plenty of territory and possession
but we failed to trouble them or the scoreboard. Then, as is often the
case with France, they turned on the style when they needed to and
pulled clear early in the second half.

At home to Wales a week later was almost the exact reverse. Shane
Byrne scored a couple of tries, as did Drico. For one of them, Drico
had about three guys on him, but he wriggled and squirmed over the
line, placing the ball down over his head. Only he could have scored it.

Darce had played in Drico's absence in Paris, and now he played alongside him for the first time ever. Darce's arrival also meant a real change in our style of play, putting much more width on our game. That stretched defences, which gave Darce and Drico more space to attack. They certainly carved Wales up that day.

Like Drico, Darce isn't overly big or tall for a centre, but he's one of those players whom you hated to tackle, in games or in training. You think you've tackled him, but he just keeps on going. He could break through a ridiculous number of tackles. He resembled Wally in that regard, with his leg strength. Darce had some real pace as well. He doesn't look particularly quick but, like Drico, he is such a balanced runner and he could pass while running at top speed. Great feet too, and his ability to get us over the gain line was crucial over the next few years, as was his partnership with Drico. Each seemed to know instinctively where to find the other.

That Wales win set us up for Twickenham. England were world champions. They'd destroyed us the previous year in the Grand Slam decider in Dublin. It was their Twickenham homecoming; they hadn't lost at home since 1999.

We were complete underdogs, going into their backyard with nothing to lose. Perfect for the Irish psyche.

Eddie also devised a wide-wide game plan specifically for England. The day before the game we had our captain's run at the not-so-glamorous venue of Roslyn Park FC. There were quite a few of the general public around watching as we began our warm-up. We formed a huddle in the middle of the pitch and Eddie decided that we'd better not give any clue to our intended plan for the following day. So we practised a fifteen-man pick-and-go style of play, in an attempt to throw off any English spies.

The actual game plan worked perfectly. Off set-piece we went wide to the far touchline, with the three front-rowers working to the middle of the pitch and the back-rowers staying on the edge where the line-out took place. The second-rowers roamed between the edge and the midfield. If Rog needed to go to scrum-half, I'd fill in as out-half. This gave us the option of either hitting up with the front-rowers in the middle, or going behind them to the back-rowers on the touchline.

We'd identified that England had quite a big pack and defended quite narrowly, so we wanted to move them around. Credit to Eddie, his game plan worked on the day, particularly for Girvan's try. I've watched it so many times. Off a maul, we stretched them the full width of the pitch and Darce made a great break from outside our 22. When Darce was tackled, he offloaded to me and I went down the short side and brought T-Bone, Tyrone Howe, in on the switch.

We went wide right off the ruck, with Shaggy, Mal and Axel carrying into their 22. Joe Worsely, on his way back from our side, tripped me. All you see on film is me sliding along the ground, and the commentator saying I'd lost my footing on the greasy surface. I complained to the referee – briefly – before then remembering the ball was still in play. I passed to Darce, he skip-passed two forwards to Drico, who did the same with a long pass to T-Bone on the edge, and Girv slid in by the corner flag. Just as we'd practised – wide-wide – and the accuracy of passing, skill and clearing out couldn't have been any better had we done it in training. It won try of the season. The whole team contributed.

We celebrated as if we'd won more than a game. We were so proud to be on that pitch. To beat England at Twickenham is very special. 'Headquarters', as they call it. You're also conscious of the many Irish living in England and how much those victories mean to them. It gives them twelve months of bragging rights wherever they live or work. From the post-match function, where you'd meet friends and family, to everywhere else, you'd hear this all night from expats: 'You've no idea what it means to us to be able to go in to work for the next twelve months having this victory behind us.' We'd hear it in the team hotel, in the Hilton in Park Lane, at the post-match dinner and in the bars around Mayfair. That night Irish jerseys were worn with pride everywhere, including some of my old school friends working in London.

Woody was in the residents' bar of the Hilton, where the Hothouse Flowers led a sing-song into the early hours of the morning. Knowing Woody and his contacts, he probably arranged it. It was one of those nights we didn't want to end.

It also set us up for a Triple Crown shot against Scotland at home on the final weekend. First we had Italy at home the week before. The wind was horrendous and played havoc with my passing: I'd pass to Rog and see the wind take it completely off course. That was also the day their hooker, Carlo Festucia, took a quick throw on his own line, straight to Mal. I've never seen a try like it.

I grew up in an era when the Triple Crown was a big deal. I'd watched Michael Kiernan's drop goal clinch Ireland's last Triple Crown in 1985, when I was seven. Winning a Triple Crown was important to our group, who had won some big games but no silver-ware. Although a trophy wouldn't come into existence until 2006, this was still silverware in our eyes.

We were more nervous against Scotland than for any other game that season, but we also had confidence in that wide-wide game plan. As is usually the case against the Scots, the ruck was an absolute night-mare. I rarely got clean ball. They'd pile guys in and grab me, or kick the ball through. But we capitalized on back plays off set-pieces.

We identified Dan Parks, who was making his debut, as a weak defender; their centre Andrew Henderson might be protective of him and defend tightly. We'd practised a back-row move to tie in their scrum-half, and then use Shaggy as first receiver to run at Parks – which tied in Henderson. That gave us a complete backline bar Shaggy to attack their outside centre, wing and full-back; I passed to Rog, he skip-passed to Drico, who missed Girvan to hit Geordie. We scored in the corner. Straight off the playbook and almost impos-sible to defend.

After half-time they drew level, before we scored three converted tries in the last twenty-five minutes. Wally was back for his first game since before the World Cup. Attacking the south terrace end, he was the only possible receiver, so I popped him the ball.

From a standing start, one of their players went low, the next went high, and he brushed both off. A third tried to tackle him, and he brushed him off too. A fourth was attempting a tackle as he went over. In other words, typical Wally.

The next try was probably my most important in an Irish jersey. Attacking the south terrace again, from a scrum under their posts, I hit Drico, who did a switch with Girv. After two pick-and-goes by

Marcus and Hayes, the ball was perfectly presented for me. I picked and managed to sneak in under Scott Murray and their winger. I dotted the ball down and, while still on my knees, flung the ball in the air in celebration. I'd scored in front of that little schoolboy section near the old Wanderers pavilion where I'd watched Ireland so many times with my mates from Pres. It was a great feeling.

Darce sealed it with his second try. For large periods of the game, the crowd were singing and there'd been a real sense that the day would end with a Triple Crown for the first time in nearly twenty years.

I was taken off with a few minutes left. Along with the other six who had been replaced, we could watch the end and soak in the occasion. Humphs kicked the ball off the pitch, and we began our lap of honour to U2's 'Beautiful Day'. The noise and the atmosphere were pretty special. It's rare enough that you actually get to walk around the ground having won a title, and rarer still at Lansdowne Road.

Winning something gives a team belief that it can win again.

That night in Dublin is a little blurry in the memory, even for a non-drinker.

The Paekekariki Express, Christian Cullen, had joined Munster that season. He was the most talented rugby player I'd ever seen. Seven years before, I'd watched him score three tries on his New Zealand debut against Samoa, and four a week later against Scotland, including one from his own goal line.

He was the most well-balanced runner I ever saw. Even at full pace, he had the ability to change direction without breaking stride. Most of the time he didn't look to be going at full pace, but he was just so quick. Unfortunately, he arrived at Munster with a shoulder injury from his farewell game with Wellington. Still, it was unbelievable to have him as a teammate. When I first met him I half thought I should ask for his autograph.

Christian is quite shy, but once you get to know him, as with a lot of New Zealanders, he's a super fella to hang around with, as well as train and play alongside. At the time he was such a superstar and I think he felt, for his own head space, that he had to get out of New

Zealand. It had been just so intense for him, and he didn't enjoy the media attention.

When he was fit and well, he gave us another cutting edge, which we needed when beating Stade Français 37–32 in the Heineken Cup quarter-finals. That earned us a fifth semi-final in a row, and the first at home. Although Lansdowne Road wasn't actually our home, it looked, sounded and felt like a different ground against Wasps – like an enlarged Thomond Park. For internationals there, the crowd don't wear much green, but no matter where you looked that day there was red everywhere.

We threw it away.

Rog went off early, but we were still ten points up with ten minutes to play. We should have held out and won. I'll never forget those final ten minutes, and their match-winning try by Trevor Leota.

I firmly believe that it wasn't a try. John Kelly and I tackled him and I tried to rip the ball from him. To this day I am certain that I dislodged the ball and he lost control of it before he grounded it. The TMO disagreed.

What a bitter way to lose. Again we felt like we'd let so many down, the 50,000 there and those watching it on big screens and at home.

Wasps had a very good team and they did a lot of good things to grind out the win. Lawrence Dallaglio told me recently that it stands out as one of the best wins of his entire career, because of the atmosphere, the occasion and the game itself – a 37–32 reversal of our quarter-final scoreline. The other side of Laurence's coin is that it was one of the worst defeats I've ever known.

My first trip to South Africa was a tough, tough tour, even though we only had two Tests. The first, in Bloemfontein, was also my first at altitude. There isn't much to the place, and we were based in Cape Town until the Thursday, the theory being that a quick 'in-and-out' visit was better than taking a full week to adapt.

We never adapted.

At that altitude, your breathing is quite different. I remember coming in at half-time and my lips and the side of my mouth were bleeding, because of the thin, dry air.

The wide-wide game plan worked in that it stretched them, and Drico cut through their midfield for a try by Shaggy. But they pulled clear in the second half.

Although we were closer to them in the second Test in Cape Town, 'back at sea level', they had the ability to up the intensity and pace of the game when needed. I didn't have a great match, and Rog and I were taken off ten minutes into the second half.

That night we decided to arrange a stag night for Hayes – a 'forced' stag as Hayes himself wouldn't have wanted anything to do with it. Any excuse for a party. Colin Farrell, who was in South Africa at the time making a film with Salma Hayek, attended the game and visited our dressing room afterwards. He also came along to our end-of-tour court session, which took the attention off Hayes a little. Colin's initiation to the team was to drink a pint of the most horrendous concoction I've ever seen – vodka and sambuca, topped off with Baileys and Kahlúa for that curdled effect. He had to knock it all back.

We went to Bobby Skinstad's bar, Billy the Bum's, down the road from the hotel, and Colin had two bodyguards/minders with him. Half an hour later, the two lads could not stand him up.

Our night was just beginning, but his was over.

12. Hunger Unquelled

After the second Test in South Africa on 19 June, my next rugby match was on 3 October. Along with several other internationals, I'd have to watch the first three league games from the stands: there was a view that we needed a rest after the tour, followed by a long pre-season. Mentally, that is quite a challenge. Extended pre-seasons are better for the body than for the mind.

Nowadays, pre-seasons have been condensed into six weeks or so. Coaches trust players to look after themselves during holidays more than they used to. Most enjoy a week of doing nothing, followed by a week of what's called 'active rest' – walking and swimming. A two-week lead-up follows, incorporating a fitness session every second or third day. Players are provided with manuals at the end of a season, which they are expected to follow. In those days, though, guys would rock up for pre-season, having done nothing for four weeks, and would have to begin again from scratch. I was a bit different: bar one or two days, I always trained during the off-season anyway – with a two- or three-week build-up, unlike other guys. I didn't mind training during the summer. But I did mind missing matches.

I still managed to start eighteen games for Munster, only subbed once – which would be unheard of now. Ireland was similar: I played all ten Tests, starting nine, and played eighty minutes against South Africa and Argentina, and all but four minutes of the Six Nations.

I've been asked if I ever became complacent during those years when I was first choice for country and province. When you're consistently playing eighty minutes for your province and your country, as I was in those years, you feel privileged, you try to savour every minute. You push yourself at training. You always look at the challengers behind you – players wanting to take the jersey from you. But it's probably human nature to think that the jersey is yours.

I wasn't alone. With both Munster and Ireland, the team was very settled, with the core together for seven or eight years from 2000 onwards. What drove us was a craving for success. There'd been a Triple Crown and a Celtic League title, but this had been overshadowed by losing a Grand Slam shoot-out and a World Cup quarter-final, as well as two Heineken Cup finals and three semi-finals, in the previous five years. A lot of near-misses.

Had Munster won the finals of 2000 and 2002, or had Ireland won the Grand Slam in 2001 or 2003, would the motivation and work ethic have been as strong? Would I have bounced out of bed at 7.30 a.m. to drive from Cork to Limerick for training with the same burning desire?

To come that close to silverware keeps a team and its players hungry.

Not that it showed particularly in 2004–5.

That said, October was good. Munster won five games. I played eighty minutes in all five. We beat Scarlets, Glasgow and Cardiff in the League, and in that second half against Cardiff we clicked. We only led 19–15 at half-time. Then we just ran riot.

Christian Cullen's two tries against Cardiff, plus a drop goal, took his tally to eight in six games. That season he played twenty-one games and scored ten tries. The messiah had arrived. He'd only played ten games the season before, after recovering from that shoulder injury. He'd played just three games the next season. You think of his time at Munster as injury-plagued, and I'd forgotten myself how good he was in that 2004–5 season. His value was particularly important when some of us were away on international duty during the November window and the Six Nations. He brought so much to the set-up.

He was a brilliant finisher, whether creating something himself or from someone else's break. He was so good at reading the game. He had a really blasé attitude. You could mistake this for arrogance, but scoring tries just came instinctively to him.

A week after Cardiff, we started our Heineken Cup campaign with a 15–9 win at home to Harlequins. Although Woody had retired, Quins had a sizeable Irish contingent: Gavin Duffy, Simon Keogh

and Jeremy Staunton, with Andy Dunne and Mel Deane on the
bench.

It was Jeremy's first game back at Thomond Park; he kicked three
penalties and was yellow-carded. I'd played a season at Under-21s
with Jeremy. He was really talented, but maybe didn't fulfil his potential. He could show moments of real brilliance and had a good turn
of pace, but mentally he could lose the rag. He'd then try something
outrageous which might come off or might not. A maverick talent.

I remember one day in training when he sprained his finger during
a fifteen-a-side session. He ran off to get some treatment, and Deccie
shouted at him, clearly annoyed by Jeremy's attitude.

'Where are you going? What are you doing?'

Jeremy held up his finger, not as an insult, but to indicate he'd been
injured, and continued towards the changing room. I don't think
Deccie was too impressed.

But it's easy to forget Jeremy carved a good career in England,
with Quins, Wasps and Leicester, over an eight-year period. And he
won three Premiership medals and a Heineken Cup.

When we won away to the Ospreys, 20–18, a week later, I scored a
try which I'd re-enact a few years later. Their left-winger, Shane
Williams – hedging his bets on the blindside of a Munster scrum –
inched infield a little. Rags, on the right wing, encouraged him by
inching infield as well. I watched Shane from the corner of my
eye, head down as if about to pass to Rog. Their blindside, James
Bater, was stuck to the scrum, so I ran around the blindside and dived
over, untouched.

The Ospreys had come together only the season before, an amal-
gamation of Swansea and Neath. They'd assembled a squad of
big-name players. I'd watched plenty of rugby on S4C as a kid, when
Swansea and Neath had been the powerhouses of Welsh club rugby.
When Swansea came over to play Dolphin in a friendly in the late
1980s, I asked Anthony Clement and Richard and Paul Moriarty for
their autographs.

The Ospreys have always had very talented teams, but although it
was a full house at the Gnoll, over 10,000, it still felt like a contrived
marriage. The two sets of supporters had been bitter rivals for years.

(Years later, the internal rivalry was still intact. In November 2011, I sat on the bench at the Gnoll for Munster 'A' against Neath in the British & Irish Cup, with a couple of hundred present. An announcement that the Ospreys had been held to a draw by Treviso in the Heineken Cup prompted a huge cheer. For some, clearly, the marriage never worked; perhaps more so for the diehard Neath fans, who felt Swansea had hijacked the Ospreys with the move to the Liberty Stadium.)

The November internationals began with a rematch against the Springboks, our third clash in six months. The rivalry from the June tour was quite fresh. It had been Ireland's first tour to South Africa since 1998, and so a first tour there for the entire squad. We had experienced the Afrikaaner mentality and aggression at first hand, supporters and players alike. There's no tougher place to tour.

They arrived in Ireland, expecting to bully us, to beat us up. Ireland had beaten South Africa only once, back in 1965; we desperately wanted to scalp a powerhouse of world rugby.

That was also the week when Jake White said only Drico would make the Springboks' team, and Paulie might have made the bench. The quote was displayed in the team room, and it added fuel to the ill-feeling from June. But, to be honest, the idea of South Africa being in Dublin would probably have been enough anyway. Real Test match rugby, in every sense.

I've watched all three games in full. Whether it was part of their game plan or not, in my ninety-eight Tests the South Africans were the ones who allowed me the least time on the ball. As I bent down, they anticipated my pass and came through on me. Much of the time I had to give Rog little scoop passes just to get the ball away before getting hammered.

Their back rows in particular were a real nuisance. Schalk Burger was at the peak of his powers. He was yellow-carded that day, and had been the week before when South Africa had beaten Wales 38–36. He played on the edge and was absolutely everywhere that day. He'd make a tackle and be straight over the ball. This was before tacklers had to release the man, so there was less time to clean the tackler out, especially a player as strong as Burger. And that's what

his game was about. When he was yellow-carded, he looked absolutely battered: a swollen eye, blood coming from his mouth and
nose. He took a hammering every single time he played and just kept
coming back for more. Bakkies Botha and Victor Matfield were also
at their peak, and they had a big front row with Os du Randt and
John Smit.

It was such an intense game. Against the Springboks it's never any
other way. We were still trying to play our wide-wide game, with
Rog sending Drico out on what we called an 'overs' line. An 'unders'
line is when the receiver comes short and looks to attack inside the
defender. An overs line is when the receiver takes the pass on a drift
and looks to attack outside the defender.

Drico had gone through them with that overs line for Shaggy's try
in Bloemfontein, but at Lansdowne Road we struggled. Jake White's
game plan was to pressurize us at the breakdown, slow down our ball
and use their line speed in defence to stop us from hitting those outside channels. They filled the pitch and came up so hard. Even Shaggy,
at inside centre, was getting man and ball, although he crashed up a
ton of ball for us that day.

We defended in much the same manner, and were all over them. It
was a frantic game. No one gave an inch.

The game's only try came from a bit of opportunism by Rog. It
was South Africa's fourth or fifth infringement in a row, and we'd
been kicking penalties to the corner. They'd have died rather than
give up a try to our maul. They defended so aggressively, coming in
from the side, even running around the back of our side of the maul,
to pull it down.

Drico said to the referee, Paul Honiss: 'That's a lot of infringe-
ments in this area, ref,' hinting at a penalty try. Honiss warned Smit,
and told him to pass on the warning to his players. Smit called in his
forwards, and had his back to us, when Rog quick-tapped and went
between their winger and Botha to touch down in the corner. Smit
and some of the other Springboks forwards appealed to Honiss. I'll
never forget the smirk on Rog's face; we weren't going to score a try
any other way.

They squandered about three try-scoring opportunities in the first thirty minutes alone, a three-on-one and a four-on-one, but a few passes didn't go to hand, and Geordie hand-tripped Percy Montgomery. We defended for our lives and ground out a 17–12 win, Rog scoring all our points.

I heard a story recently about that match. I don't know how true it is, but someone told me that he heard Jake White at a speaking engagement, and White recounted a game against Ireland when he was coach of South Africa. It concerned the analysis which the Springboks did on me: they noticed that I liked to break off the side of the scrum and go down the short side. White told Schalk Burger: 'Just put your head down, and if you keep it down Stringer is going to go on the short side.' So apparently Burger kept his head down and was ready for me. He tackled me straight into touch and followed through with an elbow into my head.

Nigel Owens was touch judge and I was waving my arms in the air, complaining. 'I was hit late. I was hit on the ground. Someone put an elbow into my face. Nigel, did you see that? What are you going to do about it?'

'What I'm going to do about it now is, next time there's a scrum I'm going to advise you not to go down there and be tackled by the wing forward.'

Eddie made nine changes for the USA game, shifting me to the bench. I was on forty-nine caps, and I'd like to have started, and maybe lead out the team. Soon after I came on, we were attacking the corner of the pitch by the East Stand and north terrace. Taking a little pop off the scrum from Axel, I rounded their blindside. There's a great photo on the wall in Mum and Dad's house of me in mid-air as I slip out of the tackle of their number 13, Paul Emerick, and touch down.

Then another grudge match, this time against Argentina – a sixth meeting in five years. They were unchanged from the team that had beaten France 24–14 a week before in Marseilles – where France normally win. We played into a breeze in the first half, and the weather deteriorated as the game wore on. They scored an early try and were 10–0 up, then 16–6 at half-time. Like France, you don't want to give them a lead. You want them chasing a game, becoming ill-disciplined, to pick off your points.

A niggly match. Always was with Argentina. This time they were bitter about their fixture scheduling at the World Cup and the suspensions of two front-rowers. Their entire front row had a go at me individually, within the space of a few seconds: one pushed me, the next guy pushed me in the chest, and the next grabbed my throat. Mike McGurn, our strength and conditioning coach, had to step in and break it up.

We seemed to get under their skins that day. We were disciplined, stuck to our game plan, didn't panic, didn't try too much off the cuff. We didn't want to give them targets. Rog had the cool head for the day that was in it, using the wind and rain, playing the corners to turn them, and pick off the points.

Still, we were 19–15 down with five minutes remaining, when Rog opted to kick a penalty. With a minute to go, Shaggy crashed up the middle off a line-out. Normally, with a drop goal routine, you'd like to do it on your terms, but the ball shot out of a ruck before we could build phases. I had no option but to hit Rog, and he had no option. But like the Welsh game in 2003, he kicked a snap drop goal with a couple of feet to spare. Again we'd ground it out, 21–19, and again Rog had scored all our points.

The grudge match could not have had a more pleasant, easy-going referee than Spreaders – Tony Spreadbury. I loved it when he was referee. A very jovial, cheery, animated Englishman. If anyone tried to complain to him, he'd say with a smile: 'Ah, lads, calm down. Calm down.'

He had a job on his hands that day. 'Relax, lads. The game's been going really well. Let's not throw a spanner in the works. Let's calm down.'

He clearly enjoyed his time on the pitch, but in this game particularly he was like a character out of a Monty Python sketch – a high-pitched, happy voice totally at odds with all the animated anger around him.

With about fifteen minutes to go, Geordie put up a garryowen which was a little over-cooked, and Felipe Contepomi had plenty of time to catch it, and call a mark, but he dropped the ball in doing so. Spreaders had whistled too early in giving a mark. I ran up to him, incensed. 'He dropped it. That should have been play on.'

'Sorry, I got it wrong. I've given the mark,' he said. You can't argue with that.

Still, by the end of the game, there was a river of bad blood between the two sides. Drico had complained of eye-gouging during the game, and Pichot had responded that we'd been 'like babies'.

Back to Munster and back-to-back grudge matches again, this time with Castres. Our seventh and eighth meetings in the Heineken Cup already. No matter where I turned, we seemed to be playing the same teams again and again. They beat us 19–12 at the Stade Pierre Antoine to leave them three wins from three, before we beat them with a bonus point in Thomond Park.

Justin Fitzpatrick was playing for them, and was yellow-carded at Thomond Park again. He didn't shy away from any confrontations with us. Four of our five tries came from rolling mauls to put us three points clear at the top of the group.

After we beat the Ospreys at home in the Celtic League, the internationals travelled with the Irish squad to Club La Santa in Lanzarote for a mid-season warm-weather break in the week before Christmas. Two sessions a day, weights at 10 a.m. and a skills session at 4 p.m. Nice weather, and plenty of time to relax by the pool.

As a result, I was one of those rested for our fixture on 27 December – a second consecutive 3–0 victory over Connacht at the Sportsground. I got a few days with the family instead. Happy Christmas.

We beat Leinster at Musgrave Park on New Year's Day – Deccie's first game in Munster as Leinster coach. The IRFU had not renewed his contract as Irish assistant coach and had offered him a position in the Under-age structure. He had considered that role, before taking over as Dragons coach. When Leinster sacked Gary Ella, they moved for Deccie, and he left the Dragons after three months.

We went into that game thinking no opposing coach, or team, had ever known us so well. I wonder whether Deccie ever fully bought into being Leinster coach, or they into him – an established Munster man who had coached us for years.

We then beat the Ospreys again at home in the Heineken Cup. I still have the Waterford Crystal trophy for my Man-of-the-Match award. It was my fiftieth Heineken Cup tie.

A week later we faced Harlequins in Twickenham in front of 33,000-plus – a record attendance for a pool match. But Twickenham at less than half capacity feels half empty rather than half full.

It was our fifteenth win in sixteen games, but a frustrating one. We never really found any rhythm, couldn't get over the gain line or generate go-forward ball for our backs. We fell two tries short of the bonus point we needed for a home quarter-final. Instead, we'd be away to Biarritz in San Sebastian.

Expectations were high for the Six Nations. We had a settled team, were the reigning Triple Crown holders, had won three in a row in November, and had England and France at Lansdowne Road. Perfectly set up, in theory.

We began in Rome, still intent on playing wide-wide: me passing long to Rog, and him passing long to Drico on that overs line. Drico ran that line so well. Twice the ploy saw him skin the Italian midfield. The first time, he put Geordie over in the corner. The second time, he hit Denis on the edge, who passed to Shaggy. Just as Shaggy was about to be bustled into the hoardings behind the touchline by about three Italians, he threw an overhead Hail Mary pass inside. I was running a support line; no one had expected Shaggy to do that, and it fell into my hands. I ran in untouched from about five yards. Without Drico, we would have struggled to make those line breaks and score those tries.

Darce and Drico both injured their hamstrings that day. Darce tore his, and wouldn't play again for the rest of the Six Nations. Drico only strained his but didn't play a week later in Murrayfield. Our midfield was Maggsy and Shaggy.

Matt Williams was Scotland's coach and they came charging out of the blocks, as we started slowly again and went 8–0 down. But Paulie and the pack upped their physicality, we settled down, got hold of the ball, kept it tight. Mal and Paulie had scored tries by half-time. Denis and Hayes added two more in the second half, before Gavin Duffy scored the last on his debut off the bench. 40–13. Two wins from two away.

England arrived at Lansdowne Road after defeats to Wales and France. Again we fell behind early on to a Martin Corry try. This was becoming a habit, a dangerous habit. They also had a couple of tries disallowed, and an opportunity late on to win.

If you can achieve an early lead, you don't need to rely on your star players digging you out of holes. But Rog, winning his fiftieth cap, kicked us 12–10 ahead by the break and then Drico delivered yet again, after Geordie created space for him.

But it was quite nerve-racking at the end. Matt Dawson had come on to spark them into life. Leading 17–12, we were relieved when their pack mauled over our line and Jonathan Kaplan didn't go to the TMO. Ben Kay also failed to gather a cross-kick from Charlie Hodgson that might have led to a try.

Now there was talk of the Grand Slam when France came to Dublin. We were three from three, but not a convincing three from three. France, too, scored early, with a brilliant try that Christophe Dominici finished. We were 18–9 down, turning into the wind, but we fought back well. Drico nearly rescued us again with a moment of magic when beating three tackles to score under the posts. But Dominici's second try killed us off.

We still had a Triple Crown to defend, but Wales were four from four, so they had a shot at their first Grand Slam since their glory days in the '70s. The Millennium Stadium rocked. Max Boyce helped whip up the crowd. 'Bread of Heaven' and 'Land of My Fathers' were belted out. Red everywhere, with smatterings of green.

Contrary to form, we started quite well. They were nervous. But once they sneaked ahead, when Gethin Jenkins scored by charging down a kick by Rog, their confidence soared. Gavin Henson was at the top of his game. He kicked a drop goal and a huge penalty either side of that try; the Welsh crowd went crazy. We scored a couple of late tries but were well beaten, 32–20.

They had a bigger prize to aim for. Whereas we were on a downer from the previous week, they were buoyant. The sun shone and they stayed on the pitch, singing and celebrating, for ages. We watched them receive their trophy. It's not pleasant losing what is effectively a final. It's a very uncomfortable feeling. Your teammates are standing alongside you, but you're alone. No one is talking. You literally don't know where to look. You've only your own thoughts for company, on how you played and why you lost. As soon as they lift the trophy, you're off the pitch. It was their moment. Although we weren't to know it then, there's no better place for a party than the Millennium Stadium and Cardiff.

A couple of weeks later, Munster's season was effectively over as well. The day after Leinster lost at home to Leicester, we lost 19–10 to Biarritz. We were never really in it, 16–0 down at half-time. Rog had been injured away to the Dragons a week before the quarter-final and was a big loss to us. No disrespect to Paul Burke, but Rog was a big-game player, and crucial to us.

San Sebastian is lovely. I've been there a few times. Ireland had a training camp in Bilbao before the 2003 World Cup, which included a day trip to San Sebastian. It was a very warm, early April day. We gave it a go, and Wally did his bit, leg drive and score; but we weren't creative on the day. They beat us more comfortably than the score-line suggests. We had failed to reach the semi-finals for the first time in six seasons.

As against France, Dimitri Yachvili kicked his points. I've played against him plenty of times without ever getting to know him at all off the pitch. He's a typically French scrum-half, with the responsibilities of a goal-kicker and the ability to play at 10; like Freddy Michalak, Jean-Baptiste Elissalde, Morgan Parra and others. And like those other 9s, Yachvili always seemed such a natural footballer. Everything he did looked effortless.

The scrum-half is the star player in France, as opposed to the out-half. It was the same with Pierre Berbizier and Fabien Galthie.

Mike Prendergast told me after he moved to Bourgoin that not only did he have to learn French to fit in, but he also had to adjust to the idea that the scrum-half called the line-outs and much more.

French rugby has become more of a heavyweight game in

recent years. Traditionally, they had more freedom to throw the ball around, which also allowed players to swap positions during matches, especially the half-backs. That gave them more vision, perhaps; a different perspective on the game. It probably would have opened my eyes, to have done that. I've swapped positions at half-back occasionally but, because it's not so much part of Irish rugby, I don't feel comfortable standing in at first receiver. It's an alien position for me. Then again, I wouldn't change anything, given everything that's happened to me.

A week later, on 11 April, Clive Woodward announced his forty-four-man Lions squad for the tour to New Zealand. On the evening of 10 April, I was in my parents' house on the Douglas Road, waiting by the phone nervously, not expecting to be named, but hopeful. Our poor finish to the Six Nations was preying on my mind.

My phone rang. It was Eddie O'Sullivan. My heart began racing. I ran up those stairs as I'd done so many times as a kid, into the spare bedroom, closed the door and answered.

He said: 'I've been pushing you hard for this. I've been in your corner fighting for you. Unfortunately, selection hasn't gone your way.' He named the four chosen scrum-halves: Matt Dawson, Dwayne Peel, Chris Cusiter and Gareth Cooper.

I was gutted. Dwayne Peel had done very well that season. No complaints there. Matt Dawson was experienced, had been a Lions' Test winner, so again no complaints. Chris Cusiter had been getting good reports during the Six Nations, but he'd had a bit of a blip against Wales, when he didn't play particularly well. Gareth Cooper wasn't even on the bench when Wales played us; maybe he was injured. Cooper remained on the bench against Scotland, came on for twenty minutes against Italy, ten minutes against France and twenty against England. I'd hoped they'd have taken note of the last few seasons, of my eighty minutes in virtually all of Ireland's games. I thought I'd been in with a shout.

The Irish contingent included three second-rows, two front-rows, an out-half, first centre, second centre, two wings and a full-back. I had been an integral part of the Irish team, part of the cog that made things tick. You'd like to think that would have counted, based on the success we'd had with Ireland.

Munster saw out the season by finishing second to the Ospreys in the League, after which the top eight went into the short-lived Celtic Cup. We beat Edinburgh to earn a semi-final against Leinster at Lansdowne Road, when I suffered the worst concussion of my career.

We were losing 17–16 with about six minutes to go when their out-half, David Holwell, caught me with his knee at the side of a ruck. The video replay didn't actually reveal what had happened, but the touch judge, Richard Hughes, saw the incident. On his recommendation Holwell was red-carded by the referee, Nigel Whitehouse.

I played on – but I don't remember anything of the last few minutes of the match. Sitting in the changing room a good ten minutes after we'd come inside, I suddenly came around, and had to ask the Doc to explain what had happened.

Later, I watched the video on my laptop. A point behind, we worked our way into the Leinster 22 and I had a pick and go myself, gaining a few yards. I laid the ball back; Axel picked and scored under the posts. We'd won in the last minute. I saw myself celebrate with the guys, shake hands with Leinster players and applaud the crowd. Then I must have walked down the steps in the West Stand, turned left to the away changing room, gone to my place and sat down. Ten minutes later, I effectively woke up.

I'd functioned on instinct for those last six minutes; your body works, you do all the things you've trained yourself to do for years, and yet have absolutely no recollection of doing it.

Thankfully, the game has changed with the obligatory protocols now in place for concussion. I've probably had about three concussions in my career. The first occurred in a schools match. I played on, finished the game, returned to the Pres changing room and looked up at the hanger with my clothes – which I didn't recognize. I was also definitely out for a few seconds in one game against Wales, and again played on.

But that Celtic Cup semi-final was the worst. As there were no return-to-play protocols, I played in the final against the Scarlets six days later. It would have just come down to me saying: 'I'm fine.'

Deccie had finished his stint with Leinster by then, to return to Munster for the 2005–6 season. Our win over the Scarlets meant Alan Gaffney finished on a winning note.

Just 11,500 were in Lansdowne Road for the final, which we won 27–16. The Celtic Cup was never played again.

Three days later, the Lions assembled in England. I went with an Ireland squad on a two-Test tour to Japan – a welcome distraction.

We brought an inexperienced squad and a coaching staff who were quite relaxed. Michael Bradley was head coach, Niall O'Donovan forwards coach, Mark McCall assistant coach and Joey Miles manager. It wasn't the most intensive tour I'd known. We expected to win both games and did. We had some good nights out, and enjoyed ourselves. Nor was it the same familiar faces, as there were six new caps. After the disappointment of not making the Lions, I bought into it.

In our down time or in the evenings, Tokyo was amazing, with Japanese street food and the buildings reaching into the sky everywhere you went. I love tech stuff, and the shops were filled with gadgets that had yet to reach Ireland.

It was really hot, with dry, hard pitches for training. When we ran the first Test XV against the rest of the squad, Michael Bradley had to fill in on the wing. He soon pulled his hamstring and had to hobble off.

Humphs went off in the first Test, and I took over the captaincy for the only time in my career. Unfortunately, this also meant the after-dinner speech was thrust upon me at about five minutes' notice. I managed a few words, thanking our hosts.

Although the attendances – 12,000 and 15,000 – were lost in the two stadiums, the Japanese took their rugby very seriously. Plenty of Japanese fans waved Irish flags, and we were taken aback by the hundreds who hung around for autographs and photographs. Even more amazingly, many even seemed to know who I was!

Yeah, yeah, I was big in Japan.

13.   'He's fooled them all!'

I dreamed of scoring a try the night before, and woke up on the morning of the final, wishing that it had been a reality.

I'd also pictured another scenario – literally. I had a simple Nokia 6230i, the first decent camera phone on which you could watch video clips. Our video analyst, George Murray, had put together clips of Biarritz and I converted them into the correct format for my phone. The screen measured about a square inch, the tiniest screen imaginable. The day before the game, on the bus journey back to our hotel from the Millennium, I showed it to a few of the lads. I was showing off, because they'd have to wait until we arrived back at the hotel to view the rest of the video analysis on computer.

I had noticed from my analysis that their left-winger, Sireli Bobo, had a tendency to drift infield from the blindside at scrums. I hadn't mentioned it to anybody. This was my thing and nobody else needed to know about it.

But by the day of the game I'd forgotten about it. I was too busy with my own calls, how we'd play, what patterns we'd use.

Then, in the thirty-first minute, with the score 10–10, a scrum went down about ten metres from their line to the right of the posts, leaving a corridor of about ten metres on their blindside. I realized it was on. Time seemed to stand still, although it all happened in less than half a minute.

I put the ball into the scrum and as I moved to the base I saw, out of the corner of my eye, that Bobo had started to inch infield. I turned my back on their scrum-half, Dimitri Yachvili, as if intending to pass across my body to Rog. I had to keep my eye on the ball, not turn my head for another look. For all I knew, Bobo had gone back to the short side and was eyeballing me through the back of my head. But I couldn't risk checking.

Those couple of seconds at the back of the scrum seemed like an eternity. *Will I go for it? Will I go for the safe option? Will I hit Rog or what will I do? Will I go for it? Will I go for it?*

In the previous five seasons we had come up one play short in two finals, and in two semi-finals, and then been well beaten in a quarter-final. Three one-point defeats. A missed kick. A try wrongly ruled out in the last season before a TMO was introduced. A try wrongly given, despite the introduction of the TMO. Every time, one play or one moment.

You begin to wonder: 'Are we ever going to win this thing?'

There was a Munster supporter who used to walk his dog, a black-and-white sheepdog, around the grassy hill surrounding the pitch in UL. He must have walked that dog there for ten years. The dog regularly used to run down on to the pitch. There's a picture of me somewhere doing laps in UL, recovering from an injury, and that dog is running with me.

He loved chasing a rugby ball. The owner apologized about the dog but, chatting to me, he'd say: 'This is your destiny, this is the Holy Grail.' He was talking about the Heineken Cup.

It was the same anywhere we went. All anyone could ever talk about was that we had come so close, that we'd reach our Holy Grail one day. The supporters, too, were obviously on a journey with us, and had shared in the heartache.

We started the 2005–6 season with our usual pre-season optimism. That's the only way to begin a campaign.

Deccie was back in his second spell as head coach and for the most part he was an excellent man-manager, probably better than he was a coach. The squad and the public as a whole were generally glad to see him back. After his year with Leinster, it seemed like the right fit, for him and for Munster. The ship had become a little unsteady. We still had a core of great players and leaders and, in combination with what Deccie brought in, in those years it worked.

Without the talent and leadership in our squad at the time, I don't think Deccie would have been recognized in the way that he was. It was an exceptional Munster generation. To portray Deccie as the man who completely transformed us would be false.

Tomás O'Leary broke into the team that September against the Scarlets. Then I missed the Leinster game after straining my medial knee ligaments in a tackle during training on the bottom pitch of Cork Con. Tomás had a good game when we beat Leinster 33–9, as I watched from the stands in Musgrave Park, two weeks before our Heineken Cup opener, away to Sale. You want the team to win but you never want the guy in your position to play too well. That's just human nature. You want your place back.

Deccie phoned me in the week of the Sale game and asked about my knee.

I said: 'My knee is fine,' and asked him: 'Am I involved?'

'You are. I put you on the bench.'

I questioned that, but he kept referring to my injury. It seemed like an excuse.

I could see strengths in Tomás. I could see weaknesses as well. Tomás brought something different from what I offered; in fact we were at opposite ends of the scrum-half spectrum. He looked to take the ball on around the fringes but was not an overly good passer.

In any case, it was the second time in my career, along with the Irish game against Scotland in 2001, when I felt that I had been dropped. It seemed to me that if it was really about my fitness, Deccie wouldn't have had me involved in the squad at all.

As had often been the case, we started away to the in-form team in England. With Philippe Saint-André in his second season as coach, Sale were riding high in the Premiership, and would later thrash Leicester in the Twickenham final in May. Saint-André had brought in several French players, including Sébastien Chabal, Sébastien Bruno and Lionel Faure, and they'd won the European Challenge Cup the previous May. They had a big pack, which also included Andrew Sheridan and Ignacio Fernández Lobbe. Edgeley Park was jammed, and it was a horror night for us: they beat us 27–13. Worse than that, Quinny did his shoulder and would be out for virtually the rest of the season. That night was also the start of Frankie's neck problems, which ended his season.

I played just seven minutes off the bench, but the following week I was back in the starting fifteen against, naturally, Castres at home – our ninth Heineken Cup meeting. Trevor Halstead was back from injury for his European debut. Trevor was brilliant for us: not a quick guy by any means, but so strong. Playing in the centre, he had that ability to bump guys, to cross the gain line and get our forwards into the game. He could also stay up in the tackle and offload.

A very quiet, humble guy. He worked so hard in training, always doing extras. He scored our fifth try in a 44–19 win and would prove to be a huge influence that season.

Paul O'Connell was injured that autumn, and Ireland and Munster missed him badly. In his absence, Munster lost at home to Ulster at the start of December, but beat the Dragons at home and away in the Heineken Cup, before his return from injury for the win over Connacht at Christmas.

Then, on New Year's Eve, we lost 35–23 to Leinster at the RDS.

For us, there was no worse place to lose than in Leinster. They were our biggest rivals. Felipe Contepomi scored twenty-five points, including two of their four tries, and practically jumped into the RDS crowd to celebrate. There was always an edge to the rivalry between Felipe and Rog; one up for Felipe.

That one hurt all of us, badly. It happened to us a lot during those years. We might have had a few shaky starts in the first few months up to Christmas, a kick in the ass to get our season going. There was no bigger one than getting an absolute hiding from Leinster.

We came off that pitch in Dublin a wounded animal. There was no hiding place, least of all in the changing room. I sat next to Axel, who was captain, and said: 'This does not happen again. We don't forget the hurt and pain that we feel here tonight. But it changes now. This does not happen again.'

We packed our bags and left for Limerick and Cork. You don't want to dwell too much on a defeat like that, but we'd made a pact. We'd always refocus in January. The make-or-break month.

We beat Edinburgh away by a point, and headed to Castres on a Friday night. French games are often absolute dogfights; but sometimes they're wide open, and this was one of the latter. Trevor and the forwards were getting us over the gain line. Rucks were so quick and we scored seven tries. Paulie scored two and Tomás came off the bench to score two from the wing.

The more we scored, the less interest Castres showed, and we just kept going. In those days we never took our foot off the opposition's throats. When we got on top, it was part of our mentality to up our work rate. Every bonus point, and every try, could be crucial in the pool stages.

A week later, against Sale at home, we needed a mini-miracle – a bonus-point win – to finish above them and earn a home quarter-final. The turning point came early, in the twelfth minute. Charlie Hodgson had made it 3–0 and Rog kicked off. As Chabal caught the ball, Paulie caught him. Donners followed and, with other forwards joining in, they drove him back at least twenty metres. Had Chabal gone to ground straight away in the tackle, then it would not have been a big deal. But pride can mess with your mind. He tried to stay on his feet. Even as big and as strong as he was, Chabal would never reverse the momentum against those guys. He was driven back and that got the crowd going. From there on it was another of those brilliant Saturday nights in Thomond Park.

The atmosphere that evening was pretty special. At one point, at a break in play for treatment to one of their players, the crowd produced a perfect rendition of 'The Fields of Athenry', from start to finish. As soon as it was finished, the injured player got to his feet and the referee restarted. The timing was perfect. I remember thinking to myself, 'I don't want the play to start until I hear the rest of the song.'

Axel scored an early try from a rolling maul, and that was the night two young, home-grown backs, Ian Dowling and Barry Murphy, announced their arrival with tries before half-time. They worked so hard to develop their skills and hone their fitness on the pitch and in the gym. Without the work ethic of guys like that, we'd have won nothing.

Iain needed to lose a bit of weight to make himself into the strong, aggressive winger he was for us that season. Whatever he did in matches, he did in training too: head first into everything. He suffered his share of injuries and had to retire prematurely.

Barry, one of my good friends, had incredible talent. He was slight for an outside centre, but had a great turn of pace. That night, for his try, he collected a loose ball fifty metres out, rounded Jason Robinson and just kept running. No fear. Later that season Barry would injure his ankle, and although he went on to have a good season in 2007–8, he never quite regained the form he had shown that autumn.

Funnily enough, the Sale press officer told me years later that he was sitting behind Saint-André that night in Thomond Park. After the second Munster try, Saint-André's message on to the pitch was 'not to panic'. Munster still needed another two. Then when Barry scored the third try, Saint-André turned to him and just raised his eyes to heaven.

Rog kept spiralling long kicks into the corners, and Paulie destroyed their line-out. Years later, Mark Cueto told me that they'd lost so much confidence in their line-out that he tried a quick throw by the low wall on the west side of the old Thomond Park. A spectator leaned over the wall, as they did in Thomond Park, and grabbed him by the back of the shorts to stop him from taking the ball.

Our sixteenth man!

We had three tries and led 24–9 at half-time but, typical Munster, didn't get our fourth until the eighty-second minute, when Wally did his thing. Quite a valuable try. He deserved a bonus in his pay packet that month. Playing until the final whistle was a Munster trait. I think you either have that quality or you don't. It's not something you can coach. You can tell someone to work for eighty-plus minutes, run faster, or work harder, but if he doesn't want to run those extra ten metres to cover the inside shoulder of another defender, he's not going to do it. We were fortunate to have so many players who wanted to do it. I'm not claiming everybody in the squad of forty had this mentality. But even from those pre-season training sessions you could see which guys were digging in and willing to push themselves beyond their physical and mental limits. We were lucky to have a core group of players who were simply willing to work hard.

★

Coming back after the Six Nations, we had a league game away to the Scarlets. But about an hour before kick-off, the match was postponed because the Stradey Park pitch was waterlogged. The prospect of a Heineken Cup quarter-final the following weekend quickly focused our minds, and we decided to stay in our gear and find a park, somewhere in Llanelli, to train.

The bus parked beside a small green area, just a patch of grass where people walked their dogs. We carried the tackle bags and cones, and replicated a game among ourselves to get something from the trip. Conditions were absolutely horrendous, but once we'd bought into it, we didn't hold back. The easy thing would have been to say: 'Ah, I don't think this is the right thing to do. Let's just get on the bus and go home and start again.' Instead, we left Wales having done something.

Our home quarter-final was played at Lansdowne Road. Earlier that Saturday, Leinster had won away to Toulouse to ensure their place in the semi-finals against the winner of our game. Knowing that Leinster were waiting for us added plenty of motivation.

In the week before the Perpignan game, Conrad O'Sullivan passed away. Conrad had been in our squad, and that was a very emotional time for all of us. The church was packed with mourners, and we all stood outside afterwards in complete shock. It was totally devastating for everybody. Mick O'Driscoll was a first cousin of Conrad's, and had been very close to him from an early age.

Conrad had been living with Frank Murphy. He was only twenty-five, at Pres a couple of years behind me and also a Cork Con boy, like myself. He was a centre who had played out-half in school. He'd been a real talent; tipped to go all the way. A really skilful player.

I didn't know Debbie, my future wife, at that stage, but she would have been very good friends with Conrad as well, and the church is in her local parish of Cloghroe.

There was a minute's silence before the Perpignan game, and guys had Conrad on their minds. It was a blustery old day and Perpignan showed up.

It wasn't a very memorable game. We got through it, we got the job done, and that was probably all we needed to do, to try and get over that tough couple of weeks.

A three-week build-up followed to the semi-final against Leinster. We'd warned each other that there would be more distractions than ever: more hype, more demand for tickets. It was the only topic of conversation, but that's what gets you excited: playing against your biggest rivals for the first time on the European stage, in their home city.

We knew we'd have pretty good support, but I'll never forget the colour of Lansdowne Road that day. It was phenomenal. Red everywhere. I don't know how our fans got their hands on all those tickets, and that was probably the last time Leinster allowed it to happen.

I'd been injured in training on the Thursday at Musgrave Park. One of our wingers was tackled and I was the first player there to protect the ball. Someone came through on my upper back and I had no bend in my knees; I felt my hamstring nearly pop. I was helped off the pitch, and all I could think about was the game on Saturday. For two days I iced and flexed it constantly at home to get the blood flowing through it.

Deccie said he'd give me every opportunity, but he brought Frank Murphy, Mike Prendergast and Tomás O'Leary to Dublin, so we had four scrum-halves at Lansdowne Road. I'd had the hamstring strapped, felt comfortable, and was pain-free through the warm-up.

We went into an early lead, and everything went our way. Our pack dominated theirs. Contepomi had a nightmare after missing an early kick from in front of the posts.

The hurt and pain from the game in the RDS helped drive us. Without a doubt it was one of the best days I've ever known, given what was at stake, who we were playing, and the venue. Mick Galwey always used to say: 'No team beats Munster twice in the same season.' If ever there was a day to ensure that statement held true, that was the day. Losing to Leinster wasn't an option. It wasn't that we had a divine right to be in a semi-final, or final. But for them to get to one at our expense, and maybe win the Heineken Cup before us, would have been too much.

So, with all that in mind, we came out of the blocks firing, and they weren't up to it physically. We just had a sense from their body language that we would dominate them that day.

We had four weeks to prepare for the final. I played the third of the three League games in between, the rearranged match against the Scarlets. Enough to be ticking over.

As with the semi-final, the final was the only topic of conversation, this time for four weeks. Flags fluttered around Limerick and Cork, as part of the push to turn the province red. This included an enormous poster of the Munster team covering the Bank of Ireland building on the South Mall in Cork.

We were probably more level-headed for our third final than we were for the first two. We knew not to become too emotionally charged in the build-up.

The final against Biarritz couldn't have been set up any better. We knew that at the Millennium Stadium we'd have eighty to ninety per cent of the crowd with us – effectively our third 'home' game in a row, away from Thomond Park!

We also knew from the previous two finals, when we scored eight points and nine points, that we needed tries.

We stayed in the Vale of Glamorgan, arriving on Friday, before a run-out at the Millennium Stadium. Open-roofed and empty is very different from a closed roof with nearly 80,000 spectators. There was a strong echo: you could hear each other from one end of the pitch to the other. Come match day, trying to communicate with Rog or Jerry Flannery, making line-out calls, meant literally having to stand beside them and shout in their ear. You had to rely on all that season's training, all the cohesion and calls, instinctively. A final at the Millennium with the roof closed is not the place for spur-of-the-moment decisions. It's just not going to happen.

I was the usual giddy Peter Stringer on the morning of the match, and poor old Wally, as usual, was as white as a ghost with nerves. I remember jumping on the bed with excitement and all Wally could respond with was, 'How are you not hating this feeling? I feel sick and there you are jumping around like a kid.' He wouldn't even speak to Aileen, his then girlfriend and now his wife, or to his family, on any match day. It was very bizarre. Even in the hotel, he didn't want to see them before a game. Wally was Wally, and I just tried to transfer some of my energy to him. Polar opposites.

Come match day, on the short journey in to Cardiff, our bus drove on the motorway for a while. I sat next to Hayes, as usual; the fourth seat from the front, by the window on the left. The bus then swung in by the Castle, down the start of Mary Street, before turning right towards our entrance. Mary Street was crammed with people, packed shoulder to shoulder. When they saw our bus with the Munster sign at the front, the whole place went absolutely crazy. It was a moment that sent shivers down my back, the sort of moment you dream of. Thousands and thousands of people have travelled for this game, and it then hits you what's at stake. What it means to people and what it means to us.

This is the day. This is the day when it needs to happen. We're never going to have ninety per cent of supporters in a stadium for a final again.

We heard crazy stories. Two guys on a motorbike making their way across Europe to Cardiff. Fans who bought tickets in Biarritz and flew there to jump on board a Biarritz charter for the final. And loads more. Nobody wanted to miss out.

I felt good in the warm-up, and I sensed a confidence in the team. Sometimes you can see the nervousness in guys' eyes. Instead, some guys were grinning. That's what you want to see. *OK, these guys are ready. These guys are prepared. Come the kick-off, I don't have to worry about guys freezing.*

Inside three minutes, Biarritz scored. Bobo danced along the touchline to touch down, and Yachvili converted from the touchline.

If you're going to concede a try, you might as well concede one with seventy-eight minutes left, rather than seven or eight minutes left. We were disappointed, but it was so early in the game we didn't panic.

Our forwards dominated that day. They were really effective at picking and going, sucking in their tacklers and clearing them out. Instinctively guys knew what they were supposed to do. We were never scratching our heads, thinking, 'What do we do now?' It just flowed.

Maybe having some new players that season helped. They had less baggage. As well as Barry Murphy and Ian Dowling, that was Jerry Flannery's breakthrough season. Fla was a great competitor, like another back-rower. He was one of those characters who stood out in pre-season. You knew he would not stop running. Even if his two hamstrings were falling off, he'd keep going until he was dragged off. They're the kind of guys you want.

I'd played with Jerry in UCC. He'd been a little insecure then, doubting himself. But, more than anything, he wanted to be a professional rugby player. He trained so hard all through his career. Even with the calf injury that eventually forced him to retire, he kept trying new things to get it right. No one could have tried harder.

In UCC he'd overcome some demons with his line-out throwing, and was quite temperamental. To have travelled with him along that journey, to see him turn into the player he did, was a privilege. He became one of the best line-out throwers I've ever seen: the different speeds he could use, and the accuracy and quality of the throw. Fla was up there with the best. Around the pitch, his fitness levels and work ethic were also up there with the best.

He's also highly intelligent, and a deep thinker about the game. Like Donners, he'd go into incredible detail, almost too much at times. But the detail of his preparation and analysis helped make him what he was. His intensity drove him. It's what made him always do more, unlike the guys who looked to cut corners.

He would also demand the ball. He'd come around that corner off a ruck with such pace, try a little spin or side-step or swerve, to avoid a head-on collision. He had the strength and the ability to do that.

That day in the Millennium Stadium I felt I always had options, guys willing to take a pop from me and carry, and Fla was as good as any I've played with. Lots of guys contributed to our first try. After Hoggy had latched on to a chip by Rog, it was Fla and then Paulie who took it on in turn. That gave us the go-forward quick ball to move it across our backline. When the ball reached Trevor, he probably could have shipped it on, but he assumed the responsibility to tuck it under both arms, ride the tackle, bump their winger,

18. Jake Boer of Gloucester swallowed me up in our Heineken Cup group match at Thomond Park in January 2003, but we pulled off a miracle scoreline to advance to the knockout stages. (*Morgan Treacy/Sportsfile*)

19. When we went to Leicester for the 2003 Heineken Cup quarter-final, we were facing the two-time defending champions, and a side who hadn't lost at home in Europe in four years. But the Red Army was there in force, and there was mayhem on the pitch after we won. (*Billy Stickland/Inpho*)

20. The try I scored on the day we beat Scotland to secure the 2004 Triple Crown was probably my most important in an Irish jersey. (*Morgan Treacy/Inpho*)

21. Celebrating the Triple Crown with Rog. (*Patrick Bolger/Inpho*)

30. Finally: the holy grail.
(*Inpho/Getty Images*)

31. It was a rainy
day in Limerick when
we came home with
the Heineken Cup, but
nobody seemed to mind.
(*Billy Stickland/Inpho*)

32. One of my rugby regrets is that I never beat the All Blacks. Here, Ma'a Nonu bounces me in the first Test in June 2006, which New Zealand won 34–23. (*Inpho/Photosport/Hannah Johnston*)

33. On the day we played England in Croke Park in 2007, Donncha O'Callaghan, Paul O'Connell and I were all pretty emotional during the national anthem. (*Dan Sheridan/Inpho*)

Jean-Baptiste Gobelet, and score. We needed that. We were dominating them, but we needed something on the scoreboard.

Rog converted. Yachvili made it 10-all. And then came THAT scrum.

Will I go for it? Will I go for the safe option? Will I hit Rog or what will I do? Will I go for it? Will I go for it?

If I had run into Bobo, or their blindside flanker Serge Betsen, I would have looked like a fool. But at that moment, when I bent down, my body took over. I went for it.

I knew that my first few steps had to be towards the touchline. Otherwise, regardless of whether Betsen was expecting me or not, I'd have just run into him. If he wasn't expecting me, I'd be able to beat him, once I straightened up. As soon as I turned my shoulders around, I sprinted. What I'd hoped would happen did happen. Bobo had wandered infield and Betsen was stuck to the scrum.

Nobody touched me.

An unbelievable feeling. One of the best feelings of my life on a rugby pitch.

I didn't show any emotion. I didn't celebrate. I knew only half an hour had gone. I didn't want to be jumping around. No matter who scored tries on my teams, I'd always turn immediately and run back for the kick-off. I was never one for celebrating back then.

I haven't seen Donncha O'Callaghan in a while, but ever since that day his opening line to me every single time, in his best Ryle Nugent accent, is: 'He's fooled them all, he's fooled them all.'

And I love it when Donners says that. I get so excited reliving that moment. He doesn't let me forget it and I'm truly grateful for that. We are due a catch-up.

We went in at half-time 17–10 ahead, and felt good. We had scored two tries. We wouldn't be chasing the game. We didn't need to change anything. Our pack were on top and Rog was kicking well.

Soon he made it 20–10. But time began to drag slowly again, so slowly that you started thinking, 'Is this ever going to end? Is this ever going to happen?'

You need to be brave to win a game, and maybe some doubts crept in during the second half, as if we were expecting something to go wrong, for them to score a try and shatter the dream.

After forty-eight minutes: Yachvili penalty. 20–13.

After fifty-one minutes: Yachvili penalty. 20–16.

After seventy minutes: Yachvili penalty. 20–19.

You could feel nervous tension building around the stadium.

Between Yachvili's last two penalties, one of their players went down injured and the big screen showed the scenes in O'Connell Street in Limerick, where tens of thousands were watching. They reacted by cheering and waving their flags, and the crowd in the stadium reacted to them.

I saw it. We all saw it. It snapped us out of a kind of nervous daze. We'd been like a boxer against the ropes, just soaking up their attack, but it gave us a boost of energy. It kick-started the last ten minutes and made us keep playing. But ten minutes is a long time. We needed to make something happen.

After Yachvili's last penalty, we got hold of the ball, worked through a few phases. Census Johnson came in from the side and Chris White awarded us a penalty. It was a tough kick, but Rog nailed it.

They came back at us. When Federico Pucciariello went down to have his shoulder treated, there was just over a minute left. 'The Fields of Athenry' reverberated around the stadium, and the picture of tens of thousands in O'Connell Street in Limerick came up on the big screen again.

They reacted again, and the crowd in the stadium did the same.

Defending a four-point lead, as opposed to a one-point lead, changes your whole mindset and approach. We went into tackling-for-our lives mode. They had to score a try, a penalty wouldn't be enough, so we could gamble a little, take a few risks and shoot up hard or contest the breakdown.

Bobo ran into one of his own players and White awarded us a scrum. Then Yachvili was penalized for offside.

I saw the clock hit red as White raised his arm. That was the first time I really believed that we could win, that we actually had won.

I kicked the ball into touch.

I jumped into Rog. I sank to my knees and put my head on the ground. I was in tears. We had won. So many emotions. The dominant one in those seconds was disbelief. Then relief. Then happiness. Then complete elation.

The best feeling I've ever had on a rugby pitch.

Everything that I'd done as a rugby player since the age of six was for that day, twenty-two years later. Everything: your diet, your training, your fitness, your pre-season. All for that moment when a final whistle goes in a Heineken Cup final. Floods of emotion. For all of us.

I've watched images, in slow motion, of Hoggy standing on his own and pointing to other teammates. Of Fla going absolutely crazy, red-faced and tears in his eyes. Paulie in tears. Donners in tears. Paulie and Donners hugging each other. And Quinny. He had defied medical opinion by making it back two weeks before and playing the last four minutes. It meant a lot to him after what he'd been through.

Thousands were waiting at Cardiff Airport to cheer us. You saw faces you'd never seen before, and some you had seen on the journey.

Getting on that plane, you realized a little more clearly that you had done it. The guys began to have a few drinks. Quinny took the air hostesses' microphone to start a sing-song, which lasted the whole flight.

Shannon Airport was mayhem, absolute mayhem, although there probably wasn't much difference in numbers between that night and after the first lost final in 2000. It's a pretty special feeling when you know that these people will be with you in good times or bad, and they were. Subsequently, you see that documentary with video clips of the supporters in the Millennium Stadium at the full-time whistle, breaking down and sitting in their seats, heads in their hands and tears rolling down their faces. It's amazing to see the effect a game of rugby can have on people.

Whenever I see or hear the word 'Heineken' I have flashbacks of that day. Years later, when I moved into a new apartment, the landlord had left a full crate of Heineken in the fridge. Obviously I didn't drink it, but just seeing that word instantly brought me back to that day in Cardiff.

Wherever I go, people remind me of that day. I won't be allowed to forget it and I'm very thankful for that.

That day will last for ever. No one can ever take it from us.

14. Silverware in Twickenham

That 2005–6 season ended pretty well for Ireland, too, but it started badly. In our November internationals, we would normally take at least one southern hemisphere scalp or at least put in one really strong performance. In November 2005 we didn't.

Paulie and Drico were both injured that month. We had a fairly experienced and settled team, but minus our two main leaders, against two of the best teams in the world, we struggled. New Zealand beat us 45–7, and Australia won by 30–14, before we beat Romania in the last match.

Drico provided our creative flair and Paulie our leadership up front. I'd have no hesitation in saying that Paulie was the best forward and Brian was the best back I've ever played with.

Paulie will never settle for second best in anything he does. He doesn't let anything slip by. He will do absolutely everything in his power to ensure that he and the team are prepared. If something isn't right he will not let it be brushed over. He's totally committed to what he does, in training, in his own preparation and in games. He is narky at times, but needs to be. That's his character. It's helped him in the role he's played over the years as a leader and being in control of so many situations, both on and off the pitch. You look at him in the dressing room and he doesn't even have to say anything. Your game raises itself. It's just his presence. He will be missed incredibly by Munster and Ireland. I can't speak too highly of him.

Although both were back for the Six Nations, the November hangover lingered. In our opener at home to Italy, we tried to play our wide-wide game, but our pack struggled and their defence easily kept us under wraps. Despite our line-out problems, a steal by Paulie led to Fla scoring on his first Test start. But they led early in the second half until Tommy Bowe scored a try from a cross-kick by Rog.

The grounding looked dodgy. Even then Rog didn't kick us two scores clear until the last five minutes.

Confidence was low as we headed to Paris. The game that unfolded was unbelievable, like one you'd dream of, or have nightmares about.

We owned the ball for most of the match, played nearly all the rugby. But Tommy Bowe slipped for their first try. Geordie Murphy and Denis Hickie collided for their second. Rog was charged down for their third. Geordie's pass was intercepted for their fourth. We'd also missed many chances to score ourselves. They led 29–3 at the interval.

In the dressing room, nothing was said for a while. Then it was very much a case of OK, this can go one of two ways. We can either be on the receiving end of an eighty-point hiding or we can come back and try to prove ourselves.

There were no raised voices. We knew things hadn't gone well. But we'd nothing to lose in the second half; just go out and play.

The second half didn't improve matters initially. Soon we were 43–3 down, facing Ireland's biggest defeat of all time.

But, as with Munster, when Ireland generated quick ball we were a different team. We had the players to create things, and in that second half in Paris the ball was lightning-quick – one-second rucks. Wally seemed to be making breaks everywhere. Drico began to cut them apart. It was like a training match. Tackle, offload, tackle, turn and spin, pop out of the tackle, and sometimes just draw the defender and pass before contact. Keep the ball alive at all costs.

Rog scored a try. Darce scored a second. Donners scored a third. Andrew Trimble a fourth. We had a couple of chances to add a fifth, which would have put us five points behind going into the last five minutes. Had there been another five or ten minutes, there was only one winner, and it wasn't them. But they held on to win 43–31.

At the final whistle the French fans in the Stade de France started booing; an absolutely deafening booing from the home supporters after a home win! They'd put forty-three points on us, but I have rarely been in a match where we played so well. Obviously there was no pressure on us in the second half. We had nothing to lose. But I don't think I've played a half of rugby so fluid and continuous without the ball being knocked on or kicked into touch. And it turned our season around.

A fortnight later we beat Wales at home easily enough. Losing Stephen Jones was a big blow for them. Gavin Henson came on. Years later, when we were at Bath together, he told me he'd been brought into the squad late and didn't know any of the calls. This was after he'd been banished from the squad and had had to apologize to his teammates for comments in his book, *My Grand Slam Year*.

When he made a couple of mistakes, the crowd really got on his back. In injury time at the end of the match, he was at the edge of a ruck and tried to tackle me, but I wormed my way under him to score. I slagged him about it at the time, but I felt bad about it when he told me years later that that day at Lansdowne Road had been one of his darkest days in a Welsh jersey.

I got a better sense of Gav as a person when we were teammates at Bath. We had been on a team social one day, and after a few hours in the Thatchers cider brewery there was a row, and Gav was knocked out by a teammate after some drunken comments. Gary Gold, our director of rugby, asked me to room with Gav on our pre-season camp in Spala. He had the idea that, as a senior player, I would be a mentor with whom he could discuss any issues he had been dealing with. Gav seemed to settle down over the season and was able to contribute positively to the club. I found him to be a really nice guy. He was also an incredibly talented player, world-class when he was at his best.

We beat Scotland 15–9, five penalties to three, on a windy, wet day in Lansdowne Road. There's a DVD of that season, of about an hour and a half, and the Scottish match takes up about two minutes.

Half an hour of that DVD is reserved for the final game, against England at Twickenham, with another Triple Crown at stake. In the first five minutes we let them in for a try. Old habits die hard. But Shaggy soon scored from a chip ahead by Drico.

We went into virtually the last play trailing 24–21. From a scrum on our 22, Rog and Drico produced a bit of magic. Rog chipped over, Drico read the bounce of the ball and offloaded to Shaggy, who went flying down the touchline. Lewis Moody made a hell of a tackle in the corner to stop Shaggy, a few metres short of the line. We recycled and went infield again. The noise was unbelievable.

From that ruck I'd seen that they pushed up hard on the short side rather than drift towards the touchline. I dummied a pass to the first receiver, which brought them up even more, then threw a perfectly weighted looping pass to Shaggy on the touchline. Lewis Moody had turned his shoulders in slightly, which made it a bit more difficult for him to tackle Shaggy. Still, Shaggy's finish remains one of the best I've ever seen. You can see him keeping his ankles together as Moody tries to drag his feet into touch. Shaggy's studs are stuck in the ground and won't budge. Then that one-handed reach. I think only Shaggy could have scored it.

The referee, Nigel Whitehouse, referred it to the TMO, and at the time I wasn't sure whether the try was good. So I didn't want to waste time going all the way back to our half. I wasn't far from Nigel, and I could hear him say back to the TMO: 'So I can award the try?'

Then came the roar from the Irish fans.

Sweet.

We'd won another Triple Crown, and at Twickenham. The Irish expats in England could live off this one for another year. And this time we really did have silverware, as a Triple Crown trophy was introduced that season. Drico lifted it. A small thing, but it made it even better and meant that the Irish fans had the stands pretty much to themselves.

I grew up watching FA Cup Finals, starting in 1985 when Liverpool played Everton (I'm a Liverpool fan!). The moment when players and fans are waiting for the captain to be handed a trophy is a magical one. The crowd quietens and then raises the noise levels for the roar to peak with the moment when he lifts it above his head. You want that to last for ever. That's why you play the game.

As a non-drinker, I of all people should remember what happened that night, but I don't remember anything. Not a flipping thing.

People don't think of the 2006 Six Nations as another Grand Slam that got away, but when you watch that game in Paris again, it actually was.

15.   Hope and History

In the summer of 2006, for really the first and only time on a tour to New Zealand, we competed properly in two Tests. Historically we'd have given it a right good go in the first, New Zealand being a bit rusty. Then they'd get their act together for the second.

The first Test in Hamilton slipped from us. We'd scored good tries through Drico and Trimble in each half, led 23–15 with half an hour remaining, and were still ahead by a point going into the last ten minutes. Even when 34–23 down, we created a couple of pitch-length moves, but Luke McAllister intercepted a pass by Paulie.

The Waikato Stadium was quite dry and their sand-based pitch is probably the best I have ever played on. Walking the pitch beforehand was amazing. It's like a snooker table. It's odd that New Zealand, with weather so similar to ours, can produce pitches of that quality.

Eden Park a week later was a different story. The weather didn't allow either team to throw it around. It lashed rain from start to finish. Graham Henry had billed it as a trial match for the All Blacks, which really grated with us. We'd come down for a serious Test match and he was using it to showcase a few players. That was mentioned quite a bit in our team talks.

Perhaps because of those comments, it was quite a niggly match. They scored a couple of tries through picking-and-going to lead 17–0, and we were in big trouble. Then we adopted a similar tactic, using the forwards in those tight channels. Paulie smashed through Byron Kelleher, got back to his feet and scored. We kicked a few penalties into the corner, and the pack mauled over for Fla to score. When Rog kicked a penalty with half an hour to go, we trailed 20–17. But their scrum was on top and McAllister killed us off with a try. Eleven-and ten-point margins suggest comfortable wins for them, but they weren't.

Australia in Perth a week later was a different story again. We did turn an 11–3 half-time deficit into a four-point lead with tries by Rog and Neil Best. But if the Wallabies get a sniff, they're lethal, and one try led to a second, a third and a fourth. We were beaten 37–15. After a long season, when most of the Irish squad had played into the later stages of the Heineken Cup, it was a game too far.

Munster began the 2006–7 campaign as reigning European champions. Now we were a more prized scalp than ever.

The beginning of the league campaign was shaky. As the IRFU's player-management protocols prioritized the national team, most of our front-line players sat out a number of early fixtures, and it took us a while to find our rhythm.

The coming of the Heineken Cup pool stages concentrated minds. The fact that our first opponents were Leicester, at Welford Road, concentrated minds even more. In an interview before the match, Rog said it as he saw it. He talked about how Sky Sports had over-hyped the English Premiership, and said: 'I honestly think that, both for Munster and Ireland, we've got more talented players than the English in many positions.'

He talked the talk, and then he walked the walk as well. It was a horrible day but we started quite well. Donners, being Donners, made a fifty-metre break to score. Wally added a second to put us 15–6 in front. But in the second half Leicester were dominant in the scrum and fought back to lead 19–18.

When Shane Jennings threw the ball away after conceding a penalty in the last minute, it moved our penalty forward ten metres to about fifty-two metres out. Rog reckoned that brought it into his range. Despite the muddy conditions underfoot, he nailed it. Our second win at Welford Road.

On the back of that we beat Bourgoin at home the following week, 41–23. Mike Prendergast had moved to Bourgoin, and the turning point was his yellow card: we scored two tries while he was in the bin. He wouldn't have been too pleased about that, on his return to his home city.

I like Mikey, although he must have been pissed off at sitting on the bench so often for eighty minutes behind me. I can certainly sympathize more with him now, after what's happened to me in later years. At the time I was too self-absorbed to notice.

The Springboks arrived for the autumn internationals in their centenary year. To mark the occasion, they wore old-fashioned jerseys with huge white patches on the back, big black numbers and high collars. Very old-school.

We cut them to pieces a few times and could have added to our four tries, but for their typical last-ditch tackling. We played the wide-wide game we'd used in 2004, but this time their defence wasn't nearly as strong or aggressive.

This was the season when Denis Leamy came to the fore. I knew Leams from UCC. He could be quite hot-headed; you could see he was just boiling inside. Anything could kick him off. Off the pitch Leams was quiet, even shy at times. On it, he punched way above his weight. He had huge upper-body strength, and was one of the most skilful forwards I ever played with. He had an incredible pass off both hands. Munster even tried him at centre, while Woody always maintained he could have been a hooker. And Leams did have an American Football-style throw which could propel the ball a mile. Being a Tipperary man, he'd always have the hurley and sliotar at training, and he enjoyed the banter with the Cork lads.

Against South Africa, he had such a good game at number 8. For one of our tries he broke off the back of the scrum and twice handed off Pierre Spies. It took a fourth man to bring him down eventually, and we got quick ball for Andrew Trimble to score under the posts.

For the last try, Drico eyeballed their left winger, François Steyn, then flicked a one-handed no-look pass out the back for Shaggy to score in the corner. That summed up our day. Everything clicked. They came up hard defensively, but our passing kept beating them.

A week later, against Australia, Eddie gave Isaac Boss the start at 9. I didn't see it coming, but I was told that they were looking to see what he could do in a big game, and I believed them. Bryan Young was also given a start.

Terrible conditions again – wind and rain – and Matt Giteau played 9 for them. When I came on for the last seven minutes, the game had long since been won; in fact it had been won by half-time. We'd chosen to play into the wind and were 15–3 up at the interval. Denis Hickie, also recalled, jinked over from a cross-kick by Rog. Geordie, also back in the team, scored off an inside pass from Shaggy. No one could complain about the selection.

Munster had a good December. I was a sub for the win over Connacht and played eighty minutes for our next four wins – back-to-back against Cardiff in Europe, Leinster at Thomond Park and Connacht again in the Sportsground.

The Cardiff games were tough, and that Arms Park pitch was consistently one of the worst I've ever played on. That day it was muddy, with hardly a blade of grass. It was a good advert for a plastic pitch, which they've since installed.

Darragh Hurley was called in late that day for his Heineken Cup debut. He was a really popular fella around the squad, and everybody was so genuinely happy for him.

That was also the day Donners had his shorts ripped off, and revealed his red underwear. He wanted to continue until there was a break in play before putting on new shorts, and I was standing nearest to him, with Wally behind him, ready for lifting duties at a line-out.

Wally smirked and said to Donners: 'What am I supposed to do? How am I going to lift you with no shorts on?' Hayes pushed past Wally. He didn't care if he had to lift Donncha with no shorts, whereas Wally was relieved.

Donners' jocks were donated to the Munster museum and, being red, cemented his place as a Munster legend. He's been asked about it so much I'd say he wishes now he'd just gone off and put on a pair of shorts. For Donners, though, it was nothing out of the ordinary. Get on with the job. Do whatever it takes to continue playing. If he'd had to play naked he'd have done it.

The predictable comments greeted him at the Monday morning review. 'Yeah, it was a very cold day all right. You could tell. You could tell!'

Let's leave it at that.

It was a day to acquire a lead and turn the screw with the pack. Because of the conditions, I put a number of rolling kicks over the top behind their wingers. Afterwards I chatted with Xavier Rush and he cursed me for those kicks.

Leams was still on fire, scoring the only try that day, and two of the four when we won with a bonus point at home a week later. I took great pleasure in annoying Mike Phillips all day, although he seemed to be annoyed most days. I don't really know Mike off the pitch at all, and I haven't had a chance to ask him, but he is a very tall scrum-half and I wonder whether I get to him more than other opponents because of my height. That day, from a Cardiff scrum, the ball came out at the base, and when Mike was a bit slow picking it up I kicked it down the field. He ran back and, with no other option, kicked the ball into touch on their 22. I could see Leams coming like a train twenty yards infield and I took a quick throw to him, clearing Martyn Williams with the pass; he carried two or three tacklers over the line with him to score. He was always ready for anything off-the-cuff.

In January we beat Bourgoin 30–27 in Zurich. Perfect conditions. Perfect pitch. A fourth try would have meant we'd need only a losing bonus point at home to Leicester in our final game to win the pool and have a home quarter-final. We only managed three. With the last play of the game Axel went off the back of the scrum. Their winger came in to tackle him and I was outside him, screaming for the ball. I was only two or three yards from the line, but he dummied and was tackled by the winger. I always regretted that, because of the consequences.

A week later we lost a Heineken Cup tie at Thomond Park for the first time ever. That was one of our most frustrating and hurtful defeats. We took so much pride in that record at Thomond, and we had a sense of what everybody had to bring to make sure that that record stood tall: every player who played there, every spectator who came along. We didn't want the record to end on our watch.

It was another bad day, weather-wise, and we couldn't gain any ascendancy up front. Ian Humphreys ran the show for them, sitting back and shifting the attack from one side of the ruck to the other. He kept chipping in behind, turning us and finding the corners. Shane Jennings played really well. After the penalty he conceded in Welford Road and as a proud Leinsterman, I'm sure he had a few points to prove.

As in the 2002 final, we played between the two 15-metre lines, and they just ate us up. Defensively it was easy for them. At times you have to be brave and play in those outside channels, if only to spread the defence a bit for the next phase.

The fact that we had already qualified for the quarter-finals, and were playing only for home advantage, might have worked against us. Normally in the last pool match, at home to an English team, we'd have our backs to the wall. Usually we had to win, maybe also with a bonus point, and maybe by twenty-seven points! Having qualified already didn't suit our mentality.

With Lansdowne Road being rebuilt, Croke Park became our home for the Six Nations. But first we had to beat Wales in Cardiff. We were 12–9 up, with seven or eight minutes to go, when Rog's one-handed touchdown sealed the win.

With about fifteen minutes to go, I cracked a bone in my hand in a tackle without realizing it, and stayed on for the rest of the game. I knew there was something wrong in the changing room – there was a big lump on the back of my hand.

Ireland's first-ever game at Croke Park was the following Sunday against France. The lads said: 'You'll be fine. There's nothing wrong with you.'

I thought: *Oh Jesus, I don't know.*

The scan revealed a cracked bone in my third finger. My hand was put in plaster for three days to help it settle down.

Sean Boylan, who had been the Meath football manager for over twenty years and who was also a fifth-generation herbalist, dropped some home-made poultice to the Shelbourne. It was made of bran, flour and herbs, a concoction normally used to reduce inflammation in horses' tendons and ligaments. It brought the swelling down.

On Friday I did my fitness test in Croke Park. It was my first time in that huge arena. I began with some passing, before Mike McGurn had me try and hold on to a tackle suit he was wearing. I couldn't do it.

When the test was finished he asked me: 'How do you feel?'

'Not bad, a bit sore.'

The physios were there as well and they just shook their heads.

Mikey said: 'You'll be back stronger and you'll be back for the next one. Let's just forget about this.'

On my own in the changing room afterwards I was in tears. The build-up for our first game in Croke Park was massive. The GAA's decision to allow rugby to be played in Croke Park, and the sense of history and occasion, made it more than a game of rugby. I desperately wanted to play on that pitch, in front of 80,000.

Eddie came in and said that Mikey had told him that I had failed the fitness test.

'Look, don't worry about it, kid,' he said. 'You'll be back sooner rather than later. Keep the head up. It's the right thing. If your hand isn't right then we're not going to play you.'

I knew they were right.

Drico's hamstring had ruled him out as well, so the two of us sat together in the stands. It was devastating to miss the match, and devastating to watch it.

We didn't play to our best. Maybe the occasion was a little too much. Even so, our desire and work rate had us in a winning position until Vincent Clerc intervened. You have to give the French credit. If we'd won in Paris with a try like that, it would have been replayed for ever.

Clerc has such good feet. Hayes found himself in a position where Clerc could target him and run at him. It was a great try, but heartbreaking.

After that loss, losing our next match – against England at Croke Park – was not an option. Due to the history between the two countries, and the venue, this was definitely more than just a game of rugby.

There was plenty of speculation in the press about what would happen when 'God Save the Queen' was played in GAA headquarters, the place where fourteen civilians had been killed by police and British Auxiliaries on Bloody Sunday in 1920. Chatting among ourselves in the build-up to the game, the players genuinely believed that there wouldn't be any hassle. And sure enough, when 'God Save the Queen' was sung, you could actually hear the English team and supporters singing along. There wasn't one boo around the stadium.

Our supporters had decided: 'Let them have their anthem, but by God, when we sing ours we're going to make sure that they hear it.'

I'll remember the singing of the Irish anthem that day for the rest of my life. It was as good a rendition as I've ever heard. I don't think I'll ever hear noise like it again. The Irish supporters also sang 'Ireland's Call' like I'd never heard them sing it before.

There was a delay before kick-off due to a hitch with the referee's earpiece. Both teams were ready to go, and the two-minute interlude allowed time for the crowd to break into, and finish, 'The Fields of Athenry'. Their passion and energy spilled on to the pitch in bucketloads.

We flew into rucks, tackled anything in white that moved, and we maintained that momentum through the entire eighty minutes. Our skills levels had never been better in the rain, because we mixed up our wide-wide game with our direct game so well. Shaggy's try off Rog's cross-kick – Gaelic football skills in Croke Park – crowned it perfectly. When Isaac Boss scored an intercept try, I laughed: I'd never been so happy for my replacement to score.

It was simply impossible to scale those heights again, two weeks later, in Murrayfield. Another scratchy win over the Scots, by a point, and Rog scored all the points.

I actually don't remember anything about the game. Nothing. We won another Triple Crown that day, but we'd now moved beyond Triple Crowns. We needed a championship. Ireland hadn't won the title since 1985. And because France lost to England the day after we beat Scotland, there were four teams – including Italy – in with a chance of lifting the trophy.

The final match in Rome was the one time in my life I'd have loved to know exactly how much we needed to win by – but because we were playing first that day, we had no idea. It was a crisp, sunny afternoon in the Stadio Flaminio, and it felt like a home match. The last days of the Celtic Tiger. As usual, away supporters made more of an effort to wear the colours, but then again it was St Patrick's Day. It's a small ground but the crowd created a lovely atmosphere.

France had a four-point advantage over us in points differential, and we expected them to win by a decent margin at home to Scotland, so we knew we needed a big win. Conditions were ideal for throwing the ball around. We wanted to be brave. We wanted to play with ambition, use our instincts. We didn't want to come back into the changing room regretting we hadn't given it a go. All week we were saying publicly that we were just going out to win the game, but internally there was very much a mindset of scoring as many points as we could.

We scored eight tries and could have scored more. With a minute to go, we led 51–17, and that would have left France needing to win by thirty-one. We were awarded a penalty in injury time, which we could have kicked dead. It could have been enough. But how were we to know? We were going to go for it. No regrets.

Leams took a quick tap in the middle of the pitch, was tackled, and at the resulting ruck we were turned over. Italy regained possession, went downfield and scored. It went to the TMO. It looked like a double movement, but eventually the try was awarded. The touchline conversion by Andrea Scanavacca meant France's target was down to twenty-four.

The dressing room was quiet. We felt that we probably hadn't done enough, that those last seven points could be the difference.

Our hotel foyer in the Via Vittorio Veneto, where we watched the end of the France match a couple of hours later, wouldn't have been the ideal place to become champions. But we wouldn't have cared. We would have been champions.

Right at the death, France, still four points short of their target, mauled over the line. It wasn't clear if they'd touched down, and so it went to the TMO. Simon McDowell. An Irishman. Watching it, I thought: 'No. There's no way that he could see any grounding there.'

I think he just gave the attacking team the benefit of the doubt. France won the title by three points. Absolutely devastating.

At the final whistle, the players, IRFU committee members (including the outgoing president, Peter Boyle, and the incoming president, Der Healy), family, friends and supporters dispersed and filtered away. I went to my room for a while and lay down. I thought of scores we had missed out on, or conceded, over the five games.

Perhaps if Drico and I had been fit against France, we might have won a Grand Slam. Instead, we came away with nothing. Another one that got away.

Thirteen days later, on Friday, 30 March, without having had a game together since the defeat to Leicester at Thomond in January, Munster went to Llanelli for the Heineken Cup quarter-final. For the game in between, against Ulster at Ravenhill, Deccie rested the players who'd been involved in the Six Nations. It's a tough call for a coach: he has to choose between resting tired players and giving them a chance to gel.

Llanelli Scarlets 24, Munster 15. The scoreline flattered us really, as we scored a late try. They ran riot. They dominated us completely. We went 17–0 down and were never in the game, playing as if we were punch-drunk. The atmosphere in Stradey Park was like the old days there, like matches I'd watched on TV as a kid, the thousands from the valleys roaring on a very Welsh brand of rugby.

They were more focused, better prepared as a team. We were under-cooked. We needed more game time together.

It was the second half before we woke up and realized we were defending champions. Way too late. Maybe our desire wasn't quite the same. Maybe our confidence had been dented by Leicester. But mostly I think it was rustiness. No game for three months is no way to prepare for a quarter-final.

I wouldn't play again until 16 August. I missed our last five league games with a neck injury. Then the Irish front-liners were wrapped in cotton wool to prepare for the World Cup.

16.   The Lowest Point

There had been so much hype, and all of it seemed justified.

The team of fifteen players who had destroyed England were all in their mid or late twenties and had fifty-plus caps under their belts. It should have been one of the best Irish World Cup teams ever, perhaps the best; everyone believed that, ourselves included.

My agent, John Baker, negotiated a footwear and clothing deal with Nike during the run-up. His bargaining line was, 'Imagine a World Cup final between New Zealand and Ireland, and no other Irish players wearing Nike boots except Strings against an All Blacks team entirely in Adidas.' That was how people were thinking at the time.

What went wrong? We didn't have enough rugby under our belts, me especially. The neck injury had brought a premature end to my 2006–7 season with Munster, and as the fifteen players who started the win over England were rested from the two-Test tour to Argentina before our extended pre-season, I didn't play any match from the end of March until midway through August. Four and a half months: the longest break in my life without a game.

You can do all the fitness work in the world, but nothing replicates matches – particularly Test matches. Another trip to Spala in Poland was part of our pre-season, and overall there was a heavy emphasis on physical preparation to the exclusion of match preparation.

We got our training wrong, spending very little time on what actually mattered when we went on to a rugby pitch. You can be as big, strong and as fit as you want, but if you don't have the skill set, the knowledge of a game plan and the understanding of guys around you in a game situation, then you're just not going to succeed. Come match time, you'll be pretty clueless.

That's the way we found ourselves in the warm-up games. I didn't make it back for the 31–21 defeat to Scotland in Murrayfield, but I joined the squad for a week in the town of Capbreton, on the south-western coast, acclimatizing for the higher temperatures and harder grounds in Bordeaux, where we'd be playing our first two World Cup group games, against Namibia and Georgia.

Bayonne were hastily arranged opponents on the Thursday night of that week. We needed more game time, but we didn't need the Battle of Bayonne. They were just out to cause us physical damage. That night we spent more time trying to control the outbreak of fights around the pitch rather than concentrating on our plays and looking to how we could improve on things.

That was how Drico came to suffer a fractured sinus: trying to break up a fight and being caught unseen with a punch from side-on by Makeera Tewhata. It was a cheap shot on a night of cheap shots.

I didn't think I played particularly well. Hardly anyone played that well. But when Redser replaced me I received a standing ovation. I thought to myself: 'Jesus, what the hell is going on here? Maybe I didn't play too badly.' A French supporter later told me it was due to my try against Biarritz in the Heineken Cup final, over a year previously. I'd become a cult hero to the Bayonne fans. That's how much they hated their local Basque rivals.

After the game, everybody was quite down. We'd been in a battle and gained little from the game; the 42–6 'win' had come at a heavy cost. Sitting in the lobby of our beach hotel later that night, Drico's right eye started to close while I was chatting with him, and the cheek on that side of his face was quite sunken. He was in terrible pain and unable to manage any facial expressions. Pending the results of his X-ray, he didn't know how serious the injury was, and whether it could ruin his World Cup. Thankfully, it wasn't too serious, and he returned for the Namibia game.

Eight days later, we played Italy in Ravenhill, and now the warning signs were becoming alarming. I'd struggled with a back spasm all week and I probably shouldn't have played. A scrum-half is constantly bending down and rotating, and my body wasn't really up to it that night.

We were lucky to win it. Rog was awarded a match-winning try with the last play, even though he didn't appear to ground the ball. Alessandro Troncon had to be restrained by teammates at the end as he tried to confront the referee, Nigel Owens.

The win may have brushed over the cracks a little, but we were not building any momentum. We were quite clueless at times. There was a hope that things would somehow click when the pool games started, two weeks later, because we had a good team that had played well in the Six Nations.

We were based in a lakeside hotel on the outskirts of Bordeaux, which may sound pretty picturesque and serene but was far from that. The lake was small and man-made, and the area was mostly an industrial estate, a long way from the city centre, and there was nothing much to do. The squad was meant to have stayed in a new five-star hotel in the centre, but it wasn't completed in time for the World Cup, which meant a late change of venue and a completely different experience for us. Bordeaux is lovely, but our place on the outskirts had the grim atmosphere of an airport hotel.

The food was poor. We filled up on flatbread and Nutella.

There was no gym in the hotel. Mike McGurn had to set up a makeshift gym in a relatively small function room, next to our team meeting room, with a few dumb-bells and squat racks and benches, on a carpeted floor.

These are no excuses for our poor results in the World Cup. Our performances just weren't good enough. But when the preparations aren't right, the environment isn't right and the performances aren't right, it can create a vicious circle. If performances had been better we might have taken more taxi rides into town, enjoyed the shops and cafés and the atmosphere of Bordeaux. But the games against Namibia and Georgia didn't encourage us to get out and about, where we'd see supporters and maybe even members of the media.

The Stade Chaban-Delmas is a lovely ground. There was a full house for the Namibia match, plenty of Irish there, and we actually started well. Drico scored early, and we should have dominated them from start to finish. But whereas at training our plays and moves were coming off, we were taken aback by how aggressive Namibia were at the breakdown. We couldn't control our ruck ball. We had players standing off in wide channels, and we didn't resource our rucks sufficiently. That should have been instinctive, once we saw the rucks were going wrong, but it just wasn't there. The Namibians were good at coming through the breakdown and getting over the ball. We never looked like losing, but it wasn't the performance that we needed to generate confidence and momentum.

We won 32–17. At the previous World Cup we'd scored exactly double that tally of points against Namibia. Our poor performance brought the French 'neutrals' into the game. It had been the Irish fans making all the noise at the start, but by the end the crowd were chanting '*Allez les Bleus*', as Namibia wore blue. France had lost their opener in our group to Argentina, so the French fans had us in their sights. They became louder and louder. It had started out feeling like a home game, and it finished feeling like an away game. It was all pretty demoralizing.

After the Namibia game we wanted to keep our heads down, keep to ourselves and work on the training ground and in our analysis, to correct the many flaws. We developed a 'try harder', bunker mentality, which probably only made things worse.

If Eddie's starting team had gone well against Italy and had hammered Namibia, then he probably would have rotated the squad for the Georgia match. Instead, he decided he needed to give his first-choice players a chance to play themselves into form, and the only change saw Shaggy return from injury in place of Andrew Trimble.

Back at the Stade Chaban-Delmas on another balmy night, the Georgia match was a terrifying experience. The French crowd supported Georgia even more passionately than they had Namibia. Again we started decently, and a maul from our line-out worked a try for Rory Best. But as the night unfolded I felt like I was playing in a daze. I wasn't alone.

Nothing came easily for us. We were losing the collisions, we were being turned over at the breakdown. You could almost see everyone thinking, 'What do we do next?' We weren't talking to one another, we were arguing. No clarity. No cohesion.

We led by just 7–3 at half-time. Four minutes into the second half came my worst moment on a rugby pitch. Ever.

We were trying to play our wide-wide game. Rog went to a ruck on the left touchline as scrum-half, and I was first receiver, as we'd practised in training and done a few times in matches.

Rog passed to me. I was quite deep and took the ball standing still. Shaggy was on my outside, and as I watched the pass from Rog to me, I heard Shaggy's call to miss him. A French number 9 in the 10 position might have been able to adapt better than I did. I skip-passed Shaggy to hit Drico. I didn't see the Georgian winger, Giorgi Shkinin, shoot out of the line until I had let the ball go.

It was like watching a nightmare unfold in slow motion. Drico didn't have a chance to turn inside. Shkinin came on to the ball, intercepted, then ran sixty metres to score under the posts. Georgia led 10–7. Fear gripped me like never before or since on a rugby pitch. I was consumed by a terrible thought: *What if this is the final score? What if we lose this game because of my pass being intercepted?*

Although Darce made another break, and Drico and Fla worked a try for Girvan to put us back in front, we were never really on top. I was taken off with eleven minutes to go, after a period when Georgia were camped on our line. I've never felt as ashamed as I did that night walking to the sideline. I would have swapped the Stade Chaban-Delmas at that moment for anywhere else in the world.

When I was replaced and I reached the sideline, I didn't want to make eye contact with my teammates. At that moment I felt I didn't deserve the respect of those guys alongside me. The bottom line after every game is that you want to return to the changing room and be able to look your teammates in the eye. When you can't, it's a pretty horrible place to be. Sitting on that bench – with Marcus and Rory, who had also been taken off, and Mal, Paddy Wallace and Geordie, who hadn't been brought on – was the longest ten minutes of my career, and one of the most uncomfortable experiences of my life.

Nobody said a word. No words would have helped me, anyway, but I knew what everyone else was thinking. I felt like I'd let down, not just my teammates, but also a nation that had such huge hopes for us. When Georgia started pounding our line near the end, for what seemed like forever, I felt physically sick inside. I wanted to throw up.

Georgia were playing to their strengths. Their pack kept picking and going. Pounding and pounding at us. Five minutes left. Four. Three. The Georgians were on our line.

Then, from the bench, all we could see were Georgians jumping up and down, celebrating. I really thought that we'd lost to Georgia, there and then. Ireland had just lost to Georgia in a rugby match at the World Cup. And it was down to me.

The referee, Wayne Barnes, went to the TMO. The replay showed that Denis Leamy had somehow positioned his shovel-like hand under the ball. I'll never be in so much debt to another player.

We survived the remaining minutes, but there was no celebrating. When I threw that intercept pass, Drico threw his arms up and was raging with me. Relief, anger and embarrassment were mixed together in the changing room, and Drico was still furious with me.

I didn't have any comeback. I never mentioned that Shaggy had called for me to skip the pass. It wasn't the place. I didn't want to pick a row with Drico and I didn't want to pass the buck to Shaggy or anyone else. I should have seen their winger out of the corner of my eye.

With a six-day turnaround to the game against France in Paris, the team was to be announced on the Monday. At 7.35 on Monday morning, there was a knock on my bedroom door. My heart skipped a few beats. A horrible, sick feeling swept through me. A knock on your door at 7.35 on the morning of a team announcement is never a good sign. I was rooming with Wally, and in the seconds it took me to answer the door I figured there was only one of us who the knock was intended for, and only one man to deliver it.

Sure enough, I opened the door to find Eddie standing there. My heart sank. My stomach turned a few more times. His body language and his facial expression were clear indications as to the purpose of his early visit. He stepped inside the door.

'Strings, I have some bad news. I am going to have to leave you out of the team for this weekend.'

I'd been a regular in the team for seven years. I knew I'd never had a divine right to any jersey, and I hadn't played well against Georgia, but his words were like a shot in the heart. Until I heard the knock on the door, I really didn't see it coming. Maybe I should have.

I felt the need to question him but I was so stunned I couldn't open my mouth.

Later, I regretted not standing up for myself. I should have made it difficult for him. I had been his first-choice scrum-half for five years. We'd had plenty of success. But I felt paralysed, so I said nothing.

'Sorry,' he said. 'I have just one more thing to say to you. You're not on the bench either.'

Even in my state of shock, I'd assumed I'd be on the bench at least. As all sorts of thoughts swirled around my head, I managed to mumble: 'Who's playing?'

'Redser is playing,' he said as he inched towards the door. 'Sorry, Strings. Look, I know it's difficult. I've been really good to you over the years and selected you on numerous occasions.'

It came across as though he thought he had been doing me a favour by picking me, and as though he was dismissing almost everything that I had contributed to the team over seven years. He turned and walked out, and I closed the door.

Wally must have heard, or at any rate guessed, what had happened, but he didn't know what to say, and there was an awkward silence. Eventually he asked and I told him.

I went down to the team meeting and my head was down. I didn't know what to do. I was embarrassed and didn't want to chat with anyone.

It was a very strange feeling. I had felt so comfortable in that environment every day since my debut in February 2000. Now, for the first time since then – bar the odd injury or game I had been rested for – I wouldn't be involved in the warm-up. I wouldn't be getting psyched up for the next game.

I went to the game, along with everybody else, that Friday night at the Stade de France. I didn't want to mope around all week in the team hotel and at training so, as hard as it was, I tried to be as positive as I could in training sessions.

But off the pitch, in the team room and in the hotel, I was a different person. My normal giddiness in the week of a Test match was gone. I avoided eye contact as much as I could, especially walking past the media. This was new territory for me. I spent as much time as I could in my room.

The two other changes to the team were forced by injuries to Rory Best and Denis Hickie, meaning Fla and Andrew Trimble were called in. I was the only player dropped from the fifteen, dropped indeed from the match-day twenty-three. Isaac Boss stayed on the bench, while Redser was promoted from third-choice scrum-half to the starting team. It made no sense. I heard from Mick Riordan and my dad that there'd been media pressure to pick Redser ahead of me, and Eddie must have been feeling the pressure too after two poor performances.

Mick, my buddy from UCC, rang me when he heard the team announcement, back home. He was raging. 'What the fuck are they thinking? You've just been made a scapegoat.'

Soon, wild rumours about trouble in the camp began to spread. These included me having a go back at Drico in the changing room after the Georgia game and punching him. This explained why I had been dropped altogether from the twenty-three, as a disciplinary measure.

In the days afterwards Mum rang me and told me that our performances had been debated on *Questions and Answers*. After all the expectation, it was a national crisis. I had to assure her that, no, I did not punch Drico in the changing room, and no, I was not having an affair with Rog's wife, Jessica. Nor had Geordie to be hauled back from the airport when on the verge of flying home. None of these rumours, or any of the other ones, was remotely true.

The next two weeks were the worst of my career, watching us lose to France and Argentina and wondering where my career was going.

What's going to happen?

Is my international career over?

Are they going to look at me again?

Is this it?

I didn't want my last game for Ireland to be that horror show against Georgia, and for the supporters to have the intercept pass as their final memory of me in an Irish jersey. It felt like I'd let my people down.

Match day. No warm-up. No psych-up. Nothing. I felt so empty, arriving at the ground in my blazer, shirt and tie, carrying a few bags and water bottles into the away changing room. I felt irrelevant, both then and sitting in the stands watching the game. On the substitutes' bench, you're on the edge of your seat, waiting to be called on and analysing how you can make a difference; looking at the opposition, where the space is. In the stands, there's nothing you can contribute.

The changing room after the Argentina match was deathly quiet. Players stared emptily at walls or the ground, as if in another world or hypnotized, or just in utter disbelief. Normally, those outside the twenty-three might offer a few consoling words, but nobody could say anything to anybody to make them feel better about it, so nobody tried.

The players showered and changed in their own time, then walked out to the bus, which drove us back to our hotel. We all felt a sense of shame over how we had performed.

Returning to Munster was like returning to a family environment. It was a comforting place. A place you knew well.

There was some slagging. Axel texted me regularly to say he'd made sure that he had all the Shannon line-out calls and backs' calls ready for me when I returned to play club rugby after the dismal performances in France. In another text, he said that we weren't the first Irish team to disgrace the nation and we wouldn't be the last.

The slagging was good. You have to have a tough skin to survive, and you didn't want it any other way. Back in that Munster environment nobody tip-toed on eggshells. Get it out in the open. But deep down you knew that your teammates, your friends, had your back covered, and would welcome you back with open arms. It was quite refreshing.

Rua Tipoki had arrived that season to play alongside Lifeimi Mafi in midfield. Mafs had a good step, but Rua had the best footwork and best side-step I've ever seen. Tackling him in training was almost impossible. You would be a hundred per cent convinced that Rua would step one way and, without fail, he would step the other way and round you every single time.

He arrived with a reputation back in New Zealand as a hard man, and he was. Hard as nails. I don't think I've ever played with a more passionate rugby player, either. He bought into the whole Munster set-up, too. He chatted with me one night, saying he'd watched the 2006 Heineken Cup final on DVD and had been blown away by what he'd seen. He told me he wanted to win something with Munster: 'I'm going to be there for you on the pitch.' He was so emotional, I wanted to play a game for him right there and then.

He and Mafs played so well together. Neither was a big man, but Mafs' offloading and Rua's passing skills gave our back play another dimension.

In the Heineken Cup, we were in another Group of Death. Wasps, the holders, first up away, followed by Clermont at home. Again, we started off with a defeat in England, but only by 24–23 to Wasps in the Ricoh Arena in a game we could have won.

We beat Clermont 36–13 at Thomond, which was being redeveloped and was at only half capacity. They rotated their squad but still had a good team. John Smit, the Springboks World Cup-winning captain in France, had just joined them and he played that day. So did Aurelien Rougerie. But our forwards dominated Clermont and we had some really good back play. Brian Carney had joined us from Rugby League and also gave us something extra. They may not have been at full strength, but not many teams beat Clermont by that kind of margin.

Our game away to the Scarlets in December was played in probably the worst conditions I have ever experienced. A hailstorm at one point during the game was so severe Wayne Barnes had to bring the two captains together to stop the game. He even considered sending the two teams inside for a while.

We were desperate to win that game, having lost in the quarter-finals on the same ground the previous season; so desperate that when we were defending a 29–16 lead late on, we went through a zig-zag pattern of pick-and-go or one-off runners for thirty-three phases. I had two pods of four forwards to hit on either side, and some of the backs joined in, probably to avoid hypothermia.

That kind of win is as good for morale in the changing room as a high-scoring try-fest. There's no better feeling than coming into a dressing room where everybody knows they've given everything for their teammates. A week later we beat them again, at home, in another tough game.

Clermont were brilliant against us in January. They had scored eighty-five points in beating Wasps and the Scarlets at home. They went 23–6 up, but critically we hung in for a bonus point, thanks to a try by Mafs. They had a couple in the bin and we ran it from everywhere, looking to offload. Our prop Tony Buckley, aka Mushie, charged up the touchline at one stage, brushed off a couple of their players, and passed outside to Mafs, who ran in from about thirty metres.

In our last pool game we needed to beat Wasps, and deny them a bonus point, in order to top the group above them and Clermont. It was the 2006 winners against the 2007 winners. It was a wet, cold, dark, muddy day. And even in a half-built Thomond, the atmosphere was cracking.

Leams, Simon Shaw and Lawrence Dallaglio were all sin-binned by Nigel Owens. Our pack destroyed their line-out and Rog had us 12–3 ahead inside the last ten minutes. Then we went through twenty-one phases, kept things nice and tight and waited for our opportunity. I passed to Rog going down the east side of the ground and, as their defenders pushed up, he went through the gap and fed Leams, who stepped inside and scored.

The crowd went crazy. That game marked the introduction of 'Stand Up and Fight'. The choir had sung it before we came out and the supporters adopted it after that try. The players already knew it: whenever we won on the road, our manager Brian O'Brien would go to the front of the bus and sing every inspiring verse.

The Six Nations was new territory for me.

Redser started all five games and I was given very little game time. I came on for the last six minutes in the opener, at home to Italy, stayed on the bench for all eighty when we lost in Paris, got nine minutes against Scotland, was left on the bench for eighty when we lost 16–12 at home to Wales, and then played the last nine minutes away to England, when we were beaten 33–10.

I generally have good memories of playing under Eddie, barring that season. But the hangover from the World Cup wouldn't go away. Confidence was low and we finished fourth with three defeats out of five – our worst performance since Italy joined the Six Nations. A bad World Cup had become a bad season. It wasn't a case of a bad performance here or there. We had played consistently below par for eleven matches. Inevitably, the England game was Eddie's last in charge.

Three weeks after Twickenham, Munster were back in England to play Gloucester away in the quarter-finals of the Heineken Cup.

During the Six Nations, I played for Munster against Edinburgh and Cardiff, sat on the bench against Ulster, when Tomás started, then started against Connacht a week before Gloucester. I desperately wanted to make a difference in those Munster games, perhaps too much so. My confidence had been dented by the World Cup and then being left on the sidelines in the Six Nations. Every minute I had on the pitch suddenly seemed magnified, and I had the feeling that my every move was being analysed by coaches.

I thought I needed to do more in order to impress them. My thinking became muddled. Reasoning that my own game had seen me dropped by Ireland, I began trying things I might not normally have tried. I tried to reinvent myself. It was the first crisis of confidence in my career. In later years, I came to terms with what I'm good at, what had served my teams and me well. If a coach wanted to try different combinations, I didn't over-react. I didn't have to take it as a sign that I needed to overhaul my game. I merely needed to have confidence in my own ability and keep working hard.

My international career never again reached the heights of 2000–2007, but I don't have any regrets about my form or my attitude towards the game. I became more professional than I'd ever been, and more at peace with myself.

But back then my head was in turmoil. The Ulster game had been the first warning sign. Then, when Deccie dropped me in favour of Tomás against Gloucester, it was a major shock to the system.

I'd started all six pool games, controlled the tempo really well in the wins over the Scarlets and the games away to Clermont and at home to Wasps. I'd enjoyed being back in the environment, and was enjoying my rugby again. But I wouldn't play one minute of Munster's three knockout games.

Not one minute.

Before the team was announced to play Gloucester, Deccie rang me.

'I'm going to go with Tomás, seeing as he's been doing well while you've been away. He's been doing really well for us.'

There was nothing I could say. I had been penalized for being away with Ireland and not getting enough game time with either team. It's happened to other players and will happen again. Still, the shock and disappointment was a bitter pill to swallow.

Tomás played well in the win away to Gloucester, but he didn't have a great game against Saracens in the semi-final. As the second half wore on, I thought surely I'd get a chance to come off the bench and show what I could do. But I was left on the bench and, when the final whistle went, so too did my chance of playing in the final against Toulouse.

Returning to Cardiff, where I had such incredible memories of the final, two years before, was strange. I looked at that number 9 jersey hanging in the dressing room – the jersey that had been mine for nine years at Munster – and felt gutted. For that eighty minutes I was lower than I should have been. I would have loved to get called on but sensed I wouldn't be, and I was right.

When the full-time whistle went, my emotions were mixed. I felt happy for my mates, for Munster, for the supporters, but I'd played no part in the win, and didn't feel I belonged in the celebrations. As we walked around the pitch, Paulie handed the cup to me. I felt awkward and embarrassed. I hadn't done anything to deserve lifting the cup to the supporters. I lifted it, faked a smile and felt empty inside.

Deccie hugged me and said: 'Thank you, you're a really special person.'

I had absolutely no idea what way to take that comment. It left me stumped. I didn't really return the embrace. I turned and walked away. He hadn't used me for one minute in those three knockout games. Clearly, his estimation of me had gone down. Worse still, he'd been chosen to succeed Eddie as Irish coach.

★

Michael Bradley was interim coach for the Tests against the All Blacks and Australia on our summer tour. The training was short and sharp, high-intensity forty-minute sessions, and we had a go.

We led the All Blacks midway through the first half in Wellington after a try by Paddy Wallace, and were ahead again and still level in the last twenty minutes. But Dan Carter was brilliant that night and set up a try for Ma'a Nonu. By the time I came on for the last ten minutes, we were 21–11 down. I tried to up the pace, change the way the game was being played. It wasn't enough, but I loved being out there again.

Brads recalled me for my first start since that Georgia game, against Australia in the Telstra Dome, a week later. It felt like my first cap again after being out in the cold for so long.

Talking with journalists the day after I was recalled, I became quite emotional. I had thought I might never start another game for my country.

Seeing that number 9 jersey in 'size small' hanging up in our bag man Rala's room the night before the game meant the world to me. No one else had the 'size small' 9. That was mine.

It was a good game. We were competitive for eighty minutes. Again we had opportunities, but, as the All Blacks had, Australia pulled away at the end. Another disappointing tour, two losses out of two.

Emotionally, 2007–8 was the worst of my career. I'd lost my place with Ireland and Munster. For the first time, I questioned my own ability and my self-worth. I had to dig deep, and I finally realized I had to crack on with what I was doing, work on every aspect of my game, and my fitness, like never before.

My career maybe never scaled the heights of the previous years ever again, but I've never given up. I can hold my head up high. I can be proud of my achievements, of the decisions that I've made. I can wake up in the morning and go to bed at night knowing that I couldn't have done any more. Whatever comes on the back of that, so be it. As long as I can live with myself, I'm happy.

17. Grand Slam

I came back for the 2008–9 season feeling better about myself, my game, and life in general.

Tony McGahan had taken over from Deccie as Munster head coach. I hadn't got to know him well in his one season as defence coach, but he did his job efficiently and effectively.

The pre-season training camp took place at Harvard University in Boston. Normally we had pre-season camps in Spain, France or Portugal, so it was a welcome change to go further afield, and everyone bought into it. The trip included a game against the USA Eagles in Connecticut, but those of us who had been on the Ireland tour to New Zealand and Australia were rested. The set-up at Harvard was incredible. We trained on their American Football pitch, a 3G surface. The gym was state of the art, with an eight-lane running track and an array of weights and squat racks on either side – ideal for squad training.

Having not played a minute in the three Heineken Cup knockout games at the end of the 2007–8 season, I wanted to make an impression. So it was frustrating to be rested and then left on the bench for the first couple of Magners League games. I started against Cardiff but was then back on the bench again for the game against Leinster at the RDS, replacing Tomás for the last seven minutes. We were already 18–0 up, but I wanted to show what I could do, and bring my own intensity to the game. Coming on to defend a lead, the obvious tactic might be to slow the game down, but I wanted to make every minute count.

I was the 9 against Glasgow on a wet night at Thomond. Two minutes into the game I gathered a poor kick from one of their players, found touch in the corner and followed up to prevent a quick throw. One of their players threw the ball over my head – not difficult, I suppose – but John Beattie spilled it and I dived at his feet to score. I needed that confidence boost, and we went on to win 25–17.

Tomás was injured for the first European Cup match, a Friday night game at home to Montauban, so I started again. They were making their debut in the competition, picked a supposedly second-string team and had nothing to lose. A nervy night, with tough weather conditions again. They actually went ahead with three minutes to go and we needed a late penalty from Rog to scrape through.

Tomás was back a week later when we won 24–16 in Sale, playing better. I know, because I watched it for eighty minutes. Paul Warwick scored a try and a drop goal that night. Paul had played for the Australian Under-21s and 7s, which meant he was ineligible for Ireland. He had joined us the season before as back-up out-half after three seasons at Connacht and had also become a really effective full-back for us. He was such a talented footballer, with a turn of pace and exceptional skills.

He had an almost unique drop-goal style, which enabled him to land them from halfway on the run. He dropped the ball from quite a height, at an angle, tilted towards him. That decreased his margin for error, but it also increased his distance. A typical Aussie back, he loved running with the ball, attacking space and having a go at defenders. He was a well-balanced runner with superb footwork, and was accurate with his kicking. He scored six tries for us that season as well, some very important ones.

Paul and I became good friends. When I moved to Bath, he was playing in Worcester – living in Cheltenham – and then stayed on, coaching there for another season. Debbie is very good friends with his wife, Carol, who's Irish, but they're moving to Australia, where Paul will have a teaching/coaching job in a school in Brisbane.

We sent a second-string team – including me – to Ravenhill. Mike Prendergast replaced me after fifty-one minutes, which tells its own story. I didn't play well that night and we were well beaten, 22–6.

Deccie's first game as Irish coach was at Thomond Park, a 55–0 win over Canada when Keith Earls scored on his debut. I played the last twenty-five minutes as a sub for Redser in horrible conditions, and I tried to up the tempo, being as professional as I could.

The following week, against the All Blacks, I wasn't even in Croke Park. Deccie chose Tomás to make his first start for Ireland, with Redser on the bench. It was not a huge surprise that Tomás was first choice – I had feared that Deccie would continue to favour him after moving from Munster to Ireland – but it was bitterly disappointing to be out of the squad entirely.

I was to get a chance to play the All Blacks that autumn – but for Munster, at Thomond Park. Munster hadn't played for three weeks, so we had a training match against UL Bohs behind closed doors in Thomond to prepare. We won by five or six points. The UL Bohs lads were up for it, and we struggled. Had any supporters been there, they'd have expected New Zealand to put a hundred points on us, and we wouldn't have argued with them. We'd done all the training, we couldn't have been fitter. It was just an attitude thing.

Maybe that training match was the scare we needed, because fear certainly motivated us that night against New Zealand – and some of us had a few points to prove. There were a number of things that contributed to the atmosphere in Limerick in the run-up to the match and on the night itself. The match came just nine days after the tragic murder of Shane Geoghegan. Limerick being a small city, and Shane being a rugby man and a Garryowen man, his killing rocked the whole city, including the rugby community.

There was also the memory of 1978, when Munster had beaten the All Blacks. That win had put Munster on the global map. Such fixtures had become pretty unusual in the professional era, so it was a rare thing to have the best side in the world come to Limerick. The match also marked the official opening of the newly built Thomond Park.

For our pre-match lunch in the Clarion, management had invited the team of 1978 to eat with us and present us with our jerseys. I was sitting alongside Donal Canniffe, who had been the scrum-half and captain in '78, and Olann Kelleher, the sub scrum-half that day, whom I know well. They talked about how things had changed over the years. The players had full-time jobs back then, and were accustomed to having a few pints the night before the game.

The hotel foyer was crammed with supporters. A special night was brewing.

We were missing ten Irish internationals and, as in '78, it was very much David v. Goliath. You compare the two teams and you wonder how we competed with New Zealand at all on the night. Timmy Ryan made his one and only start for Munster at tight head. Donnacha Ryan made one of his first starts in the second row. We lost Leams early on, with Billy Holland replacing him. We were a team of misfits, thrown together. I don't think anyone gave us a chance, but it's amazing how fear of a hiding can motivate a team.

All the pack had played in the AIL that season, but the commitment and effort that everyone showed on the night was phenomenal, and I don't think I've ever experienced an atmosphere like it at Thomond Park.

Rua Tipoki had led the haka with NZ Maori teams and was very passionate about it. He and Dougie Howlett, who had won sixty-two caps with the All Blacks, were in favour of putting together some kind of response Munster haka. After considering getting the whole team involved, we eventually agreed that our four New Zealanders should perform it: Mafs, Rua, Dougie and Jeremy Manning. They practised it in private, so we didn't know what to expect. We were told to line up as a squad before the four guys would step out to do their haka.

How many people in their lifetime get to witness a haka against a provincial team, much less two on the same night? The two hakas fed into the crowd, which fed into the team, and the intensity, the roaring, never stopped except for kicks at goal.

Paul Warwick was on fire for us that night, landing two penalties, including one from halfway, and a drop goal. We were 10–9 down coming up to half-time, when we had a scrum inside the All Black 22. The scrum was rock-steady, James Coughlan fed me and suddenly we had a two-on-one on the blind side, with Barry Murphy in space on the wing and only Hosea Gear, their big winger, in a position to stop us. Earlier, Barry had been dazed by a clash of heads, and as he got to his feet I'd accidentally kicked the ball straight into his face. But he recovered from that, and when I drew Hosea Gear and passed to Barry, he had an easy run-in. I needed treatment after the crunching hit I took from Gear, but it was worth it! Barry was the only player to score a try against New Zealand on that tour – something Scotland, Ireland, Wales and England all failed to do.

With five minutes to go, we led by 16–13 when Joe Rokocoko scored in the corner for them. Complete silence. Everyone was stunned.

In the changing room afterwards, heads were sunk in hands. Guys were in tears. All the lads who had been involved in the Irish camp came into the dressing room. They would have seen that we'd nothing left. Emotionally and physically we were absolutely drained. Of course there was pride in the performance, but what a victory like that would have meant!

All night supporters repeatedly told us: 'You didn't let us down' and 'It was as good as a win'. You appreciate what they're saying and how much the performance meant to them. But it's never as good as a win, especially when you come that close. It's actually even harder to take than a more one-sided defeat.

After that, it was very much a case of back to normality. Tomás was in good form, and this was limiting my game time. Against Clermont away in the Heineken Cup, Tomás started and I stayed on the bench. Marcus scored a great try to help us escape from there with a bonus point again – we lost 25–19, whereas it had been 26–19 the previous season.

The following week, at home to Clermont, I was brought on with seven minutes to go, not long after they had taken a 13–11 lead with fourteen men. Tomás hadn't played too well, but he made a great tackle on Benoit Baby under the posts after he'd broken through our defence. Jamie Cudmore had been red-carded for punching Paulie, who had been yellow-carded for retaliating. Julien Malzieu scored a brilliant try from far out to put them ahead and Thomond fell eerily quiet. It was as if fear had gripped the supporters and you could sense that on the pitch.

We needed something special, and Marcus provided it with another try, before Niall Ronan sealed the win and denied them a bonus point by gathering his own chip-ahead and running in to score. He had the ability, as a good Gaelic footballer, and he had the balls to try something like that, especially on the big stage.

We came down to earth with a thud in our Christmas derbies. First Connacht beat us 12–6 in Galway. We had plenty of possession and opportunities, but they defended for their lives. They were all over us and didn't give us an inch.

I was supposed to be on the bench for the match at home to Ulster, but Tomás pulled out after his back problems flared up again, and Tony rang me to say I'd be starting. I was at home, and sick with food poisoning. Debbie and I had been in absolute bits over New Year. I could barely get out of bed, never mind start a game, but I didn't want to pass up the opportunity. I went down to Limerick, still not feeling great, but I didn't say a word to anybody. My energy levels were pretty poor, and I probably didn't do myself any favours. We were well beaten.

Tomás started away to the Ospreys, and scored a try. He started at home to Sale and away to Montauban in the Heineken Cup, and scored again. I came on for the last twenty-four minutes. He played well in those games, which made it increasingly difficult to watch from the bench.

That Montauban game had been rescheduled from the Saturday to the Sunday owing to wind and rain, and the pitch was horrendous, but we got the job done with a bonus point, to secure a home quarter-final against the Ospreys.

I was back in the Irish squad for the Six Nations.

The November series had not gone too well. We'd beaten Argentina with a late Tommy Bowe try to secure a top-eight seeding for the World Cup draw, but there was still a hangover from the disappointment of the previous season. Then the squad had a get-together in Enfield over Christmas at which Rob Kearney made his famous comments.

He was very honest. He stood and admitted that what we'd done in Munster was unbelievably special. He said he'd be lying if he didn't admit he was jealous, which was brave in front of Leinster teammates. Then he asked us if playing for Ireland meant as much as playing for Munster.

It was the elephant in the room. It prompted a very open and candid discussion that cleared the air and probably brought the squad that bit closer. Having said that, honest discussions were common enough in those team-building meetings. I don't think as much would have been made of Rob's intervention, had it not been for the results that followed.

We had France first up. They had beaten us seven times in a row since our win in 2003. They had a team full of stars and they went ahead through a brilliantly worked try by Imanol Harinordoquy. But we responded by going wide off a line-out inside our own half, and then going back, left to right, for Jamie to score. It was every bit as good a try as Harinordoquy's. Croke Park went crazy. The players went crazy, jumping all over Jamie. It was as if a huge weight had been lifted off the team and the supporters.

Even sitting on the bench, I could sense that that try gave us the freedom to play – and of course that only made me more desperate to be a part of it. But I was left on the bench as we closed out the game brilliantly, Darce scoring on his comeback and Drico adding another with an outside break past Lionel Beauxis. In one game, maybe in one moment, the hangover had been cured.

The following week, in Rome, we started poorly and were a point down when Rog was sin-binned nearing half-time. I came on for the last five minutes of the first half as a blood replacement for Paddy Wallace. He had taken some hammering on his nose and eye and looked as if he'd been twelve rounds with Tyson. Tomás went to 10, and again I tried to bring a new level of intensity with my introduction. We went through nineteen phases before Luke scored. We never looked back, winning 38–9. I came on again for the last ten minutes and at least felt I had contributed.

We had no fear of playing England, particularly at home. Things had turned since 2003. But the game was scrappy, the ball saw plenty of air, and Rog had a rare off day with his kicking at goal. The key moment came in the second half, when Drico was laid out by a late hit from Delon Armitage. As he was being treated, Paulie and Rog opted to go for the corner. England looked like they wished we'd gone for the posts. The crowd loved it and Drico dragged himself to his feet to burrow through for a try.

When I came on for the last fourteen minutes we were 11–6 up. Then there was a moment of madness from Danny Care, who'd come on only a few minutes before me. Marcus was slow getting away from their side of the ruck, but he was nowhere near the ball when Care shouldered him in the back. Care was sin-binned and Rog kicked the penalty, which meant Armitage's late converted try wasn't enough for them. We had ground out the win, our fifth against England in our last six meetings.

With three wins from three – including wins over France and England – there was no escaping talk of the Grand Slam. We had Scotland and Wales left, both away, but two games we believed we could win. The Slam was in our own hands.

Dangerous territory.

Deccie had picked the same team for the three wins, and everyone – including the players – expected he'd do so again. It was a strange one for us when he brought in Rory for Fla, Leams for Jamie, Darce for Paddy Wallace and me for Tomás.

More often than not, coaches stick with the same side in those circumstances. Why change a winning team? To be honest, I didn't see it coming – my first start for Ireland since the Australia game nine months before, and only my second since the Georgia game, twenty months previously.

Deccie's thinking was clearly to keep guys on edge and motivated. I was thrilled. I thought: 'I've an opportunity here, if I play well. Who's he going to pick the following week against Wales? I'm going to make sure I ask them that question with my performance.'

It was my first Six Nations start in two years, and I was both proud and emotional. That week I was intensely aware of the talk around the squad and in the media. Two words dominated: 'Grand' and 'Slam'.

We treated the match as a semi-final and, like all semi-finals, it was a nervy affair. We simply had to win. We couldn't let a shot at a Slam slip by. Having been so close so often, we knew this was a massive opportunity – our best so far. It would have been unforgivable to throw it away.

Our defence was phenomenal that season. After outscoring France by three tries to two, the only other try we'd conceded had been that late try by Armitage. Deccie had added Les Kiss to the coaching ticket, and he'd brought our defence to another level. He introduced the choke tackle and worked on our line speed and aggression in the tackle. Players were encouraged to bring more line speed if they saw an opening for an aggressive hit, and others would then swarm in to close any gaps. It was very much about defending together rather than as individuals.

It was our defence that kept us in touch in a tight match against Scotland. Ten minutes into the second half we were 12–9 down, when we got a line-out on their 10-metre line. The call was for the throw to go to Jamie – who had come on for an injured Leams in the first half – and for me to pass to Rog. But as the ball came down to me I spotted a gap between their 7, John Barclay, and their big lock, Nathan Hines. Completely off the cuff, I put the foot down and ran at Mike Blair, stepping one way and then the other, before doing a 180-degree turn. Blair fell over and injured his back – he had to be replaced straight afterwards. I heard Jamie roaring for the ball and thankfully my pass went into his hands. As he headed for the line he jabbed a finger into the air in celebration, holding the ball one-handed. I thought to myself: *You better not drop the ball, after all my hard work here!*

Rog landed a drop goal soon after, and then a penalty, to seal a 22–15 win. We were one step from heaven.

I was the Man of the Match that day, and coming off the pitch I felt I couldn't have done any more. No regrets; I was content with myself. Heading into what could be the biggest week ever for Irish rugby in the modern era, I'd put it up to the coaches. I had put my hand up for selection.

But on the Tuesday, Deccie restored Tomás, along with Fla and Jamie. He spoke to me that morning before announcing his starting side. 'I'm just going to put Tomás back in there,' he said. 'You played really well last week, but Tomás has been there since the start of the Six Nations and I can't dismiss that, either. He's done well for us and I'm going to put him back in.'

Disappointed as I was, if I had been in Tomás's position, having played well for Munster and also in the first three Six Nations games, winning them all, I'd have been devastated to be dropped for the last two games.

It was a bizarre selection policy, but it worked. Although I'd have loved to start that game more than any other, it wasn't the week to drop the head. There was a Grand Slam at stake with only a week's turnaround. The whole squad had to remain really positive and get the preparation right. We'd fallen short a few times before, losing a Grand Slam shoot-out with England in 2003 and missing out on the title on the last day in 2007. This time we had to get it done.

Leams and Rory were in the same position as me, back on the bench after the Scotland cameo, and we all had to see the bigger picture: Ireland hadn't won a Slam since 1949, and that was a hell of a long time ago! All of those near-misses made us realize how difficult it is to actually win a Grand Slam. We were aware that we didn't have any divine right to win this competition.

The whole week was incredible. Players were flying in training, as if we were all running on air. We just wanted to be in Cardiff. The Millennium Stadium had been a good venue for Irish teams over the years. We also had a better record against Wales in Cardiff than we had in Dublin, and it probably did us no harm being in Cardiff from the Thursday onwards, to get away from the hype and the demand for tickets at home. It's a massive rugby city, with the stadium as its heartbeat, especially on days like this.

Once again the roof was closed. They belted out 'Land of My Fathers' and 'Bread of Heaven', but 'Ireland's Call' echoed off the roof too, and 'The Fields of Athenry' followed, about ten minutes into the game. There was a huge Irish presence in the ground.

Sometimes it's possible to be quite relaxed on the bench. Not that day. In a final you don't want to slip up, and certainly not with a Grand Slam at stake. You need to be ready. So everyone was clued in.

The pack played well and we had a ton of ball, but we weren't able to do enough with it, and Stephen Jones kicked them into a 6–0 lead at half-time. But then, early in the second half, Drico burrowed over again. The referee, Wayne Barnes, was one of the few people in the ground who had seen that it might have been a try, and the TMO confirmed it.

From a scrum almost immediately afterwards, Rog chipped in behind them for Tommy Bowe to gather and beat Gavin Henson on his inside. When Tommy first arrived on the Six Nations scene in 2006, he had a few hairy moments in games. Eddie was frustrated with him and he could easily have faded away, but Tommy became one of the most improved players I've seen in the Irish set-up. Strong, quick, so good in the air, he could beat defenders, and had a huge work rate: in a short time he turned himself into a match-winner. One of the good guys in the game as well: always had a smile, was great to be around and was genuinely liked by everyone in the squad.

Tommy's try put us 14–6 up. Daylight. But Wales quickly started pegging us back, with penalties on fifty and fifty-five minutes.

As the minutes ticked along, I began to recall how Deccie had left me on the bench for the entirety of the 2008 Heineken Cup final. Same coach, same venue, same scrum-halves, another huge prize at stake. Just as I was resigning myself to the same fate, he brought me on with twelve minutes to go, along with Geordie and Rory. Making so many changes at a late stage when narrowly ahead was pretty ballsy, I suppose, but the three of us had plenty of experience.

Not long after I came on, I gathered a long kick and passed inside to Geordie, but he'd looked away. The ball went along the ground and he re-gathered it. So much for experience! That's the kind of moment when one thought goes through your head: *Don't be the one to fuck this up!*

They had a line-out and Mike Phillips came through the middle of it, handing me off. I wasn't up to speed with the game yet. He beat another couple of players, but I got back to tackle him before the line. After they recycled a couple of times, Jones landed a drop goal: 15–14 to them.

Their supporters went wild. It was all so frantic. I just wanted us to get hold of the ball and gain some control.

We still had five minutes left. No need to panic. Get the forwards picking and going. Keep it tight. We made it to their 22, on the left-hand side. At all costs control the ball at the back of the ruck. Don't pass to a forward if he's on his own and allow him to be isolated. Make sure that players are on their feet. Not a time for my usual kind of high-tempo game. Make sure we keep recycling. Work it into range for a drop goal by Rog.

Marcus, Donners and Wally took it on. The forwards kept recycling. The moment had come.

Rory Best was in my way for a moment, and then Paulie came around from my blind side as I went to pick up the ball. Back then, there was no 'use it' call from the referee to play the ball after five seconds. So I took my time, waited for Paulie to pass by and take up his position on the far side of the ruck to act as a blocker on their chargers.

My feet were in the right position. The ball was nicely placed – no forwards' lazy, trailing feet obstructing it. This wasn't like Rog's drop goal here in '03, when the ball trickled back to me from a tap back and we had no option but to go for it. We were very much in control. My left foot was placed behind the ball, in a strong position for a powerful pass. Wales knew what was coming, and they'd be charging flat-out as soon as the pass left my hand – so I put everything behind it. That's the scrum-half's job. You're expected to be able to do it. The challenge is to deliver when you are under intense pressure in a cauldron of noise and there is so much at stake. It needs to be quick and on the money. You've one opportunity to do it. Any bit off, and the chance is gone.

I've looked at the video a few times, that motion of getting my shoulder over the ball and my full body in behind the pass. If I was to be over-critical about it, the pass was probably fractionally high. I was looking to hit Rog in his lower chest, and I hit him a few inches higher.

More importantly, though, the pass was on the correct line: it arrived at the right-hand side of his body, so he didn't have to move his feet, perfect placement for a right-footed kicker. If it had been slightly on his left, he would have had to turn his shoulders and adjust his whole body, eating up another split second, and the kick might have been charged down.

He didn't have to adjust his feet or his body position. His first step was to kick the ball and, under pressure, he nailed it, as he's done so many times over the years.

It takes a rare mentality for a player to put himself in that position, to attempt something like that. Most players would be afraid to put their hands up in case of failing. Not Rog. He always had the balls to take it on. He wasn't successful every single time, but he never shirked it.

We had three minutes to see it out. The parallels with that crazy finish in the same ground in 2003 were uncanny. At a Welsh ruck on halfway, I couldn't believe my eyes when I saw Wayne Barnes with his hand held out to signal a penalty against Paddy Wallace for off-side. I genuinely expected Stephen Jones to slot it.

Years later, at Bath, I chatted with Gavin Henson about it. He had a longer kicking range than Jones, and he told me he'd stepped forward to take the kick, but Jones had the ball and wasn't handing it over. Knowing the range of his kicking, I think Gav would have landed it.

It's amazing how many thoughts you can cram into a few moments like that, as Jones placed the ball on the tee and lined up the kick. Had the ball gone through the posts it would have been devastating. Everything that we'd worked towards, starting with the French game and the three wins that followed, would have seemed worthless.

Jones got under the kick a little, but it was dead straight, and there were an agonizing few seconds as the ball hung in the air. You're hoping and praying that it doesn't make it. Geordie and I were under the crossbar and we were probably the first to realize that it was coming up fractionally short.

Geordie called for it, caught it, touched it down and then ran along the in-goal area and kicked the ball into the crowd.

We'd won a Grand Slam. Something that hadn't been seen in our lifetime.

As a kid I'd watched Mick Kiernan kick the winning drop goal for a Triple Crown and a championship in 1985, the last time Ireland had won the title. But none of us had ever seen Ireland win the Grand Slam. We'd been on a journey, most of us, for years. Some of us since 2000. Ten Six Nations campaigns. To have walked away from our careers without a Grand Slam would have left a hollow feeling for the rest of our lives.

We gathered on the podium in the middle of the pitch, lights dimmed and Drico was last up, to be handed the trophy by President McAleese. That's why you train seven days a week. That's why you play. Moments like that. Lifting the trophy into the air in front of your supporters.

President McAleese always appeared to have good time for me. Before the English game in Croke Park she'd said to me: 'Here's my boy.' That was her stock line to me, and always with that smile. We went to the Áras a couple of weeks later and I had a good chat with her and her husband, Martin. A lovely, lovely lady.

Unlike the Heineken Cup final in the Millennium Stadium, I felt no embarrassment. I'd been part of winning that Slam. I felt unbelievably proud. This time I deserved to lift that trophy, instead of thinking: *I've nothing to do with this, I had no part to play in it.*

I had played a part, and had done it to the best of my ability.

The Hilton in Cardiff was packed to the rafters with Irish supporters, sharing in our elation. Arriving back in the hotel to those crowds was unforgettable. We had a real sense of what we'd achieved when we walked through the guard of honour formed by the crowd.

The atmosphere was electric, but there was no time to soak it in. We were ushered away to prepare for the post-match meal. We were always given about thirty minutes to get into our suits. Plenty of time for us, less so for the wives and girlfriends, who were never happy about the quick turnaround!

Debbie greeted me in the room. I sat on the edge of the bed and had a moment to take it all in before getting dressed and taking the glass lift down to the ballroom for dinner.

Dinners always follow the same script – speeches by the respective presidents of the two unions and the two captains. They can be an ordeal, but this was different. Everyone was on a high. The lads were settling into the evening with a few beers.

Debbie and I were one of the first couples to leave the festivities. Next morning, coming down to breakfast in the team room, it was clear that the festivities had continued until the bacon and eggs were being served! Geordie and Leams, to name but two, were still in their tuxes, and a little the worse for wear. They had to be shepherded

upstairs by Ger Carmody to pack their bags and prepare for the journey home.

There were a few sick heads on the bus ride to the airport. We were
ushered through security and waited to board the plane. It was an
Aer Lingus charter flight for the team and partners. Gordon D'Arcy,
never a fan of flying, was not feeling a hundred per cent. The turbu-
lence, coupled with the sick head from the night before, were not a
good pairing.

As we came in to land, we could see the fire brigades, with sirens
on, lined up in readiness for our arrival. There didn't appear to be any
other planes in the airport. The doors opened to huge applause from
airline staff and baggage handlers, all waiting, cheering and clapping.
These are moments that you never forget.

It was obvious how much this meant to everyone. We knew we
had been fighting hard for a Grand Slam, and it seemed as if all of
Ireland had been as well. The arrivals hall was crowded. I stopped to
sign some autographs and have photos taken with fans. I was also
handed a few babies. In the mayhem I became separated from most of
the boys, who had already made their way outside to the waiting bus.
Eventually a garda escorted me out through the crowd.

The squad travelled in one bus with the wives and girlfriends following in a separate bus. It seemed like the whole of Ireland was on
the streets of Dublin. We arrived at the Mansion House for a reception and some food. I think most of the boys were happy to be off
that bus. They were as green as the Irish flags hanging in the function
room. Food was a welcome sight. Clear the cobwebs.

A stage had been set up outside the Mansion House for the homecoming, and the street was full of people of all ages. We had done it,
and the country was sharing in our success. We all hung Tommy out
to dry by letting him sing 'The Black Velvet Band' on his own, and
he's had to sing it wherever he's gone ever since. I'd say that song has
become the bane of his life.

That night we went back to the Fitzpatrick Castle Hotel in Killiney to continue the celebrations with a meal and a chance to catch
up with family and friends. My brother George and his wife Isabel came
to join us, along with Síle Seoige and a friend of hers. An after-hours

party in Krystle nightclub on Harcourt Street followed into the early hours of the morning. I instantly regretted bringing Debbie, Síle and her friend along after the lads pointed out the party was 'boys only'.

Debbie and I took the train back to Cork the next morning. Rog was also on the train. Moments like that, seeing Rog and Debbie a little the worse for wear, remind me how happy I am to be a non-drinker!

18.   Hitting the Wall

In the summer of 2009, Ireland made a brief tour of North America. As is generally the case in Lions years, it wasn't the most intense of tours. I loved my time in Vancouver, where we played Canada. We had sunny weather, probably about 26 or 27°C, ideal for strolling around town in shorts, a T-shirt and flip-flops. One day we took the cable car to the top of Grouse Mountain, only to discover that the temperature was dramatically lower up there, and there was snow and ice on the ground. In the Grouse Mountain Refuge for Endangered Wildlife there were bears, grey wolves and stunning views of the city – but we were a bit underdressed!

The game took place in the Thunderbird Stadium on the University Endowment Lands, west of Vancouver. Supporters were enjoying the sunshine and drinking beers on the sidelines and it had the feel of an AIL final in early summer. However, as I was waiting to receive the kick-off, some Canadian fans began hurling abuse at me, commenting on my age and how I was past it. This has happened to me a couple of times in my career – only in the States and in Canada – and I found it quite strange.

Our side had a lot of unfamiliar combinations, and the Canadians were fired up, seeing an opportunity for a major scalp. But Barry Murphy scored on his debut, as did Ian Whitten, and we won 25–6.

The USA game was played in a soccer ground, Buck Shaw Stadium at Santa Clara University in California, on a 3G pitch, on a baking-hot afternoon. The Eagles team, then coached by Eddie O'Sullivan, trained there before us on the Friday. As I walked on to the pitch with my boots in my hand, Eddie passed by. We shook hands and briefly chatted. No ill feeling. He'd been through a tough time of it as well, and I don't like holding grudges.

We won 27–10 and were now officially on vacation. After the game I flew down to San Diego with Barry, Ian Dowling, Chris Henry and a few of the other guys for a bit of R&R, then on to Vegas for three or four days. Debbie then flew out to Los Angeles to meet me, and from there we flew to Cabo San Lucas in Mexico for a week, and then on to Chicago for another week. I loved Chicago. It's like a smaller, cleaner New York, with good food and a really nice vibe. From there, we flew to my parents' place in the south of Spain for another week, before going back to Cork. I always feel like I need to get away for my four weeks off. It's great to be able to escape from the game mentally as well as physically and be in an environment where nobody knows you.

The previous summer, Debbie and I had become good friends with Anne Pennefather, who worked with Universal Music in Dublin. Her job consisted of looking after touring acts from the moment they arrived in the country to the time they left. She invited us to go and see Lady Gaga in concert at Cork's summer music festival, 'Live at the Marquee'. Some of Lady Gaga's security team had been rugby players in the States, so we brought a selection of unwanted XXL Munster training and match jerseys to the gig as a little memento of their trip to Cork. After the gig, Debbie and I were brought backstage to Lady Gaga's dressing room. I presented her with my number 9 Ireland jersey from the match against the Eagles, with 'USA' embroidered below the crest. She tried on the jersey while we chatted, and it fitted perfectly! We had an interesting conversation, and she mentioned that one of her first boyfriends had played rugby. At one point she came right out and asked: did Irish people regard her as good-looking? Did I find her attractive? Of course I said yes. She said a lot of people in the States didn't think she was attractive, and didn't really understand her as an artist. I gave her the jersey to keep. Who knows what she did with it?

Soon after that, Anne rang me to say she'd be looking after Kanye West when he came to Cork to play at the same venue. She invited Debbie and me along for dinner with him, before his gig in the circus tent at the Showgrounds. We had actually spotted Kanye, and his girlfriend at the time, having breakfast at the next table in The Original Pancake House on Bellevue Place in Chicago. Before leaving, we introduced ourselves and mentioned that we were looking forward to seeing him perform in Cork in a few weeks' time.

I arranged a quiet, secluded table at the back of the restaurant for Debbie, Anne, Kanye, two of his minders and me. Kanye talked about his clothing line, which he was bringing out with Gap. He also talked about his dislike of the music industry in general, other performers, and his annoyance over MTV awards he hadn't won. Even though we were relative strangers, he didn't hold back!

Kanye's manager asked me to recommend somewhere for a drink after the concert. I rang a friend of Debbie's called Stevie Grainger, a DJ who was part owner of a bar/club in Cork called The Pavilion, and explained the situation. We met Kanye and his entourage there, and he performed a few songs on their stage.

I wasn't long back with Munster before there was an ominous portent of things to come. Munster had brought in a Kiwi scrum-half on loan, Toby Morland, as Tomás was injured. Morland was on the bench against Glasgow and Cardiff, and then started against the Scarlets, when Tomás was back on the bench. Just before the end of his loan spell, Morland was on the bench when Tomás started against the Dragons. Sitting in the stands, I just couldn't get my head around that one.

I was on the bench for the next five games before the autumn Tests. On 31 October, against Ulster at home, we won 24–10. Tomás played and I was left on the bench for the eighty minutes. I understood that the Irish management wanted Tomás match-fit for the autumn series, but neither they nor McGahan were doing me any favours.

I hooked up with the rest of the Irish squad in Dublin a week after the Ulster match. Deccie asked me if I'd play for the Ireland 'A' team, the Wolfhounds, two days before Ireland played Australia in Croke Park. I was disappointed at being left out of the senior game, but I thought OK, fair enough: I hadn't started a match in seven weeks. I didn't expect to saunter into the match-day squad, considering what had been going on in Munster. Deccie's words were simple: 'I just need you to play this Wolfhounds game, to get you some game time. Trust me on this.' It wasn't the game I had wanted to be involved in, but after my chat with Deccie I saw it as a stepping stone to getting back to where I felt I deserved to be.

So I made my debut for the Wolfhounds on 13 November in

Ravenhill against Tonga. Two days later, Tomás started against Australia, with Redser on the bench. A week later, Redser started against Fiji, with Tomás on the bench.

. The following week, Ireland played South Africa. I'd pushed Deccie hard to be involved. I had pointed out that I'd played in the last four games of the Six Nations, started the two Tests on the summer tour and reminded him of our conversation prior to the game against Tonga.

At the end of training in Donnybrook on the Monday before the South Africa game, Deccie had a conversation with Redser in the middle of the pitch. Redser didn't look too pleased with whatever was being said. That gave me some indication I might be back in. I was. Tomás started, I was on the bench . . . where I remained for eighty minutes.

It was, admittedly, a tight game against South Africa, which Ireland won 15–10; one of those cold, foggy winter evenings at the end of November. The coaches obviously didn't want to mix things up too much. Rog didn't get off the bench either. A week after making his international debut against Fiji, Johnny Sexton played the full eighty.

Between October and the game on St Stephen's Day, against Connacht, that Wolfhounds match was my sole start. I played eleven minutes in the league against the Ospreys, was left on the bench in the 24–23 Heineken Cup win at home to Perpignan, and played three minutes when we won away to Perpignan by 37–14, the following week. Being second choice to Tomás at Munster meant I was losing any chance of being second choice to him at Ireland.

They were the worst three months I'd known with Munster since I'd broken into the team in 1998. And January wasn't much better. I played in the defeat to Ulster, had the last twenty minutes against Treviso, and was left on the bench for the win over Northampton.

I was named in the 2010 Six Nations squad, along with Bossy, Redser and Tomás. The Wolfhounds had a game against England Saxons a week before the Championship began and, once again, Deccie put me in the starting fifteen, explaining, 'It's the same situation as before in the autumn, I need you to get some game time again.' I was glad: it was a chance to play rugby.

Deccie told me to play my normal game and not to feel like I had to go and prove myself. That was fine. I was playing a match. I was excited again.

We lost 17–13 at the Rec in Bath. It wasn't a great game. I played OK and was happy enough with my performance.

In the changing room afterwards I felt pretty good. Deccie came in, everyone sat down and he named the guys who were to meet up with the senior squad the next day in Dublin, to prepare for the first Six Nations game, at home to Italy. I waited for my name to be read out but it wasn't. I was devastated and it suddenly hit me: for the first time in ten years, since making my debut in February 2000, I wasn't in the Ireland squad for a Six Nations game.

Then Deccie named the squad for the Wolfhounds game against Scotland 'A', for the following Friday in Ravenhill. I was down to start, with Bossy on the bench, again. At least it was another game, a chance to show what I could do.

I got sixty-five minutes in a 34–19 win, and was really happy with the way I played. Debbie drove to Belfast for the match, and afterwards we drove back together to Dublin, where we stayed with my brother George and his wife Isabel. The next day I hung around the apartment and watched Ireland beat Italy. A difficult afternoon's viewing. My head was all over the place. I didn't know where I stood, but I took Deccie at his word.

On the Sunday, Debbie returned to Cork. I stayed in Dublin, as the full squad was assembling out in the Fitzpatrick Castle Hotel in Killiney that evening. I waited around George's apartment for the day, itching to get back into camp and out on the training pitch on Monday morning.

I went around the corner to a shop to buy food for dinner with George and Isabel. Someone tapped me on the shoulder. I turned around to see a small, frail lady, who said: 'I'm sorry to hear that you have not been included in the squad.'

I said: 'Sorry? What do you mean?'

'I just heard it on the radio. They announced that you were not involved in the squad for the game coming up against France.'

Initially I was lost for words. All I could think of saying was: 'Oh, yeah. Yeah. It's disappointing all right.' And I walked away.

I pretended I knew about it. I didn't want to admit I hadn't heard anything. I put the stuff back on the shelf and walked back to the apartment.

I rang Debbie. She was on the train, on her way back to Cork. She'd just seen online that the squad had been announced but that I wasn't in it. It seemed everyone had known before me. I phoned Deccie. He fell silent, before eventually muttering: 'Oh, someone should have rung you.'

I would have expected *him* to have rung me. I was raging. After ten years in the Ireland squad, I thought that out of common courtesy he should have told me. I shouldn't have had to hear it from a stranger in a shop. I'd understood, from our previous conversation, that I needed game time. I had no issues with that. I'd played the two Wolfhounds games. And then I'd been left out without so much as a phone call.

It was an awkward conversation, all the more so because it happened over the phone. He asked me to come out to Killiney the following morning, so that we could talk, face to face. Initially I thought to myself, *What is the point? He's not going to change his mind.* Then I realized I needed to have it out with him; I needed to stand up for myself. I arrived at the hotel around 9.30 a.m. and met him in one of the suites upstairs.

I said: 'You told me that I just needed to get those two games under my belt. You said the same would happen as it had in the autumn, and that you'd have me involved in the squad.' It felt to me like I had been given false hope.

His head was down. He explained that he hadn't intended to suggest that I'd get back into the squad automatically. He apologized for the way he'd phrased it and the way he'd treated me, not phoning me to let me know where I stood.

He said that I would have to have played in a certain percentage of games in each section of the season or else he couldn't pick me. I wondered whether the IRFU had put this policy in place, or whether it was just something he was saying, there and then, to justify his decision. To the best of my knowledge, having subsequently researched the matter, I can find no evidence of this policy being in place at that time.

My relationship with Deccie went back to our days together in

Pres. From 1998, when he gave me my Munster debut, until 2008, our relationship was good; after that, it deteriorated quickly. Of course, I was grateful for those early opportunities in my first season with Munster. He stuck his neck out and made the ballsy decision to pick me ahead of the two Irish internationals at the time, Tom Tierney and Brian O'Meara.

I felt better for finally having fought my corner with a coach, but it still wasn't a pleasant drive back to Cork that Monday morning.

I'd played in ten consecutive Six Nations campaigns. I'd been first choice in the first eight of them, and been involved in the last two. This would be the first time in eleven years I'd be watching it from the outside.

Not that I could bring myself to watch much of it. We were beaten 33–10 in Paris, we beat England in Twickenham 20–16, beat Wales in Croker, when Earlsy scored a couple of tries, but then lost our farewell game in Croker to Scotland.

I watched the beginning of all of them, but I couldn't stay with them. Even seeing the lads come out and stand for the anthems was difficult. Looking at their faces as the camera panned along, seeing them arm in arm, was the moment that really hit me, because I loved being out there for anthems, as the atmosphere built. Instead, I was sitting on my couch, watching and wishing I was there.

The one positive of being left out of the Ireland squad was playing three games in a row for Munster in March. But then in April, when the Ireland players returned, Tomás played eighty minutes against Leinster, and I played just the last two minutes against Northampton in the Heineken Cup quarter-final.

Munster's season ended with defeats in both semi-finals. In the Heineken Cup we lost 18–7 to Biarritz in San Sebastian. Their scrum dominated ours and we struggled massively to get decent possession in their half. We were really poor that day – so poor that Tony McGahan gave me seven minutes. Other players were being brought on around the sixty- or sixty-five-minute mark, but in Tony's mind we clearly had to be in deep trouble before he turned to me!

I came back into the changing room, completely disheartened and angry. Sometimes it's hard to look a coach in the eye and have respect for anything he says. You'd like to think you were picked on the bench for a reason, that you were an option, that you could do a job. But I felt Tony never really respected me or believed that I could play the role he wanted.

Meetings with Tony were futile. I always felt that he was just telling you what you wanted to hear, fobbing you off by offering you something to go away and work on. Like they'd have a list and run their finger down the options before picking one. They might as well have had their eyes closed. It never seemed like a genuine conversation to motivate you to be a better player.

In the Magners League semi-final we lost 16–6 to Leinster. Without Paulie, our line-out struggled, and again we lacked a cutting edge. They deserved to win. I played the last fifteen minutes.

I was selected for an Irish fifteen against the Barbarians in Thomond Park, and I was included on the tour of New Zealand and Australia. I watched the All Blacks game in my suit from high up in the stands of Yarrow Stadium in New Plymouth. Jamie was red-carded early on and it was a disaster to watch. We lost 66–28.

The following Friday night we played a non-Test match against the Maoris in Rotarua. I was picked on the bench, with Redser starting. I played the last seventeen minutes. I didn't make the match-day squad against Australia, when we were beaten 22–15 in Brisbane.

New Zealand and Australia are nice places to tour, but you're only really there for one reason: to play Test rugby.

For the first time since my debut in 2000, I hadn't played one Test in the entire 2009–10 season. I came on as a replacement in five Heineken Cup matches, for the grand total of forty-five minutes.

I was demoralized. I began to question my own ability and whether I could ever get back to where I had been. I wanted answers to those questions from the coaches, but they just wanted a certain type of player, i.e. Tomás.

I was in a pretty bad space, coming away from that tour. I needed a break, to reassess my own value and what I wanted from the game.

Debbie and I went to Sardinia for a week, and then to visit friends in Monaco. After a few days there, we returned to my parents' place in Spain for another week. We finished off our holidays at home because Debbie's sister, Ciara, was getting married, in Kinsale.

My career had seemingly hit a wall. I was very down after the season, but I kept fit by working hard in the gym and getting my conditioning done every day.

I was still hugely motivated by what rugby had to offer and I had a genuine love for the game. It wasn't something I was willing to give up on, based purely on some coaches' decisions not to pick me. It didn't take me long to realize that I did have confidence in my own ability to be able to relaunch my career.

19.   Ninety-eight and Out

I came back to pre-season feeling good, refreshed and excited about the new challenge. The past was the past. I didn't dwell on it any more. My goal was the 2011 World Cup. But first I had to fight for my place with Munster.

I needed to get decent game time under my belt, and I started the first two league wins at home to Aironi and away to Edinburgh. But then normal service was resumed: two minutes against the Ospreys, fourteen against Glasgow, and eighty minutes on the bench in the defeat to Leinster at the Aviva. But Tomás's back was troubling him that season, so I started the first Heineken Cup game, away to London Irish, where a minute's silence was observed beforehand for the legend Moss Keane, who had passed away that week.

I wanted to make the most of the opportunity, not dwell upon how I'd got there. Enjoy the game and relax into the position that I'd held for the best part of ten years. I felt confident and comfortable. I was starting a Heineken Cup tie again. This was what I'd been brought up on, these Heineken Cup games.

London Irish scored a breakaway try off an intercept just after half-time, and then their tails were up. They were right up for it and defended very well. Hosting Munster in the Heineken Cup was a big, marquee game for them. We were 23–12 down with less than seven minutes to go when Rog kicked through for Sam Tuitupou to gather and score for a losing bonus point. It was something.

Although Tomás was fit for the Toulon game, I was picked to start: back-to-back Heineken Cup games for the first time in three seasons. I felt in control of the number 9 jersey again.

A lovely sunny day in Thomond. The pitch was perfect. They came with a decent enough side – with their squad, they couldn't put out a weak one. But everything clicked for us in a really open, flowing game. I was like the kid who made his debut in 1998. Flying around the place. I found myself in rucks, getting through on the opposition scrum-half, energized by being back in Thomond and starting a big game. We didn't give them an inch that day.

Felipe Contepomi started, and that also energized the crowd. Over the years he'd caused us a few problems with Leinster, but he could be quite hit and miss, and always seemed a little rattled when playing at Thomond Park. He could be a superstar or quite fragile. The crowd got to him again that day. He missed a few kicks, and when Paul Warwick counter-attacked off one of them, we nearly scored a pitch-length try.

Sometimes you get a feeling on the pitch, a confidence and belief that things will click for you, and this was one of those days. After their early try, I set up our first for Leams, and we went on to score six. We fed off the energy of the crowd.

Back in the league we beat Treviso at home and Ulster away. I started both games, playing the full eighty against Ulster. We went into camp with Ireland for the November matches with those four consecutive games under my belt – the game time the IRFU and Deccie wanted! My game was better for playing them.

South Africa were first up in the new Aviva Stadium and I was back on the bench. It was an incredibly physical game, as it usually is with the Springboks. Just after they went 23–9 ahead, I came on with Rog for the last fourteen minutes. We tried to increase the tempo. Nothing to lose. Tommy Bowe scored off a cross-field kick by Rog, who then put Rob Kearney over. Unfortunately, Rog's touchline conversion hit the post and we came up two points short.

Another disappointment was the attendance at Lansdowne Road, due to a fiasco with the IRFU's ticket pricing. The Union then had to admit they'd got it wrong and apologized for their ludicrous prices. The country was in a mess at the time. Supporters voted with their feet, and it was such a shame to see so many empty seats at all the games, something that would have been unthinkable before.

Even so, it was exciting to be back, and Rog and I started the following week against Samoa. I played almost the whole game and played well, and we won 20–10. My confidence was back.

Redser returned against New Zealand, and I dropped to the bench, but I understood that he was the starting scrum-half at the time. It was up to me to push for the starting place. We were still in the game at half-time before they pulled clear. I was given another fifteen minutes, although by then the game was out of reach, and they won 38–18.

The New Zealand game also had the best atmosphere of the four autumn internationals, by a long way, such is the All Blacks' magnetism. We played ambitiously and, when I came on, the pace of the game was very fast. We had nearly all of the ball for those last fifteen minutes but, as is usually the case with New Zealand, they absorbed all our pressure.

Drico scored a cracker and Fez, Stephen Ferris, scored our other try. He really announced himself that month. He was just what we needed at the time: a big, physical, ball-carrying back-rower. You look at the four sides we came up against that autumn, and they all had players like him.

Fez had unbelievable leg strength, similar to Wally, to get his team over the gain line, as well as making big hits. He was immense that month and brought another dimension to our back-row play. Always putting his hand up for ball carries, playing the role that Sean O'Brien does now. Having a player like that, to break tackles and help generate quick ball, is absolutely crucial.

Stephen's other nickname is Horse, and that's exactly what he was: a workhorse. He's also a great lad; he loved playing the game, always had a smile and was great to have around the squad. He'd tell a story, instinctively laugh at his own jokes, and it would become infectious. He played through serious problems with his knees and shoulders for a long time, before finally his body said no more.

I started the following week against Argentina. The short coach journey took an age because of snow. It was quite sunny, but cold. The footpaths were lined with snow, as were the four sides of the ground, but the pitch was in pristine condition.

We won 29–9. I played nearly the full eighty minutes and was pleased with my performance. It was my first – and, as it turned out, only – start with Johnny Sexton. Everyone knows Johnny is cranky. He demands the best and, like all good 10s, he sets high standards and expects his teammates to play to them.

He liked playing a wide game and flat to the gain line, and I loved that – zipping the ball out to him. He was very vocal and left you in no doubt about what he wanted. From my point of view, the sooner I heard those calls from the 10, the easier it made my job.

With Johnny that day, before I'd reach a ruck, I'd know exactly where he'd be, as he'd already called for it. We had plenty of ball and moved the Argentinians around with a wide game. Johnny always wanted the ball and to play at a quick pace. I really enjoyed playing alongside him. He's gone on to bigger and better things since then, and this has in no way surprised me. He is a world-class out-half and has the ability and the attitude to stay at the top for a long time.

After the autumn internationals, I felt like I was back to where I'd been, and this set me up for the return to Munster.

Paulie was back after a nine-month absence for our win at home to Cardiff. The roar which greeted his return as a second-half replacement almost shook Thomond Park. By then Tomás, fit again, had come on for me too. A week later, at home to the Ospreys in the Heineken Cup, he had the 9 jersey once more; I was back in number 20. I didn't get to dirty it, either, as I stayed on the bench for eighty minutes once more. Here we go again.

It seemed that, regardless of my performances for Ireland, I would be back on the bench for Munster, once Tomás was fit.

In the return match at the Liberty, I came on with twenty-four minutes left – Tomás's back was at him again. Having lost our opener to London Irish, we knew we had to do the double over the Ospreys, or else we'd have to win in Toulon to have any chance of qualifying from the group. But the Ospreys were in the same boat. They were also hurting from the previous week, and their scrum caused us huge problems.

It's always difficult playing a good team back-to-back, and even more so when the second game is away from home. We'd done the double over Cardiff and the Dragons, but the Ospreys were a better side. It was a tough group, and only Toulon had recorded an away win, against London Irish in the third round, which made it even tougher.

A week later, I started against Connacht. Conor Murray was on the bench. He had some game time during the November window. I hadn't really seen him play very much, nor did I know much about him, to be honest. He'd come through the academy, and the coaches were keen to have him involved. All along I'd seen Tomás as my competition at Munster. Conor slipped in under the radar after Christmas. I could see he was a good player in the making.

I started the home league wins over Ulster and Glasgow. The New Year's Day attendance was 22,000 for the Ulster game. Great days.

I had that number 9 again, and my confidence was high. I was back in control of my own destiny. That day was as good as I'd felt in two seasons. I'd worked so hard on my game and my fitness. There'd been a complete turnaround in my fortunes since being left out of the Six Nations, almost a year before.

We were well beaten in Toulon, 32–16, which knocked us out of Europe in the pool stages for the first time since 1997–8. George Smith was immense for them, killing any momentum we managed to gain. We'd plenty of possession in the first half, but generally we went sideways. They defended aggressively. Wayne Barnes penalized us regularly, especially at scrum time. Jonny Wilkinson kicked six penalties, as well as converting both of their tries. When I cleared the ball downfield from our line, they went through a number of phases, and their scrum-half Pierre Mignoni kicked through for their winger Christophe Loamanu to score. Once they had the lead their tails were up, and they were 26–9 ahead by half-time. I was substituted after fifty minutes.

The coaches had to shake things up for the final game, at home to London Irish. It should have been one of those do-or-die, Saturday evening games at home to an English club. Thomond Park was packed. Instead we were playing for a place in the Amlin Challenge Cup.

There was a real hangover from the defeat to Toulon and our exit from the Heineken Cup. It was a huge blow for the whole organization. Moments after I came on for the last fifteen minutes, we went 14–7 down. This was Thomond Park, where we'd lost only one European Cup game. But that triggered some fight and pride within us.

We scored three converted tries in the last ten minutes – twenty-one unanswered points and a bonus point. We'd be away to Brive in the Challenge Cup. But it wasn't about the Challenge Cup. It was purely a matter of pride and, better late than never, putting in a performance for a full house.

I'm not sure that you'd get 27,000 at Thomond Park for a dead rubber now, and I'm not sure we'd have managed that late comeback if the ground had been half empty. We were at a low ebb, but the crowd helped us over the line. The supporters have always been massively important for the team.

Going into the Six Nations, I'd started six of the last eight games for Munster. For the season as a whole, I'd started eleven games, Tomás had started six. This was the game time that Deccie said was so important.

It didn't matter.

Tomás started against Italy in Rome, with Redser on the bench. I was pissed off about Tomás leapfrogging me. I had established myself as first choice at Munster. To be left out of that Italian game was a huge let-down. Watching Tomás play that season, I could see he was struggling with his back injury. I couldn't understand the coaches' thinking.

I reminded Deccie about our previous conversation, about the need for a certain amount of game time, and that over the previous month or two Tomás's game time had been very limited. He explained that Tomás was still first choice from the November games, and Redser second choice. It seemed to contradict what he'd said to me about game time.

Although we only won 13–11 in Rome, thanks to a late drop goal by Rog, it was the same story for the French game, a week later. Tomás started and scored a try, but France beat us 25–22.

I played almost seventy minutes of the Munster–Edinburgh game. There'd been no indication that I'd be involved in the week of the Scottish game in Murrayfield. Tomás was to start again, with Redser on the bench, but Tomás's back went in training and I was called in on the Thursday to sit on the bench behind Redser.

Again I told myself not to worry how I got there, and just play as well as I could. And I was thrilled to be involved in the Six Nations.

We outscored Scotland three tries to nil, but Nigel Owens's penalty count was 13–4 to them. I came on for the last fifteen minutes and we were clinging on for a 21–18 win at the end. It was quite a nervy finish to the game. Chris Paterson kicked four penalties and then Dan Parks kicked a penalty and a drop goal. Johnny came on as well, but this time we tried to slow things down and regain control.

We'd gone a little flat. We were edgy and were giving away too many penalties. One of the key roles I have adopted on the field is to continue talking to each of the forwards individually, to try to instil some energy and enthusiasm, but also some calmness and discipline. I appreciate the workload that those guys get through, from scrums and mauls to rucking and carrying into contact. It is important to have a voice that gives them some sort of clarity at times when they are struggling to catch their breath. *No more penalties* – that was the main message.

Away to Wales, two weeks later, Tomás was still out and I was on the bench again. Sitting in the stands as a replacement, you tell yourself to be ready in case you have to come on in the first minute, though it might happen only once or twice in your career.

Well, it happened that day. In the first minute, Lee Byrne tried to clear from inside his own 22, and Redser put him under pressure. When you're going for a chargedown, you should always make sure that your hands are crossed so there's no possibility of the ball hitting your face. But you don't always remember. Redser rushed up, arms flailing, and the ball caught him full-on in the face. He was concussed although, once everyone knew he was OK, he took some slagging for it.

When a squad is announced, the priority is obviously to prepare the starting fifteen as well as possible for the game ahead. The vast majority of time at training is allocated to ensuring that those fifteen guys are as cohesive as possible in everything they do on the field. The challenge you are faced with when named on the bench is to make sure that you find the time to familiarize yourself with every last detail of the game plan. You have to be prepared as though you were starting the game.

It's one thing, studying the moves on a screen or being on the opposition side at training and seeing them unfold, thinking you understand them. But until you actually run those plays, you won't have the timing or appreciate the running lines of the guys around you. Timing: that is the key to the success of the set-piece play. There is an individual responsibility on the replacements to swap themselves in and out with the starters throughout the sessions. I'd done that during the week, and even though it was only the first minute, I felt comfortable with the game plan.

I was straight into it, and relished being back. We pounded their line through phases with great tempo. I hit Tommy with a long pass and he offloaded out of the tackle to put Drico over. Within a minute of me coming on, we were 7–0 up.

We were so much the better team. We should have won, but we couldn't take our chances, and then we were the victims of one of the worst pieces of touch judging I've ever experienced. Scottish referees and touch judges! They haven't been good over the years, and I make no apologies for repeating it. They simply haven't been up to scratch.

We were 13–9 up when Johnny came on for Rog in the fiftieth minute. He sliced his first kick out on the full. The ball bounced over the advertising hoardings and into the first row of the stands. But a ballboy gave Matthew Rees a different ball, and he took a quick throw to Mike Phillips, who sprinted in for a try.

'Play to the whistle': I'd been told that so many times since my Cork Con Under-8 days. But Phillips was gone past me before I knew it, and although Tommy got close, no one could stop him. Paulie, Drico and I surrounded the referee, Jonathan Kaplan. We knew the laws: for a quick throw-in, the player must use the ball that went into touch. That is the exact wording of Law 19.2 (d). Everyone knew that law! I have always made sure I am fully up to speed on the latest laws set out in the IRB's law book. You would assume that after thirty years playing the game, there wouldn't be much else to know but, with rugby constantly evolving, new laws do come in. It's not just about playing the game; it's about knowing the game.

'Is it the correct ball?' Kaplan asked his touch judge, Peter Allan, a Scot.

'It is the correct ball, yes,' said Allan.

'It is?' repeated Kaplan.

'Yeah.'

It wasn't. The ball had clearly been kicked into the crowd about twenty metres further up the pitch. The ballboy handed another ball to Rees, right in front of Kaplan.

I cannot understand how Allan didn't pick up on that. If the touch judge is not sure, he should say so. It was so clear-cut, I was sure it would be called back.

With eighty minutes up, trailing 19–13, we hammered at their line and went wide, creating an overlap, but Paddy Wallace cut back inside with Earlsy outside him. I think it would have been a definite try if Paddy had passed to Earlsy, and we'd have had an opportunity to win the game with a conversion from the touchline. Maybe Paddy was thinking of the conversion angle. But in my view, you score the try and you back your kickers in those situations.

I was selected on the bench for the final game, at home to England. Who knows if it would have been different had we beaten Wales? I'd actually had a good game in Cardiff, had done all the basics, made all my passes.

England were seeking the Grand Slam, and were favourites on form. That was enough to concentrate our minds. In the last game of the season, we finally produced our best performance that year, by some distance. Our intensity was relentless, as it nearly always is against England.

It was our seventh win out of eight games against England. We had complete control, dominating them in every respect from the first minute. Johnny was on fire, and put Tommy over before Drico broke the Six Nations try-scoring record with a sharp pick-up and finish.

Martin Johnson had no argument with the result, and he admitted that losing that game took the gloss off winning the championship.

We were 24–3 ahead early in the second half when Steve Thompson scored after intercepting a pass by Redser. Even so, I didn't get on until the last minute – enough time to take my gumshield out of the top of my sock, miss a tackle on Danny Care and, with my first touch, take the ball from a maul with the eighty minutes up and kick it off the pitch.

For the first time since the Aviva opened, there was a truly feel-good atmosphere at a home international. It was a great day for Irish rugby, at a new stadium, and a sign of big things to come. Yet I felt pretty worthless out there: one minute and one missed tackle. I couldn't buy into it, clapping the English team off the pitch and then going between their two lines of players, under the stands and into the changing rooms. Head down, being patted on the back by a few of the English guys. I hadn't contributed anything. It would have been even worse if I'd known then that my ninety-eighth Test would be my last. Not the best way to finish.

Before the Six Nations, I'd been first choice at Munster. Tomás was still injured, yet I was back to second choice with Munster, this time to Conor. He started the next three games. It seemed as if I was being punished for having played in the Six Nations.

The third of those matches was away to Brive, a 2 p.m. kick-off in roasting heat. The pitch was superb, and the 42–37 scoreline said it all: a very open, free-flowing game that could have gone either way. I was happy to get thirty-two minutes off the bench. Soon after I came on, I took a quick tap in our own 22, as they were shy of defenders on our left-hand side. We broke downfield, Dougie kicked ahead and I chased it down. The ball bounced awkwardly for their full-back and popped up to me. I chipped it over him, re-gathered and scored under the posts. It was probably one of the best tries I've ever scored.

I wanted that 9 jersey back and I felt better, coming off the pitch. I started the following League game, a win away to the Scarlets, but that was it. Conor was back against the Ospreys and then Harlequins in the Challenge Cup semi-final defeat at Thomond Park.

Tomás was back against Connacht, before Conor started again in the League semi-final win at home to the Ospreys and the final at home to Leinster. I was on the bench for eighty minutes.

The only reason I started thirteen games that season for Munster was because of Tomás's back injury. Tony never thought of me as the starting scrum-half, or even as much of an option off the bench. That was my gut feeling.

The final was a tough enough day anyway, regardless of whether I'd been given eighty minutes or none.

Our strength and conditioning coach, Paul Darbyshire, had come to Limerick a couple of days beforehand from England, where he was receiving treatment for motor neurone disease. It would be the last month of his life. Darbs stayed in the Clarion with his wife, Lyndsey, and their little boy, Jack. I went to the room with a few of the lads to say hello.

It was an incredible shock to see how quickly he'd deteriorated. He was in a wheelchair, so frail and unable to speak. He'd been such a big, strong, physical man, and a guy we respected so much; to see him fade away to nothing was horrible. It must have been a huge effort for him. But he wanted to be there. He was in no condition to get on the bus, but he wanted to be with us one more time. When we left the Clarion after our pre-match meeting and loaded our gear bags on to the bus, Darbs was being carried on before us. To see what had become of such a fit and healthy man was gut-wrenching.

It's a short, five- or six-minute drive to Thomond Park from the Clarion: along the river, turn right and you can see the stadium. You're trying to focus on the game, but all I could think about was Darbs. After we'd changed, we went out for the warm-up, and Darbs was sitting beside the subs' bench in his wheelchair.

During the match, I glanced down every so often. Seeing a friend in a situation like that puts everything into perspective. Playing professional rugby can be all-consuming. It feels like it's everything to us. But that day it seemed relatively meaningless in comparison to life, and spending time with family. That day was very much about Darbs. After we'd won, and the podium was set up for the trophy presentation, Rog wheeled Darbs on to the pitch to sit alongside us.

Jack, his son, lifted the trophy with Paulie. Darbs was in tears. He would have known this was probably the last time he'd see us play, and to see his son lift the trophy must have been pretty special. He passed away a few weeks later, on 20 June 2011.

I needed a break to recharge and target the World Cup. For our summer holidays Debbie and I went back to Cabo San Lucas for a week. From Cabo, we flew to San Francisco, and then drove down the west coast. Really chilled out and relaxed, we stopped off in a few

places along the way, before reaching Los Angeles, where we spent
some time on the beaches. Larry Mullen from U2 had been to many
Irish games over the years, and I'd met him several times. U2 were
touring in the States that summer, and he contacted me to ask if we'd
be interested in coming to one of the gigs. I said yes, definitely. They
were playing in the Angel Stadium of Anaheim, The Big A, home to
the LA Angels baseball team. Larry arranged tickets and said: 'Make
sure you come and see me before the gig.'

I said I didn't want to be disturbing him, but he said: 'No, no, definitely come down and see me.'

After we collected our tickets, we bumped into Wayne 'Pocket
Rocket' McCullough, the Irish boxer who won silver at the 1992
summer Olympics in Barcelona, and his wife, Cheryl, whom Larry
had also invited to the gig. On the night that Wayne returned to boxing after a two-year lay-off in 2002, Larry had led him into the ring.
I hadn't met Wayne before, but I introduced myself and we got chatting. We have since met up a few times in California, where he is now
a boxing trainer in his own gym out there.

We passed by Bono's dressing room, which was absolutely full of
people, so we kept walking and found Larry's room, down by the
stadium's underground car park.

Larry was sitting on the couch on his own. It was great to see him
and have a good conversation. We told him all about our holiday, and
then Wayne and his wife came in and the five of us carried on chatting as Larry prepared to go on stage.

He and the other U2 lads loved touring the States. He was staying
in the Sunset Marquis hotel, just off Sunset Boulevard in LA and said:
'We'll catch up later and have a drink.'

We left Larry's room, and the security guy who'd brought us there
said that Bono wanted to see us, so we ended up filtering our way
into Bono's changing room as well. That was a little more hectic, but
when Bono saw us come in he made a beeline for us. We had a good
chat with him too. I hadn't seen him in a couple of years, not since the
gig in Croke Park in 2009, when we'd talked briefly. They were only
about twenty minutes from going on stage, and had plenty of people

to see, but it was great to meet them. That finished off the holiday nicely.

Great gig, too. Not an overly big stadium, but a nice venue, and a wonderful atmosphere. Americans love U2. I'd seen them in Dublin, but it was exciting to see them somewhere else. A novel experience.

The end to the season with Munster had rocked my hopes of making the World Cup.

But still, I had started thirteen games for Munster, and had been involved in the Irish set-up, playing in the last three games of the Six Nations. Coaches couldn't claim I hadn't had enough game time.

I was confident I had a great chance of going to the World Cup. I had a good pre-season, the greater part of which was in Carton House with the Irish squad, and some of it with Munster. There were originally four scrum-halves in the squad – Redser, Tomás, Bossy and me – and then Conor was added.

I'd kept training every day on holidays and was as fit as I'd ever been. The squad was breaking up on 28 July after completing our pre-season training. That was the Thursday before the first of four warm-up games against Scotland, nine days later.

At lunchtime Deccie texted me, asking me to give him a call before I left the hotel.

I rang him and he said: 'I would just like to talk to you for a bit.'

I sensed this might not be a pleasant conversation. I went to see him in his room.

We had a brief chat before he told me that I wouldn't be involved in any of the four warm-up Tests. I was devastated. I felt I'd done really well in training. I'd worked out the numbers and figured he'd be picking four scrum-halves for those games. I couldn't believe that I'd been relegated from second choice for the last three games of the Six Nations to this.

I said: 'So you mean to say that all of the other scrum-halves here will be involved?'

'Yeah, but that's not saying that, you know, you're still not in with . . .'

'Look, Deccie,' I said, 'so you're telling me that I'm number five? I'm fifth choice?'

'I'm not telling you that you are fifth choice.'

And I said: 'Well clearly I am. That's the way it seems to me. Just be honest and tell me where I stand.'

But he couldn't bring himself to say that I was fifth choice. He kept saying: 'Look, it's not the final call. The squad hasn't been named yet. The squad for the World Cup hasn't been announced yet. If things don't go well, you know . . .'

I said: 'Look, if I'm fifth choice, just tell me and tell me what I need to do, or if there is anything I can do.'

He said: 'I'd tell you if you were fifth choice.'

He just kept saying that I wasn't fifth choice, when clearly I was, given his selection of the other four ahead of me. He also said that if Tomás's back wasn't right, they'd be inclined to pick Conor as more of a like-for-like replacement. I was seriously pissed off. Before that meeting, I'd figured that, at worst, I'd be third or fourth choice, and that I'd get a chance in the warm-up matches to make an impression.

Being told I wouldn't be involved in those games, and trying but failing to get a straight answer out of him, did my head in.

I left the room believing that, in the coaches' minds, I was fifth choice. I sat in my car in Carton House car park to drive to Cork and went through in my head the four players who were now ahead of me.

Conor had come through at the end of the previous season, and had played a handful of games – none in the Heineken Cup, and none for Ireland. Tomás had his back problems, and hadn't played much rugby the previous season. Bossy had come from absolutely nowhere. That was the killer. He'd been Leinster's second choice. He hadn't been involved in the Six Nations. How the hell had he jumped above me?

Not being big-headed, but there is no way that I was fifth-choice scrum-half at that point in time. I just could not believe the selection.

I was helpless. There was nothing I could do in those warm-up games, unless there was an injury, or an absolute crisis. As they were only ever going to take three scrum-halves to the World Cup, something drastic had to happen. Ninety-eight caps counted for nothing.

I wouldn't even get a minute in Ireland's other warm-up match, against Connacht in Donnybrook. Bossy started that one, with Conor on the bench. Tomás started two of the Tests, Redser the other two. Conor had three Tests off the bench and was picked ahead of Tomás, who missed out.

Ireland lost all four warm-up matches, but I couldn't bring myself to watch any of them.

I did have one more meeting with Deccie. It was Sunday, 21 August, the day before the World Cup squad was announced. The meeting was before the final warm-up game against England. I met him in the Rochestown Park Hotel in Cork, in a conference room.

When I went in, Deccie had his head slightly lowered and did his best to avoid making eye contact with me. But I knew what was coming. He would tell me that I wasn't being picked for the World Cup squad. It was news that I knew was coming. It wasn't a shock. The main shock had come at the end of that Carton House training camp when he'd told me I wouldn't be involved in any of those warm-up games. Ever since that day, I'd known that my chances of going to the World Cup were nil.

'All I've ever wanted was to be told straight up where I stood, and I never got that indication from you,' I said to him. 'I genuinely felt that I was one of the top two or three scrum-halves. Even in the worst-case scenario I never thought that I was fifth choice. I asked you that day in Carton House, was I fifth choice, and you didn't have the balls to tell me.'

I went on: 'You've ended up bullshitting a lot of guys and telling them what they wanted to hear, and as a result a lot of players have lost respect for you.'

There wasn't much to be said after that. Silence from both of us. I stood up and left the room. That was my last meeting with Deccie, on a professional level. There's been a brief 'hello' somewhere since. Can't remember when or where.

I'll admit it wasn't a very easy World Cup to watch. I watched highlights of the win over Australia and brief highlights of the quarter-final defeat to Wales. That was all.

How times had changed. It was a long way from eagerly setting my alarm for those games in the 1987 World Cup. The last thing on my mind during the 2011 World Cup was setting my alarm to watch any of the matches.

Ask any ex-player, and most will tell you that, over time, it becomes easier to watch Ireland games and to support the team. But the hurt from not making that World Cup, and the way I was cut, was too raw.

20.   The Long Goodbye to Munster

I played in Munster's first six games of the 2011–12 season, rotating with Tomás O'Leary. But once Conor Murray came back, post-World Cup, Tony McGahan stopped including me in match-day squads.

In November 2011, frustrated at getting no rugby, I asked the coaches for a game. I think they were embarrassed about it. They didn't want to name me in the 'A' team. It wasn't what I wanted, either. But I had talked it through with my dad, and I wanted a couple of games under my belt. Any games. So they agreed to rotate Duncan Williams and me for two British & Irish Cup games. I started for Munster 'A' against Cornish Pirates on a Friday night in Clonmel. There was a howling wind, and a crowd of 500 people.

For the next one, against Neath, I was on the bench. I'd had some good days against Neath, including in the Heineken Cup. I returned to the Gnoll to sit on the bench, replacing Duncan for the last twenty-five minutes.

That was the straw that broke the camel's back. I came on in that game and was feeling as low as possible: now fourth choice, in my mind.

Soon after, I received a call asking if I was interested in playing for the Barbarians against Australia in Twickenham, the following week. Damn sure I was!

Graham Henry was the coach, and there was a strong squad, including Stirling Mortlock, Bryan Habana, Kevin Mealamu, Simon Shaw, Victor Matfield, Jerome Kaino and Adam Thompson. But some of the All Blacks hadn't quite finished celebrating their World Cup victory, and it was probably the worst performance in the history of the Baa-Baas. Australia won 60–11.

We stayed in the Grosvenor House hotel in Park Lane. The night before the game, we were having dinner in JW Steakhouse, in the

hotel, when I received a text from Phil Morrow, the former Irish
S&C coach, who had joined Saracens after the World Cup. When I
rang him back, he asked if I'd be interested in coming to Saracens on
loan for three months. Their two scrum-halves, Neil de Kock and
Richard Wigglesworth, were both injured. I told him I was definitely interested.

I hadn't previously considered the possibility of going somewhere
on loan. But I was interested: this looked like a chance to play some
rugby. I went to Tony McGahan and said: 'There's an opportunity
for me to go on loan, which I am very keen to do.'

He said: 'Well, obviously we don't know how it will work with
regard to payment.'

I said: 'If that can be organized, I just want to get an answer from
you. Are you OK with me looking into the possibility of going on
loan?'

He said: 'Yeah, if it's something you want to do, then we're not
going to stand in your way.'

That put things in motion. I went to Sarries the next week on a
three-month loan. I never spoke with Tony again. It wasn't easy leaving Munster, even temporarily. I'd been there for over twelve years,
played for them over 200 times, I'd developed a close relationship
with the fans and with teammates. You become a bit institutionalized
when you're in one place for so long. It's all you know. But I needed
to play rugby.

I knew that I still had a lot to offer as a player. I've always made
sure to move with an ever-changing game, and to keep tabs on my
own performance. I try to break down aspects of my game to the
things you can measure: fitness results, speed of pass, kicking accuracy. Nothing had slackened, nothing had changed, but I found myself
dropping down the pecking order at Munster and, as a consequence,
with Ireland.

Conor Murray had come through and had done unbelievably well –
there's no questioning that. But I didn't have a good answer for people
who said to me, 'I just cannot understand why you're not getting an
opportunity ahead of . . .' – and they'd mention Tomás O'Leary, or
Duncan Williams, or, towards the end, Cathal Sheridan.

I asked myself: *Is it just my family and close friends telling me this? Are they just telling me what I want to hear?* But I didn't think it was. I still rated myself as a player, and felt I was being underutilized by Munster.

One of the hardest things about leaving Munster was that it meant leaving teammates like Donncha O'Callaghan. As much as any other guy I've played with, he set the standards for everybody else, in the way he trained, the way he prepared and the way he looked after himself. The Munster story would never have happened without him. He was one of those who set the benchmark.

He was always one of the fittest players in the squad, every year. He worked unbelievably hard at every aspect of his game and he always wanted to learn more about the game. Donners is probably the most professional player I've ever trained or played with. It got to the point where he had to be sent away from the gym on days off, because he was just doing too much. He was the first guy to start bringing his own packed lunch on travel days – food he'd prepared meticulously at home to ensure he was putting the right nutrients into his body at all times. In those early years, he set the example, and I followed.

He's also one of my best friends. We played together from schools onwards. Like me, he doesn't drink, and so he was always one of the guys I hung out with on nights out. He's one of the best guys I've ever known.

Leaving Munster meant leaving that kind of attitude behind. Thanks to players like Donners, Paulie and Fla, Munster had it in abundance, and I wondered whether other teams had that same willingness to work hard.

Those players made it easy for me in Munster. I just had to look after my own job.

It was a tough week for me when I arrived at Sarries' training grounds in St Albans. I had to get to know everyone and learn a new game plan and a whole new set of calls for a big European game that weekend, against the Ospreys at Wembley. Mark McCall included me on the bench and said I would definitely be getting game time.

It was my first time at Wembley, and it didn't disappoint. We got off to a great start and were 10–3 up in no time. We were always two scores ahead for much of the match, which helped settle my nerves in anticipation of being called to go on. On the sixty-minute mark, I was running on in front of 40,000 supporters in a big Heineken Cup match. It felt great. We went on to win 31–26. In the space of three weeks, I'd gone from the Gnoll in Neath with Munster 'A', to Twickenham with the Barbarians, and then to Wembley!

I'd been at Munster for my entire career. I knew no other way than the Munster way. We knew our strengths in Munster and played to those strengths. It was successful and we won trophies. Consequently, I believed that this was the way you had to do things if you wanted to succeed. At Saracens I had to learn their way of playing, and quickly. They had a completely different mindset, a different structure and a different attitude towards training. One of the lessons I started to learn at Saracens was that there are many different paths to success.

Sarries were a force in the Premiership, having finally won it for the first time the previous season, beating Leicester in the final. They played a relatively low-risk game within their own half, putting teams under pressure with their kicking. I struggled for the first few weeks. My Premiership debut was against Harlequins, an 82,000 sell-out at Twickenham. From a ruck in our own half, I looked to play it quickly, but my teammates weren't ready. They didn't run the ball in their own half. They didn't even do it in training, much less in games. I had to adapt quickly.

Sarries weren't just different from Munster; they were different from everyone else, and they revelled in that. The club's CEO, Edward Griffiths, wanted to do things differently from any other team in the world, and wanted to be seen doing so. During that season we went to Abu Dhabi and Dubai for a squad-building trip. Some of the club owners are South African, and they wanted to move our Heineken Cup home game against Biarritz, on 15 January, to Cape Town. Biarritz had agreed to travel to the southern hemisphere for the game; but in the end the owners couldn't agree on whether the game should be played in Newlands Stadium, the oldest stadium in

South Africa, or in Cape Town Stadium, a football ground, and the newest stadium in South Africa. So ultimately the game was played at Vicarage Road.

The trip to Cape Town went ahead, however. We departed on the Sunday before the game, for a few days' training in Cape Town, and spent our day off, on Wednesday, powerboat-racing in Cape Town harbour.

On the Thursday we had the option of going skydiving. We arrived at the airfield and got suited up, but the skydiving was cancelled due to high winds. On Friday morning we attended a sponsors' breakfast in our hotel, the Cullinan, where François Pienaar, the Springboks' World Cup-winning captain in 1995, was the guest speaker. He spoke about his fondness for Saracens, where he was captain, coach and CEO between 1997 and 2000. He mentioned how delighted he was to see that I was now playing for them and that I was one of his favourite Irish players of all time! Very humbling words from a great man. On the Saturday, we flew back to Heathrow for the Biarritz game the next day.

This went against everything I'd experienced in my career. I had always thought you had to prepare thoroughly on the training ground in match weeks, with the minimum of disruption or distraction. We won the game 20–16.

My re-invention as a person and a player after moving to the UK started with that experience with Saracens. They say travel broadens the mind, and my time with Saracens certainly did that. I'd love to have stayed longer, but the two injured scrum-halves, Richard Wigglesworth and Neil de Kock, regained fitness. Mark McCall told me: 'I'd love to keep you, but we have three scrum-halves now, and you'd make it four. It's just not possible.'

I started the last Heineken Cup pool game away to Treviso, which we won, topping the group and earning a home quarter-final against Clermont. By April, when the quarter-final came around, I was at Newcastle. Mark rang me to ask if I'd come down and speak to the squad on the day of the game after their pre-match meal. He wanted to draw on my European experience. I said yes, and felt privileged to be asked. I spoke of my experiences in the Heineken Cup, how much it meant to me and what an occasion it would be. Unfortunately, Clermont blew them away: too physical on the day. It was disappointing to witness that. Although I was only with the club for a short time, I'd actually become really close to the guys and was almost as disappointed as if I'd been playing.

I wasn't fully aware of the attitudes of other teams and players towards Saracens until I went to Newcastle and Bath. They are not the most popular club in the UK, but they revel in that. They could abide by the old Millwall motto: 'Nobody likes us but we don't care.' They really don't care what's going on outside their club, or what people say about them. I think other players are possibly a little envious of how Sarries treat their players, the places they are taken to. During the season, their players are asked to bring their passports to a game, without being told where they might be going. They'd then be taken somewhere on a private plane for a couple of days – like a weekend at the Oktoberfest in Germany. That might grate with players outside Saracens.

Added to this, their style of rugby is seen as very negative. But when they get into the opposition territory, they are very clinical. They also pride themselves on coming away with points every time they visit the opposition 22. They frustrate teams, make them impatient, and feed off their mistakes.

Key to their game is their defence, which they call The Wolf Pack. With all the other teams I've been involved with, a defensive line is kept together at all times. If someone comes out of the line quickly to make a hit, he is singled out for criticism if doing it leaves a hole and doesn't stop the ball. But the mindset in Saracens is very different. If a player leaves the line quickly, everyone else has to keep up with him. The mantra is to get off the line as quickly as possible and put the opposition under pressure. That's the Saracens way, and it complements their no-risk approach when they have the ball. By kicking the ball so much, they frustrate their opponents, who eventually feel compelled to run from deep. That's the trap Saracens want teams to fall into. They apply so much pressure with their kick-chase and their defensive line that the opposition are forced into errors in their own half. This enables Saracens to pick up points from penalties, and tries from rolling mauls, having kicked to the corner. Their game is about having more patience than the opposition, and relentless pressure.

It's a negative approach, but the Saracens supporters don't care as long as Saracens are winning, consistently reaching the knockout stages of the Premiership or the European Cup. As they do every year.

After my stint at Saracens, Mark McCall told the press: 'I just said in the changing room if Carlsberg did loan signings, then Peter Stringer's your Carlsberg signing. He's been outstanding on and off the pitch. He's a brilliant guy and unbelievably experienced. He's brought all that experience to bear.' That was good to hear.

The plan was to return to Munster at the end of the loan period in March 2012, but then Newcastle made an offer. They'd brought in Gary Gold and Mike Ford as interim coaches with a brief to save them from relegation. I said to myself: *OK, Newcastle. Bottom of the table. But they want me to play the last five or six games of the season.* It was either that or Munster, where I'd be third choice at best.

Newcastle had been playing a very expansive game, but it hadn't been working for them. Gary had worked very closely with Brendan Venter at London Irish. Their approach was not to play in their own half, to kick downfield and use line speed in defence to apply pressure on the opposition. It was a very structured, disciplined game, which Gary now implemented with Newcastle.

It wasn't the most attractive way of playing, but he said: 'Lads, trust me. Buy into it. If we've any chance of staying up, this is the only way. The only way.'

And it nearly worked. Newcastle were at the bottom of the table by some distance when I joined, but we took it to the last game of the season, away to Wasps. If we scored four tries on the day and won, we would stay up and Wasps would go down. As it happened, we won the game but managed only two tries – I got one – and Newcastle were relegated.

I played eighty minutes in five games on the trot. That was the way I liked it. My career had always been about contributing on the field; not sitting behind a computer screen on a Monday morning, offering advice to players who could be taking your place at the weekend.

My loan spells at Saracens and Newcastle only strengthened my belief that I was still capable of playing at the top level. I knew I wasn't too old.

Around the time I signed the loan deal with Newcastle, I also re-signed for Munster for another year. New coaches, Rob Penney and Simon Mannix, were arriving to replace Tony for the 2012–13 season. I felt really good about it. I had never seen eye-to-eye with Tony; there was just a bad vibe between us. Away from the game, we'd have a good laugh and a joke together, but it was all a bit false. It's horrible when you know that you don't have somebody's respect, when you don't really feel you're a viable option.

I'd talk to him one-on-one, and ask for more game time. He'd mention some fixture and say something like: 'Yeah, we'll look at that down the line.'

A couple of weeks later, I'd talk to him again. 'What about this game? You said you'd play me.' He often seemed to forget things that had been said at meetings. I suppose that's the nature of coaches having a lot of one-on-ones with players. He eventually brought in Jason Holland, our backs coach, to sit alongside him and take notes of what was being said.

So, when he left, I thought, 'This is a good opportunity.' I didn't know much about Rob and Simon, but Axel and Ian Cosgrave were now assistant coaches and I always seemed to get on well with both of them. *OK, this is a clean slate*, I said to myself, and I looked forward to the 2012–13 season as a new beginning.

Pre-season went well. I had plenty of meetings with Rob, as he explained the new game plan he intended to bring to Munster. It was a very expansive style of play, very different from the style Munster was renowned for. But we bought into it. There were three warm-up games, away to La Rochelle and at home to Bristol and London Irish. With Conor being rested after a long season with Ireland and with Cathal injured, Duncan and I were the only two fit scrum-halves available for these games.

Duncan started, and I was a replacement, in all three warm-up

34. My worst day
on a rugby pitch:
15 September 2007,
Ireland v. Georgia
at the World Cup.
(*Billy Stickland/Inpho*)

35. Munster came so
close to beating the
All Blacks in 2008:
after the final whistle,
I was crushed with
disappointment.
(*Matt Browne/Sportsfile*)

36. I made an impromptu break off a lineout against Scotland in the 2009 Six Nations, which led to Jamie Heaslip's try. As one of four changes to an unbeaten side, I was named Man of the Match. (*Billy Stickland/Inpho*)

37. Sharing the moment of Grand Slam glory with Brian O'Driscoll. (*Stephen McCarthy/Sportsfile*)

38. Trophy in hand, flag around neck: all was right with the world. (*Stephen McCarthy/Sportsfile*)

39. Hill 16 was mostly red for our Heineken Cup semi-final against Leinster in 2009, but Leinster got the better of us that day and went on to win the Cup. (*Billy Stickland/Inpho*)

40. We won the Magners League fairly comfortably in 2009: this photo shows that it meant a lot to us. (*Billy Stickland/Inpho*)

41. Paul Darbyshire (*front and centre*) was Munster's brilliant, inspiring strength and conditioning coach from 2007 until late in 2010, when he was diagnosed with motor neurone disease. He died in 2011. Thinking of him still helps drive me on.

42. We beat Leinster in the 2011 Magners League grand final – the last bit of silverware I won with Munster. (*Dan Sheridan/Inpho*)

43. This is the moment when, frustrated at being third- or even fourth-choice scrum-half for Munster, I told Tony McGahan I was interested in going to Saracens on loan. (*Diarmuid Greene/Sportsfile*)

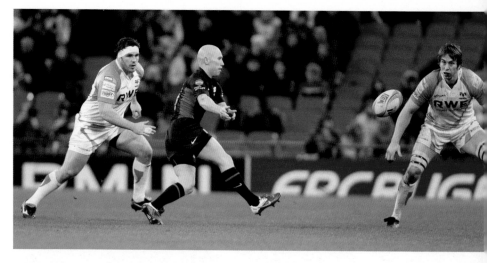

44. Nine days later, I was playing in a Heineken Cup match at Wembley Stadium, helping Saracens beat Ospreys 31–26. (*Andrew Fosker/Inpho*)

45. With Debbie at Christmas 2012.

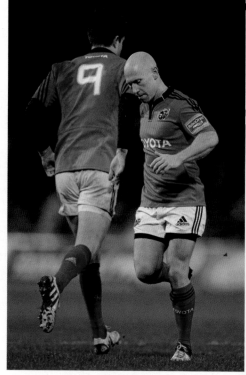

46. Coming on for Conor Murray in a league game against Ulster, 29 December 2012. I didn't know it at the time, but it would be the last time I ever played for Munster. (*Ray McManus/Sportsfile*)

7. George Ford joins me in celebrating after I scored Bath's third try in the 2015 Premiership semi-final against Leicester. (*Patrick Khachfe/Onside Images*)

8. The ovation I received from the crowd when I was substituted at the end of that semi-final – my last home game at the Rec – was one of the sweetest moments of my career. *Patrick Khachfe/Onside Images*)

49. Debbie and I got married in the Old Town of Marbella in June 2015.

50. With my parents and my brothers John, Dave and George after the wedding

matches. That seemed an odd way of looking at both of us. I was frustrated but said nothing for the time being.

The first League match was away to Edinburgh, and Duncan started again. I came on for the last seven minutes. A week later we were at home to Treviso and this time I was given the last thirteen minutes.

I went to see Rob. 'What's the story here?'

He said: 'We know what you can do. We're just having a look at other guys.'

I never regarded that as a genuine response.

'Yeah, I know what I can do as well, and I feel it's better than what he's bringing.' It seemed to me that Duncan was the only guy they were looking at. I would have liked the chance to show what I could do.

All I ever wanted was an opportunity to play. I've no gripes if I don't play well, and another guy plays better, and he becomes first choice. Fair enough.

'Leave it with me,' Rob said. 'I'll talk to Simon. We have a plan laid out for the next few weeks, and we'll see if we can get you a start.'

He came back to me the next day and said: 'I've spoken to Simon. We can get you a start against the Dragons in Limerick.'

Although I didn't know it, that match would be my last time to start a game with Rog. It went well. I was chomping at the bit. We scored two good early tries and Rog converted both. And that was pretty much it.

I was omitted from the next two games, away to the Ospreys and then Leinster at the Aviva, both of which we lost. The following week, in our first Heineken Cup match, away to Racing Métro, Conor was picked to start and I was named on the bench.

I thought, *Great, he sees me as the number two. It's something.* The first Heineken Cup pool match is a benchmark selection. It's the first real indicator, each season, of where you stand in the pecking order. The relief was huge. We arrived in Paris the night before the game and I was feeling pretty good again. In the team room we had dinner and watched the Harlequins v. Biarritz match. I was at the back of the room and Rob was sitting next to me. I felt I could chat to him a bit more easily now.

He said: 'Strings, knowing that you're here now should mean a lot to you. You now know where we're coming from, that we've selected you in the squad for this game.'

I said: 'Yeah, it's great. I'm just itching to get out there. I just want to play. I know I'm not starting, but that's fair enough.'

We began well, with our scrum on top, and were 10–0 up early on; but then we let it slip away. Conor didn't have a particularly great game. Near the end he went for a dummy inside our 22 and was nabbed. This led to a penalty that made it 22–17 for them. I thought that my Heineken Cup experience would be useful for the endgame, but I didn't get on. Every sub was used except Stephen Archer and me.

When the final whistle blew, I was both devastated and puzzled. Why hadn't Rob brought me on? We were behind, Conor wasn't having his best game, and Rog had gone off, injured, so we were short of a bit of experience.

I went into the changing room, pissed off. I'm not one for confrontations in the heat of the moment. I like my head to be clear. If I start something with somebody, especially a coach, I don't want to be caught off guard. And there was a bigger picture here. Munster had just lost. It wasn't the time or the place.

I had become particularly close to Marcus Horan. He had found himself in a similar position to mine in recent years. Players in our circumstances are drawn to each other like magnets. You each say your bit about the coach and vent your frustrations that way.

Marcus, who had been sprung from the bench, asked me: 'How come you weren't brought on?'

I said: 'I don't know.' I couldn't understand it. I decided that all I could do was turn up for training the following Monday and be positive. Be enthusiastic. I've always tried to be a motivator, to be energetic, and bring that vibe to training.

The Monday was light enough, just units and weights. Tuesday was the main rugby session at UL. Of course, I was hoping to start the next week in the second pool game, at home to Edinburgh. But realistically Conor was first choice now. I was settling for a place on the bench again.

We assembled in the team meeting room in UL before training and Rob announced the team. I wasn't even named on the bench. I'd been dropped from the match-day twenty-three, having been left on the bench the previous week. There had been no communication about it from Rob or anyone else. Nothing. Duncan was promoted to the bench. I didn't understand it.

We went through training and I was a bit down, but being my own stupid self I tried to be upbeat and put on a good face in front of the others. After the session, I grabbed Rob for a chat.

'Yeah, we're just going to go with Duncan this week and try to give him more experience in Europe.'

Over the years I've had discussions with coaches and have been unable to believe their responses. When you try to get straight answers they say things like: 'We're just giving this guy a run' or 'We're giving this guy an opportunity to bring him on'. It seems to be a standard line.

I said to Rob: 'You picked me on the bench last week and you didn't bring me on, and then you drop me. It just does not make sense to me. If you did that to another, younger guy you'd ruin his confidence, you'd ruin his whole appreciation and love of the game. He'd think, "What's going on here?"'

You know when you're trying to have an argument with someone but they won't oblige you? They might even be a little bit jolly about it, when you want them to bite back and confront you. But Rob wouldn't. He even smiled! I did not want him to smile.

He was playing it down like it was no big deal, but it was a massive deal for me. I came away furious from that meeting. It wasn't clear what else I could possibly do. There was no point in talking to Simon Mannix. He was the backs coach and sometimes had a few tips for me in meetings or on the training pitch, but I don't think I ever talked with him about selection.

As it panned out, I would never again be involved in a match-day squad in the Heineken Cup with Munster. Conor started and finished both matches in December against Saracens, with Duncan on the bench. I had to settle for a couple of League games off the bench in November.

I couldn't take much more. I went to Rob one more time. I said, 'Rob, I've constantly asked you for game time and I haven't got it. As much as I don't want to leave this place, I feel I have no option and I would like to go on loan, please. What I want is to be here, playing for Munster, and that's all I ever wanted. I would be happy to see out my career playing for Munster, but if I'm not going to have an opportunity to be involved, there's no point.'

'OK, OK,' Rob said. 'Let me look at it. Let me talk to the other coaches.'

I always had the impression that Rob was never fully in control of the day-to-day running of the team. To me he came across as being a bit clueless about the workings of the organization, and was never that dominant figure you expect a head coach to be. It was only after I had left Munster that I learned that he and Simon had to rely heavily on the input of other members of the coaching team and management to assist in their decision-making. This did not come as a surprise to me.

I started away to Connacht on 22 December and played the full eighty minutes at the Sportsground. A miserable night in Galway. I played well, and we won 16–12.

In the dressing room after the game, I had my hands over my face and I was crying to myself. Doug Howlett walked over to me. He put his hand on my shoulder and with a slight smile said: 'Are you OK?'

I looked up: 'I am.' That was all that was said.

Dougie is one of the best guys I know. An All Blacks legend, their leading try-scorer of all time. It was an incredible pleasure playing alongside this man, who gave his all every time he pulled on the Munster jersey.

I thought to myself: *Fuck it; this is what it's all about.* The Sportsground on a shitty Friday night, wind and rain, playing the game you love. Guys must have been looking at me, thinking: 'What the hell is wrong with him?' I'd been through so much in my career. I'd been lucky to play in so many big games. Over 200 games for Munster. Almost 100 games for Ireland. And here I was, crying after a win over Connacht in Galway. It just meant so much to be on a rugby pitch.

A week later, I was on the bench with Rog for the game against Ulster at Thomond Park. He went on and then I joined him for the last twelve minutes. We won 24–10. No one knew it then, not me or anybody else, but it would be the last time I ever played for Munster.

21.   A New Adventure

Whereas Tony McGahan and Rob Penney had clearly never thought very highly of me, I knew one coach who still rated me, who still believed in me. Gary Gold, who had brought me to Newcastle at the end of the 2011–12 season, had now become the head coach at Bath, with Mike Ford his assistant. While I was at Newcastle, Gary had made it clear that he was keen to keep in touch after the three-month loan was over. 'Strings, ring me,' he used to say. 'Any time. Ring me.'

It's always a dilemma to ask a coach to go on loan, because at that point you feel as if you're severing any opportunity of playing again. A coach hears that and thinks, *OK, he doesn't want to be here.*

I can also understand that if a player tells his coach he wants to leave, the coach is bound to think: *What's the point in picking this guy?*

Ideally, I'd have preferred to stay. Munster was my club. Always had been, and I had always assumed I'd be a one-club man. But I had played more rugby in six months with Saracens and Newcastle than in the last two seasons with Munster, or than I was likely to play in the next two seasons with Munster.

So, in January, I rang Gary Gold.

'Gary, this is the situation: I'm not getting game time.'

He said: 'Strings, you would not believe it. I thought about you this morning and was about to pick up the phone and tell you that Michael Claassens has just broken his thumb in training and is going to be out for six to eight weeks.'

I said: 'I was ringing you to see if there's an opportunity –'

'Strings, when can you get over here?'

'I can be over this weekend. I just need to sort out the details.'

As I hadn't been playing much for Munster, I'd been doing extra conditioning after training and on my days off, because I'd never have forgiven myself if I arrived at a club and not been fit and match-ready. There would be no excuse for that. Without making a big deal about it, I would ring the fitness coaches, Aidan O'Connell and PJ Wilson, to arrange extra conditioning work. Now, suddenly, I was getting a chance to put my preparation to work. The Saturday week after I phoned Gary, I was on the bench for Bath's LV Cup game at home to Exeter.

I was brought on early in the second half. The score was 6–6. Within ten minutes I had scored two tries, and we won 16–6. Gary came out to the middle of the pitch at the end and gave me a big hug. 'Thank God you came to us,' he said.

I'll never forget it. I had a new lease of life.

In March my loan was extended to the end of the season, and in April I signed a one-year full-time contract. I was delighted to have joined Bath and to be playing in the Premiership, but it was also disappointing to realize that my Munster journey had come to an end. A part of me wanted to believe that one day I would make it back, but deep down I knew that it was over.

We were mid-table in the Premiership that season, and our involvement in the European Challenge Cup ended with a loss at home to Stade Français in the quarter-final. I started the match, and my opposite number for Stade was Jérôme Fillol. At one point in the first half, the whistle blew and I tried to take the ball off him – par for the course between scrum-halves. But what happened next was not normal: he spat in my face!

It had only ever happened to me once before, in an Under-21s match between Ireland and France at Musgrave Park, and it was the same player: Fillol. Dad has kept all the match programmes from my games over the years, and when Fillol's name appeared on the Stade Français team sheet, I knew it was him: the same guy who had spat in my face that day in Cork. The two most despicable things that ever happened to me on a rugby pitch, and both by the same player.

The touch judges in the Under-21s game didn't see it, and there was no video footage of the incident. Athough none of the officials saw him do it in the Challenge Cup game, it was blatantly obvious when replayed on video.

The International Rugby Board chief executive, Brett Gosper, tweeted: 'Spitting on Stringer should be punished to the full extent of the law.' That would have meant a suspension of up to a year.

The ERC's independent judicial officer, Anthony Davis, said he had considered a suspension of twenty-six weeks appropriate, but had reduced it to fourteen weeks because of the 'genuine remorse expressed by the player at the hearing, as well as his exemplary record and strong character references'.

It was reported that Fillol sent me a letter of apology after the incident. Well, if he did, no one gave it to me. I received no letter.

Paul Warwick, who was with Stade that season, later told me that Fillol showed no remorse whatsoever; he was laughing and joking about it.

There was a reshuffle at the top of Bath Rugby over the off season: Gary was moved to director of rugby and Mike Ford was promoted from defence and backs coach to head coach.

Then, in December, Gary was removed as director of rugby.

It was puzzling. We had just won our ninth game in a row in all competitions. We were top of our group in the European Challenge Cup and third in the Premiership, six points behind Saracens. Gary finished up training with us on the following Monday, 9 December. When we came in on the Tuesday morning, he wasn't there. Bath issued a statement on the club website, saying that Gary's departure 'followed a restructure in the rugby department' and that the decision was made 'with the interests of both Gary and the club in mind'.

I rang Gary that day and said: 'Look, I don't know what to say.'

And he said: 'Strings, I honestly do not know what has happened. My life has been turned upside down. We are going to have to leave Bath, just as my son is getting settled in his school.' He was quite upset.

I'd love to know what the real story was, but I guess I never will. The club issued a statement the following Friday: 'It became clear that the club and Gary were not able to agree on how to define the role.'

It just shows there is no security in rugby management.

Despite Gary's departure, we continued our good run of form into the new year. Wins at Newport and at home against Bordeaux Bègles saw us top our Challenge Cup pool to ensure a home quarter-final.

The priority for Bath in recent years has been to win the Premiership. With that in mind, the club had been building a squad capable of producing results even through periods when some players were away on international duty. During that Six Nations period we competed well, with Micky Young and me sharing the duties at scrum-half. But a 19–16 loss to Harlequins in the last game of the Premiership regular season at 'the Stoop' saw us miss out on a play-off spot by just one point.

We beat Brive in the Challenge Cup quarter-final at the Rec to set up a semi-final against Wasps in Adams Park. After a tough, physical game we came out on top, 24–18.

I found myself in yet another European final in Cardiff – the only difference being that it was held next door to the Millennium, in The Arms Park, and we were competing for the Amlin Cup. Our opponents were Northampton. I had to be content with a spot on the bench, coming on for the last twenty minutes. We were outplayed in that second half, going down by 30–16. It was another bitterly disappointing fall at the final hurdle, but nevertheless there was a real sense within the organization that huge strides had been made, both on and off the pitch that season.

That June, Debbie and I went to Barbados on holidays and stayed in Sandy Lane, which is part-owned by JP and Noreen McManus. They are two of the most generous people I've met in my life, not just to us but to so many others in every walk of life. I first got to know JP and Noreen from various dinners and Munster games they'd attended. Noreen is a huge Munster fan. Their passion for sport and their willingness to help people is like nothing I have ever experienced. Just incredible people.

In Barbados we became really great friends with their son Kieran and his wife, Anne-Marie, whom I'd never met before. They invited Debbie and me to their house for dinner with their friends on the first night we arrived. It became a nightly invite.

This was during the fourth and last week of our holidays. Of course, me being me, I left it till the very last night to do the most important thing I'd planned for that summer: propose to Debbie!

I'd been thinking about it for a long time and had bought the ring. I suppose if I'd asked her on one of the earlier nights of the holiday, and she'd said no, it would have made for a fairly difficult four weeks together!

Already on that holiday we had gone through countless airports in the States. I didn't want to leave the ring in my suitcase and risk having it lost or stolen. So I kept it in my rucksack. I don't know how many security checks and scanners we went through on that trip, but every one of them was nerve-racking. I was afraid that they would search the bag, take out the box and ask me to open it up. I didn't want to go down on one knee and propose in an airport terminal in front of other people. That wasn't how I planned it.

Finally, on our last night in Barbados, I said to Kieran: 'If you don't mind, we are just going to eat in the hotel tonight.'

After dinner, we went for a walk on the beach. I didn't think I'd be as nervous as I was, but, when the moment came, I was relieved that Debbie had no idea, and hadn't spotted the ring anywhere. I was even more relieved that, thankfully, she said yes!

That capped off an unbelievable holiday, and made for an amazing year. We set the wedding for twelve months later, in June 2015, in Marbella.

Since my first loan move to Saracens, I've led a nomadic life, between Munster and three English clubs. None of this would have been possible without Debbie. She's made it so easy for me to continue my career, and to move from place to place. She has suspended her own career for the benefit of mine. She understands that I have only a limited number of years left to play, and she wants to be part of the adventure, to make sure that I extract everything I can out of the game.

When I joined Saracens, Debbie was finishing a Master's in food marketing at UCC, so she stayed at home. She said: 'There's no decision to be made here. You have to do it. I'll stay here and finish my Master's.'

When I moved on to Newcastle, she stayed in Ireland, living in our place on her own while I was over, trying to reignite my career.

But when I joined Bath in January 2013, Debbie joined me there. That made extending our stay for another year, and then another year after that, so much easier.

Living in Bath, Debbie has worked on various projects in PR, marketing and media. She's a driven, motivated and ambitious person like me, and not being able to plan our futures for more than a year ahead is still holding her career back.

I feel guilty. I feel like I'm depriving her of things that she wants to do. But she knows this won't be forever. In fact, it won't be for much longer.

I received some terrible news later in the summer of 2014. It was about the man who had taught me to fly, Denis Metcalfe.

I first met Denis in May 2011. Debbie had bought me a voucher for a flying lesson, and I'd enjoyed it so much that I signed up for a course of instruction out of Atlantic Flight Centre in Cork Airport. Denis, a lad from Mallow, was my instructor. The first day I met him, he looked so small and so young that I initially questioned whether he could be even twenty-one. *Surely he's not going to be the guy who is going to teach me how to fly a plane?*

He was, indeed, only in his early twenties, but he'd been flying since he was fifteen or sixteen. He'd been offered a job with Ryanair a few years later, but wanted to remain a flying instructor for the time being.

I spent from May to November 2011 flying with him, a couple of hours up in the air at a time. In the summer it was nearly every day, and then, once the rugby season started, every second or third day, depending on the weather. You get to know someone pretty well when there's just the two of you in a small Cessna 172 plane for a couple of hours.

Denis made the experience enjoyable, just like a good rugby coach who makes training fun; you want to work with him every day. With Denis as my instructor, I wanted to get up there and fly again as soon as possible. There were a few occasions when he wasn't working, and I would fly with different instructors. It just wasn't the same. They didn't have the same approach, the same enjoyment factor.

Denis inspired and motivated me to earn my licence – and I even got thinking about training for a commercial licence. A couple of times I met with Pádraig Ó Céidigh, the former chairman and director of Aer Arann, to get his thoughts about job opportunities in the airline industry. Pádraig is an extremely motivated person and someone who has helped me greatly over the years. As rugby has remained my main priority, I have had to put thoughts of a commercial licence on hold for a while.

In November 2011, I passed my flying test on the first attempt. I made two flights after I received my private pilot's licence out of Cork Airport – once with Dad and once with one of my friends, Michael Brennan – before the move to Saracens. I've been based mainly in the UK since then, and unfortunately have not had an opportunity to get airborne over here.

On the few occasions when I was back in Cork between December 2011 and the summer of 2014, I always said to myself, *I must give Denis a ring and get up in the air to keep my licence current.* I never did. But I kept in touch with Denis, texting him every now and then to see how he was getting on.

On 18 August 2014, I looked at the RTÉ news on my phone and saw that a young pilot had just passed away. It was Denis. He was twenty-five. He'd just taken up a job with Stobart Air. On his last flight, he co-piloted a seventy-two-seater into Shannon.

An hour later he was on the road, driving home. According to the news report, the driver of a car travelling behind him saw Denis's car swerve and slowly come to a stop on the side of the road. The driver in the car behind, who happened to be a nurse, pulled in and walked up to Denis's car. She realized that Denis had had a heart attack. She couldn't revive him and he passed away that evening.

I flew home to attend his removal in his house in Mallow. I hadn't met his family before. I walked into the house, and the coffin was in the front room. His mum, dad and sister were standing there, greeting people as they came in. As soon as his dad saw me, he broke down, crying, and gave me a big hug. His mum did the same and said that I was always one of his favourites to fly with. Denis had always said that I'd had great promise. I said it was purely down to him and his attitude towards instructing me during all those hours flying.

For such a young guy, with his life ahead of him, it was devastating. What he'd done from such a young age in flying was remarkable. The word 'tragic' is used too easily and inappropriately, but this truly was a tragedy.

In the 2014–15 season, my relationship with Fordy changed. In the past, we would have been buddies, dating back to his four years with Ireland, and he was part of the reason why I went to Newcastle and then to Bath. We got on really well at Bath, too. He repeatedly told me: 'Strings, we're a different team when we have you on the pitch.'

Then, all of a sudden, things changed. The chats stopped. He told me in November 2014 that Bath wouldn't be renewing my contract at the end of the season, and he stopped picking me. At scrum-half, Chris Cook and one of the academy players were being retained. Micky Young and I were being released. To learn so early in the season that you won't be staying at the club is difficult to take.

In February, it was publicly acknowledged that Bath would not be renewing my contract, and there were rumours that Leinster might be interested in signing me. I'd have thought the very idea of my being linked with Leinster would have been sacrilege, to both Munster and Leinster fans. But apparently not: out of everything I heard and saw, from Munster and Leinster supporters, there wasn't one negative comment. It seems Munster supporters want to see me do well because they genuinely feel I was mistreated there.

One Munster fan said to me: 'Go do it. If they [Munster] don't want you, well then go for it. We just want to see you playing. We'd love to see you back in Ireland.'

They've always been so supportive of me. I've had some of the best days – including the best day – with them, and I always loved what they bring to the occasion, because without their singing and the atmosphere they create, it wouldn't feel so special. I played fifteen seasons there. I'm Munster's third-highest caps holder, with over 230 games. I wish I'd had the chance to thank them properly. When I became aware that the Barbarians would be playing Ireland at Thomond Park at the end of May, my agent contacted the Barbarians to let them know I'd be keen to play – provided I wasn't involved in the Premiership semi-final that weekend with Bath. I just wanted one more run-out at Thomond – I'd do it for free!

As winter turned to spring, I sometimes wondered: *Is there a moment when it hits you: this is it, this is the end?*

I knew that moment hadn't come for me yet. The bottom line was, I still loved playing. There has never been a moment when that wasn't true.

My body wasn't urging me to stop. At Bath I was consistently among the squad's top three or four in fitness training, and emotionally I was as committed as I've ever been. That made it hard to contemplate stopping.

Maybe that fear of life after playing subsides with retirement. But every time I thought about it, during that last spring at Bath, the thought of not having a game at the weekend terrified me. It gives my week a structure. It gives my life a structure.

Throughout my life I've been asked: 'Where can you see yourself in three/four years' time?' I've never, ever been able to answer.

I do, however, have options.

During my time with Sarries, I met an Irish guy, Bernard Dwyer, who owns a construction company in London. He has become a good friend and mentor, encouraging me to think about life after rugby. Over the last few years I've done bits of work for him, and perhaps I will continue to do more after I hang up my boots.

Coaching would interest me. I've completed the RFU Level 2 coaching course, which means I still have a long way to go, but I think I'd thrive at coaching because I genuinely love the game, love thinking about it. When Deccie was coach at Munster and Ireland, if I was ever on the bench, I'd find it easier to analyse a game from the stands than when I was in the middle of the action. He'd approach me at half-time.

'Have you got anything for me?' he'd ask.

I'd point out things the opposition was doing and suggest things I thought we should do, and at times Deccie would use my input.

So coaching is a possibility, and I've got other options after I stop playing; but the bottom line, in the early months of 2015, was that I wasn't ready to stop playing. That's why my agent and I were weighing various possible moves for the 2015–16 season. That's why I went to Mike Ford, six weeks before the European Cup quarter-final against Leinster at the Aviva, and made the case for being involved that day. And that's why I went back to Fordy on the Monday before the Leinster game – the intervention that, I'm pretty sure, secured my place in the squad.

I just wanted to play.

22.   My Obsession

What does one do to become a rugby player? Almost all of my decisions while growing up were aimed at answering this question.

I was lucky, because there was a good structure in place for the Under-age game in Cork Con, and I had a dad who was willing to put in the hours with me. But I also worked very hard at it. I studied the game. I pushed myself to do more, be stronger, be better. When people said I was too small, I decided to prove them wrong. I never whinged about being bored, cold or wet. This is what I wanted to do. I was hungry for every aspect of the game. I think the one thing that Debbie would say about me is that, once I put my mind to something, I will do everything in my power to make it happen. That was true even when I was very young.

No matter how much I struggle, or how tired I am, I'll look for that bit extra from my body. I guess this is both my best and my most annoying trait! I don't really know how to give up.

I have always believed that it doesn't take skill or talent to work hard; you just have to want to do it.

I can remember chatting to my Munster teammate Barry Murphy after a pre-season training camp in Breaffy House. It was his first involvement with the team, and he told me how tough he'd found the training. I saw him recently, and he reminded me that I'd stopped him in his tracks by saying: 'It is never really a tough slog when it's something you love doing and are passionate about it.'

I am relentless in this and, with age, I've become even more focused and motivated. I constantly research and educate myself on all aspects of the game – nutrition, diet and fitness. Instead of training once a day while on holiday, I now train twice. I have made changes to my diet. Everything I do is to make me the best I can be.

You may think it sounds horrendous. But I love it: seeing what my body is capable of, always pushing harder and for the tangible reward at the end.

Not only is my height still a topic of conversation, but now my age is as well. I'm almost thirty-eight as I write this, and I feel in the best shape of my life.

I can't identify a specific moment when my devotion to fitness began. I think it was a natural progression from training with Cork Con on those Wednesday afternoons. I loved being active, being outside, whether it was rugby training or playing football with my buddies after school in the field behind our house until it became so dark you couldn't see any more.

After we moved to Leahurst, I remember Mum and Dad began to take in foreign students who were studying English. One of these students was a German guy called Heinz, who would go for a run on winter evenings. For some reason, one evening I asked him: 'Do you mind if I go along with you?'

Off we went. I thought it would be a leisurely jog, but he kept upping the pace, asking: 'Is this OK for you?'

I wanted to say: 'No.' Instead I kept saying: 'Yeah, that's fine.' We ran for a few miles and I finished in absolute agony.

I remember coming home and thinking: *Why did I ask to go with this guy?*

But it triggered something inside me. The buzz of training through pain. I was nine or ten at the time.

Almost ever since, a day without training leaves me filled with regret and guilt. From that first run with Heinz, I've been obsessed with being in the best possible shape, giving myself every single opportunity to be the best I can be.

Fitness was a big part of schools rugby, especially when Deccie was coaching. I'll never forget the 800-metre runs around the pitches on those cold Tuesday and Thursday evenings in the pissing rain in the Wilton training ground, which had a junior pitch, a senior pitch and some land around them.

We'd start at the corner of the Under-13s pitch, and our finishing line was called the Sandpit. Deccie would sometimes blow his whistle to signal that we were to stop, turn, and go back the way we'd come. Some guys would hang towards the middle or the back in anticipation of that whistle, so they'd be nearer the front after we turned around.

But I'd go as hard as I could, and when the whistle sounded I'd now be one of those at the back, having to overtake those who'd been behind us.

In my first year at Pres, aged thirteen, I built my own training circuit in my bedroom. I went into town and bought a chin-up bar which I screwed into the doorframe.

Then I bought press-up stands, raised about six inches off the ground. I'd mix different press-ups – feet on the ground, feet on the bed; really wide press-ups with my hands far apart and others with my hands literally touching each other. My bedroom chair saw more use for tricep-dips than for study. Later, I bought a set of dumb-bells for bicep-curls. I'd spend forty-five minutes to an hour training, pretty much every evening. It was all my own doing, my own ideas – I had no training manual, nobody advising me.

Around the same time I started swimming after school, generally twice a week, while doing my circuits the other three evenings. This was in addition to training on Tuesdays and Thursdays, and matches on Wednesdays and sometimes at the weekend. I was lucky in that Douglas Swimming Pool was two minutes' walk from Leahurst. I'd go there before dinner, or I'd finish my homework and then be there for the last slot at 8 p.m. I noticed a change in my body, in the muscle definition in my arms and chest. And that drove me to push myself even harder. I'd do fifty lengths of breaststroke at a steady pace and leave the pool feeling great after fifty minutes of non-stop swimming.

I was still small, compared with everybody else, and my added strength wasn't going to change the way I tackled bigger guys. I would still target their ankles. It just gave me more confidence in everything I did, and it meant I could carry the ball with more conviction.

Even against Dublin teams like Blackrock College, renowned for their size and physique, and boarding-school teams who trained all week and did gym work, I was still punching above my weight. It's always been that way. I didn't want to be physically dominated. I wanted to be able to look after myself on the pitch.

For summer holidays in Rosscarbery, I created my own high-intensity sessions on the GAA pitch behind our house. I'd mingle twenty- or thirty-metre sprints with press-ups and sit-ups. Along with swimming, I did some bodyboarding. I bought a Styrofoam bodyboard in Jeffers Sports shop in Bandon. If there was a breath of wind I'd go to the Long Strand with my wetsuit and stay in the water for a couple of hours. Often it was cold and raining, and there was nobody around. Naturally, that only motivated me more.

On a summer holiday in New Hampshire in 1992, when I was fourteen, I'd take a pedal-boat into the middle of Lake Winnipesaukee, dive down to the bottom, and retrieve all the golf balls people hit into the lake. I did it on my own because my brother George couldn't swim, and John and Dave were too young to do it. It served a dual purpose: I swam for ages, which was great for my fitness; and when the boat was full I'd pedal back and sell the balls back to the golfers who'd hit them there in the first place. I took further satisfaction from the probability that no other fourteen-year-old boy in Ireland, or perhaps anywhere else in the world, was pedalling into a lake at eight o'clock in the evening, swimming around and collecting golf balls.

After I left school, the IRFU's Foundation Programme introduced me to serious weight training. The Union sent Mark McDermott, a former Munster hooker, down once or twice a week to supervise the five Cork-based lads. At eighteen, I was a relatively late starter, given that most players nowadays begin at fourteen or fifteen.

I'd say I spent more time in that UCC gym than I did in the lab or lecture room! During the two years in college – before I abandoned chemistry – I trained almost like a professional. I knew I wouldn't grow another three or four inches taller. I just had to make do with the frame I had.

Even so, when I joined the Munster set-up in the pre-season of 1998, I immediately noticed I was still behind. Munster's speed coach,

Mark McManus, introduced me to running and agility drills. He was from Scotland and had a background in sprinting.

Being in Munster meant developing yourself into a complete athlete in every single way – strength, power and speed – in addition to rugby skills and knowledge of the game. I began weight training with basic lifts – bench presses and squats – and I'll never forget the sick feeling from those early sessions.

Nowadays, S&C coaches identify areas to focus on during six-week blocks, varying from heavier to lighter weights, and different numbers of reps. These variations are introduced because muscle responds to changes in training. The idea is to stimulate different muscle fibres and 'keep your body guessing'. That's how you get the best from it. So the S&C guys monitor you and keep mixing it up every four to six weeks, alternating between strength, power and hypertrophy sessions.

I am now in my nineteenth season as a professional player, and my fitness scores are as good as they've ever been. I might not be as quick in a fifty-metre sprint test as I once was. But when I train and play, my body feels no different from when I first started. Of course, I feel a bit sore when I get out of bed the day after a match, and there are times in pre-season when you feel sore the next morning. That's natural – you just have to get on with it.

I've already written about Paul Darbyshire, who joined Munster as head of Strength & Conditioning in 2007. He'd played Rugby League with Warrington before becoming their S&C coach. He demanded the best from everybody. I had no problem working really hard for him, within the demanding environment in Munster. Everyone bought into it. When Darbs had a session laid out for us, we didn't want to let him down.

In his first few days at Munster, I can remember him saying: 'Lads, I'm going to do a session which consists of ten sets of ten reps, who's in?' His exercises of choice that day were bench-press, dips, shoulder-press, curls and chin-ups. A hell of a session for the four or five of us who attempted it. He'd also throw in random sessions from day one with his usual enthusiasm. He also introduced boxing sessions, which I did occasionally with him. He'd put together a routine and after

thirty seconds you were absolutely hanging. But, again, his enthusiasm made you want to keep pushing yourself.

Pre-season can make or break a player, and a squad. But Darbs and
the players continually encouraged one another. If you had your
hands on your knees, the player next to you would say, 'Stand tall!'
This can also apply to a team's body language during games: when
you tire, you don't want the opposition to see it.

In that 2007 pre-season, and for the next three pre-seasons, Darbs
set out our stall, demanding that we work hard for each other. He
was a huge, huge influence on me. To this day, during fitness sessions,
I remember him. Thinking of him helps to drive me on.

Darbs was a major part of what we developed in Munster, in terms
of our core values. His replacement had to be somebody we all
respected. Bryce Cavanagh was appointed Munster's new head of
Strength & Conditioning in 2011.

Most of my pre-season in 2011 was with Ireland in Carton House,
preparing for the World Cup. I didn't meet Bryce for his first
few months with Munster. He was from an AFL (Aussie Rules)
background. He, too, was hugely respected by everyone. In our preparation and our training, he brought the level of professionalism to
new heights.

He believed that the two or three hours we spent training in Munster wasn't defining. It was what we did for the other twenty-one or
twenty-two hours, away from our working environment, that made
the difference, primarily with regard to how you felt every day and
for how long you could continue playing.

I'll never forget the day Bryce called Hayes, Donncha, Paulie,
Mick O'Driscoll, Wally, Fla, Rog and me – all us thirtysomethings,
basically – into our meeting room in CIT (Cork Institute of Tech-
nology). He had put together a 'book' for each of us, based around his
own research. The book was divided into different sections – lifestyle
habits, recovery, training preparation, etc. – everything to do with
giving you the tools to help you become a better athlete. He called his
book 'Project Maldini'. The inspiration was the great Milan central
defender, Paolo Maldini, who finally retired at the age of forty-one,
twenty-five years after his first season in Serie A.

Bryce said: 'Lads, you can take what you want from it. It's what I believe will ensure you get the most out of your careers.'

At first, I didn't adhere to 'Project Maldini' religiously. In recent years, however, it has become my bible. Not everything in it is for me, but it has certainly educated me on how to get the best out of my body.

I still swim. I'm not a very fast swimmer but I push myself. On holidays, I get restless and hot, lying in the sun. So I go into the water. I'll see a rock at the other end of the beach and make it a target. I'll swim there and back, but then it becomes an obsession.

I can't leave it at two widths of the beach. I have to set a target of ten widths. It sounds completely ludicrous. Even to myself it sounds insane. I can't just 'go for a dip'. I don't do 'dips'!

I read a book by Chris Hadfield called *An Astronaut's Guide to Life on Earth*, describing his lifetime ambition to become an astronaut, all the training required. It was like reliving my own youth (except the bit about becoming an astronaut). He writes about the fact that an astronaut has to be prepared for all eventualities, and that struck a chord. I have always had that same fear of being unprepared, be it for the first day of pre-season, a match or any challenge I am presented with. It's all about being ready for whatever is thrown your way.

Continuous daily training, even in the dark periods when I wasn't getting picked, meant that I was ready to make loan moves at short notice and be up to speed with my physical fitness. The easy option, during those periods, would have been to ease off training. But if I'd received those calls from the English clubs without having done all that preparation, I simply wouldn't have been able to live with myself. That regret would have burned inside me.

I train with much younger guys every day. In a squad where everyone is younger, and some are particularly young, enthusiastic and fit, I love knowing that, physically, I still have it.

Because I'm at an age when the vast majority of professional rugby players have finished playing, I'm constantly being asked about my retirement plans. When I search for reasons why I would stop playing the game I love, I can't find any. As long as my mind and body are in sync, as long as I feel good and I'm still enjoying it, then I'll keep going.

I'll be a long time retired. I'm the type of person who regrets mistakes, and I'd regret packing it in just because I'd reached a certain age. I'll need a better reason than a number.

I recognize that playing has been my reward for my obsession with fitness. But my fitness regime is now distinct from my rugby career. On the day when I finish playing, I'm certain that my attitude to fitness won't change. In fact, it will allow me to do other things.

Many ex-players take up cycling, because it's easy on the joints. I've never skied before, and I'd love to try that, be it downhill or cross-country. Maybe I'll try triathlons, or marathons, although I doubt a full marathon would motivate me that much. Recently I went with my brother Dave for a ten-mile run, which I hadn't done in many a year. I found it quite monotonous. I like variety, mixing things up.

Being a professional rugby player prevents you from doing certain things, because your main goal is still Saturday. Nothing can jeopardize that. But when I close the door on playing rugby, other doors will open.

Whatever it is, I'll probably train just as hard. It's purely me, knowing that I can continue with the rest of the day, having done my training. It will be a daily part of my existence as Peter Stringer.

I know this from my annual holidays. Every day of those holidays for the last number of years, I've enjoyed a new environment for training. I've been lucky enough to have been to Dubai, Miami, New York, Mexico, Chicago, Los Angeles and other places. Wherever I am, I get up at 6 a.m. and complete my fitness or my weights session by 7 a.m. Then I have breakfast and look forward to a full day. Come the evening, I might do another session before dinner.

In Miami I found a park close to the hotel and marked out hundred-metre runs. In Mexico it was too hot, so I found an underground car park in my hotel and used my skipping rope and the parking-space lines to do shuttle runs. Whatever the location, the terrain or the temperature, I will have a session adapted to my surroundings. In London, I've been allowed to use Fulham Football Club's gym, which I've used when taking weekend breaks with Debbie.

I can't let a couple of days pass without training. I realize that might sound a bit obsessive, but it's what keeps me sane. The idea that nobody else might be doing what I'm doing on holidays motivates me even more. When I turn up for the first day of pre-season, I've already completed a three- or four-week pre-season.

I love it, and I love the results from it, and how my body responds to it. There's no better feeling in the world than finishing a pre-season, having trained constantly for those weeks. As tough as it is, being that fit and healthy and having put in that hard work is so rewarding. For my own sense of well-being, I need to feel that I am doing the right thing for my body all the time, whether it is through my diet or my training schedule. I just can't live with myself otherwise. It has become more of an obsession with each passing year, but it is why I am still playing. It has extended my career.

It's easy when you're playing every single Saturday. Any player will tell you that. You have your routine, your schedule, your goal and your reward. You know which days to do weights. You know Wednesday is your down day. Everything is aimed towards Saturday, and so it goes from week to week. That is the easy part of being a professional player.

As I've discovered in the past four years, the difficulty is the Saturday without a game. I responded by doing twice as much training on my down day, because I haven't been exposed to those eighty minutes of intensity, or even to sixty or twenty minutes. I had to compensate for that. This also meant doing extra training after Tuesday and Thursday squad sessions, because I knew I didn't need to keep myself fresh for Saturday. Even on Saturdays, when the guys were playing, I couldn't *not* do something! Whether I was at the game or watching on television, I hated the fact that they were playing and I wasn't. I felt I needed to replicate that intensity in some way. And again on Sunday, because I didn't have to rest or recuperate from a match, I felt I didn't deserve a rest.

Recently I spent some time with a couple of jockeys, Ruby Walsh and David Casey. Ruby couldn't understand my drive to train when no one was watching me. He admitted he couldn't do that himself. He'd need somebody over his shoulder, telling him what to do and encouraging him. Everybody is different. Sometimes it comes easily to me, sometimes it's as tough as hell, but it's always worthwhile.

Ruby and David gave me an insight into the sacrifices they make to perform at their job. They need to keep their weight as low as possible, so they eat very little. For breakfast they might have only a cup of tea. They might have a sandwich for lunch, a bar of chocolate in the afternoon, and something small for dinner.

I wouldn't envy them, not one bit.

My diet has changed dramatically over the years. When I first started in Cork Con on those Saturday mornings, I used to have a fry-up every weekend. When I became a professional player, I had to cut down on fried food, but I satisfied my sweet tooth with a couple of bars of chocolate every week.

My weight has never really varied from around 72 kilos (roughly 11 stone 5 lb) for most of my professional career. I was under 9 stone (57 kilos) when I went with the Irish schoolboys to Australia, ridiculously light.

After my initial loan spell at Bath, and before my first full season there in the summer of 2013, I decided to undergo a food intolerance test. I'd been feeling really bloated and I'd been complaining about my stomach gurgling. After years of white bread and Nutella sandwiches (a guilty pleasure) I discovered that I was intolerant of yeast and cow's milk. I knew immediately that my diet had to change. Anything that affected my performance negatively had to go.

We had just moved into our flat in Bath and decided not to buy a toaster – a little thing, but it extinguished any craving for toast immediately! I eliminated bread from my diet, and this in turn eliminated the need for butter and cheese. Pasta has gone as well – anything containing wheat. We also decided to change from cow's milk to almond milk. People keep asking: 'How are you still playing at thirty-eight? How do you still have the same energy levels?' It's because of the changes I choose to make.

After I received the results of my food test I contacted Graeme Close, the Munster and England rugby nutritionist, and asked his advice. I greatly respect him, and his credentials in the area of sports nutrition speak for themselves. After his time with Munster, Graeme returned to the UK and is a lecturer in Liverpool University. The RFU have also enlisted him in advance of the World Cup to ensure the Premiership clubs are all on the same track.

Since then I have become intrigued by the science of nutrition. I'm interested because the changes I've made have all been positive. Straight away, the discomfort in my stomach vanished, but I wanted more. It took my diet to a new level, and I want to reap the benefits of eating healthily into retirement.

I've a fairly low intake of carbs early in the week. I'd eat brown rice or sweet potatoes on a Thursday or Friday before a game, to ensure I build up my glycogen stores sufficiently before the game, along with a healthy source of protein. I definitely feel better and fitter without having eaten carbs all week long.

I'd take a protein shake before bed, and another one in the morning before my weights session. Growing up, I would never have managed a weights session on an empty stomach, but in recent years I've been doing weights without eating any carbs. I've found that my body has adapted to this change in my diet and as a result I feel great.

I've learned not to be completely rigid: it's important to listen to my own body and the way I'm feeling. Professional sport puts serious demands and stress on your body, so if at times I am craving more carbohydrates, then it's not an issue for me to meet those needs.

After weights, I'd have eggs for breakfast, and maybe some salmon or turkey that I'd have packed for myself, along with a banana and a protein shake. After the morning pitch session, a big lunch: plenty of veg for fibre, along with chicken or fish, and some salad.

In the evenings I might have a bag of mixed salad leaves, tomatoes, salmon fillets and boiled eggs. At around 9 p.m. I might have some cottage cheese with tuna or turkey, and another protein shake if I knew I was doing weights the next morning.

Debbie is wonderful, and she has accompanied me on the journey. She is not as strict as I am, nor would I want her to be; but when we are at home, there is no bread, cereal, cheese or milk. No temptations.

It's not all boring. Debbie has taken up the challenge and bakes treats like dairy-free, wheat-free banana bread, pancakes and protein bars. And so far the clean eating is suiting us both.

Everyone needs a treat occasionally, and everyone who knows me knows I have a sweet tooth and would pick sweet over savoury any day. On match days, if I have played I'll allow myself a treat. Ice cream! Not any old ice cream, either. I have found an organic brand from Jody Scheckter's Laverstoke farm in Hampshire, made from buffalo milk, which doesn't affect my stomach. (This is the same Jody Scheckter who was the 1979 Formula 1 world drivers' champion.)

Training as hard as I can, and eating clean, keeps me physically in the shape I need to be in, in order to play at the highest level. That in turn keeps me mentally focused. I suppose it is an obsession. I am obsessed with fitness and what I put into my body, but there are worse addictions!

23. Farewell to Bath

After my pleas with Fordy for me to feature against Leinster at the Aviva Stadium, it was as if a switch was flipped in his head. We stood second in the Premiership and had a six-day turnaround till our next game, away to Newcastle. When the team was named, I was in the starting fifteen.

We won 29–12 with a bonus point, playing a high-tempo, wide game; all four tries came from our outside backs. Two weeks later, I started again, and we beat London Irish 43–12, with five second-half tries, in another Friday night game. The Rec was sold out.

I started again away to Harlequins a fortnight later, and we won 27–26 – Bath's first win at the Stoop in eleven years – to secure a semi-final place. A week later, I started again, and we beat Gloucester by 50–30. After one start all season, I'd suddenly become our number 9 for four wins in a row.

Semi-final week was also the week my future was resolved: I signed for Sale Sharks for a year. There'd been a couple of other possibilities in the pipeline, but Steve Diamond was the first to make a firm offer. This was what I wanted, Premiership rugby. Because of the World Cup, there will be a delayed start to the season, and then eight months of fairly full-on, intense rugby. I'd guess that Chris Cusiter and I will rotate quite a bit. In any case, I'm excited and relieved to know I will be playing for another year.

Sale publicly confirmed my signing on the Tuesday prior to the semi-final. This meant I could focus on the match against Leicester at the Rec, knowing my future was secure.

All week Bath had been more colourful than normal: flags and bunting everywhere. It is a small, intimate community, and rugby-crazy. On our day off, Wednesday, I met well-wishers everywhere.

Part of owner Bruce Craig's vision for the club is to involve all the local businesses and make Bath Rugby self-sufficient one day. Hence a company or a business sponsors every player, with their logos on each jersey. Mine has been a local project-management consultancy, Nine Feet Tall – an obvious fit for me! They have always been very generous, sending us something for my birthday and flowers for Debbie on our engagement. Huw Jones, a partner in Nine Feet Tall, texted Debbie, asking if we'd be interested in meeting for dinner, with friends of our choice. Eight of us had dinner on the Wednesday night in Hudson's steak restaurant, just around the corner from where we live.

The best steaks in Bath.

I had the fourteen-ounce porterhouse and I asked Debbie, who'd normally order a six-ounce fillet, to have the ten-ounce, so that I could eat her leftovers!

Huw also prepared a going-away package for me – a Manchester hamper. Inside were about six or seven little gifts; Manchester caviar, a can of mushy peas, an Oasis CD and more. All the gifts were very apt and appropriate for our move.

As well as a couple of his clients, Debbie and I invited one of our conditioning coaches, Jameson Mola. Every single time I texted him on a Tuesday to ask if he'd be available for an extra weights session on our Wednesday down day, he facilitated me without fail.

I also asked along our team manager, Sophie Bennett. She has made everything so easy for us at Bath, arranging match tickets for family and friends. I wanted to bring some of those who really made a difference for us in the last couple of years and who don't get the recognition they deserve. I also asked our video analyst, Kate Burke. A nice way to begin the farewells to Bath.

With all my other clubs, the physical work would be done earlier in the week before tapering off. Thursday would normally have been a session for going through plays.

But at Bath our main training day at Farleigh House was a Thursday. We'd have what we'd call a clarity session, going through our plays in the morning on the 3G pitch. In the afternoon, we'd replicate a match for about forty-five minutes. We'd leave the changing room as a starting fifteen, as if ready to play a game, with fifteen players in bibs, who'd have had half an hour warming up, waiting for us.

On the Thursday before the semi-final, our opposition had prepared some of Leicester's plays. Unusually, they were allowed to
attack the breakdown and compete for the ball. For an hour it was as
close to a full-on game as you can get. It wasn't our best hour.

In the huddle afterwards a few heads were down, but the exercise
had served its purpose. Fordy said: 'Even though you might be down,
and you might feel it hasn't gone that well, personally I think that
was the best session that we possibly could have had in preparation
for this game. Take confidence from what we are going to learn over
the next couple of days. Don't dwell on giving away penalties, because
ultimately that's behind us. The game is on Saturday, and we can
affect what will happen in the game from now on.'

He praised the non-starting guys for their attitude to the session.
Stuart Hooper, our captain, came in and said the same. There was no
negativity.

It definitely prepared us for what was coming. A light team run on
the Friday set us up. Leicester are the most successful club in the history of the Premiership, and they are end-of-season specialists. They
were playing in their eleventh semi-final in a row, having won nine
of their previous ten. They also wanted revenge for losing 45–0 at the
Rec earlier in the season.

One of the advantages of a home semi-final is that you sleep in
your own bed the night before the game – although, as usual, I was
almost too excited to sleep. I was quite late going to bed, about 1.00
or 1.30 a.m. With a 5 p.m. kick-off, it would be a long day anyway. I
used my iPad to study their players. Our staff had prepared individu-
alized videos on each member of their back line. I also went through
all the notes I'd made at meetings and videos of our training sessions
during the week.

Then I concentrated on my own role, going over the different
calls. Doing all that late at night makes it hard to sleep, but I'd generally go to bed quite late anyway, and we weren't meeting until 3 p.m.

I woke up at about 10 a.m. It was a really warm, sunny, dry day;
perfect for the kind of game that we had planned and trained for.

I made myself breakfast: porridge with strawberries, blueberries,
flaxseed and nuts. I discovered I had no honey, and wasn't inclined to

dip into the bag of sugar – I haven't eaten sugar in I don't know how long. I took a stroll to a lovely little artisan shop around the corner, The Foodie Bugle, to buy their homemade honey for my porridge.

I didn't want to change anything that I'd normally do. Not even the honey.

I gave my boots a quick clean and made sure the gumshield was in the bag – the usual routine. Debbie couldn't make the game – Rob Webber's fiancée, a good friend, had her hen party in Brighton that weekend, and Debbie was committed to it.

My mum flew into Bristol at around 12.30, then got the bus and train to Bath. I arranged to meet her later to give her a ticket for the game.

The Rec is a five-minute walk from our apartment. About two hours before kick-off, with my gear bag on my back, I set off on that stroll I'd come to know blindfolded.

There was a different buzz around Bath. The weather was beautiful and the Leicester fans had arrived in force. By law, every building in Bath has to be constructed in the local oolitic limestone, which gives it a uniformity more like a continental village; it's as pretty as any city in the UK. It's just such an idyllic place on a day like that. On that walk to the ground I was as excited as I've ever been on a big match day.

I turned left from our front door, on The Circus, and went down Bennett Street. Then I passed the Bath Assembly Rooms, down Broad Street. A local tailor, Mark Wallace, who has a couple of shops in London and has just opened on Broad Street, was making my wedding suit. He stuck his head out of the door as I passed to tell me the suit would be ready on Monday and to wish me the best of luck. Supporters, too, stopped to wish me well. It seemed everyone was wearing a replica jersey. The atmosphere was building.

I met Mum at the fountain on Pulteney Street, a meeting point we'd used before, and gave her the ticket. She then set off for a stroll around the town.

Alongside Pulteney Bridge there is a spiral stone staircase with cobbled steps that takes you down by the River Avon, and from there you walk into the entrance of the Rec.

Fordy spoke about what we'd achieved so far this season, how we'd played, having the confidence to play from within our own 22, to throw the ball around. He said: 'I want you to go out and do the same thing. If it's right to kick, then do it, but don't play within yourselves.'

Everyone was nice and relaxed. We didn't feel any pressure. We knew we had the attacking plan and the structures to open up teams and to score tries.

Our pre-match ritual is to do some weights a couple of hours before the game. All the weights – barbells, dumb-bells, skipping ropes and medicine balls – are set up for individual programmes, whatever you need to make sure you're ready for kick-off. Our latest research has shown that if you prep your body beforehand, your blood flow is up and you are more likely to be primed and ready for the start of the game.

At the backs meeting, George Ford went through the attack plan, and JJ – Jonathan Joseph – talked about defence. Then Fordy asked me: 'Strings, in your experience of big games and big competitions, what would you say to the lads?'

And I said what I would always say on these occasions. 'We've trained a certain way. Let's not forget that. Let's go out and do what we've done and, most importantly, just enjoy the occasion.' For me it's always been about enjoying it, having a smile, not being tense or stressed about it, not worrying. Try and let yourself relax. These occasions mightn't occur too often in our careers.

About an hour before kick-off, I went outside for an individual, twenty-minute warm-up. As soon as I went on to the pitch I saw Geordie Murphy, now part of the Leicester coaching staff, on the halfway line. We hugged each other and he congratulated me on my move to Sale. I wished him the best and asked him if he had any sun cream for the top of his head, as he's thinning a small bit – although, as he noted, I probably needed some myself. I don't get to see him that often; it's nice when you meet a familiar face, someone you've played with and been through some really good times with. Geordie is one of the good guys, and one I clicked with. He's a genuine fella who always played with a smile on his face, enjoyed the occasion and was fun to be around.

'Keep in touch, you have my number,' he said to me. It's all too easy to lose touch with your mates when they retire.

The Rec is normally quite a reserved venue, but the atmosphere before kick-off was unlike anything I'd known there. The whole place was just electric. This was Leicester in a semi-final, and everyone knew that Bath's first Twickenham final since 2004 was at stake.

As I finished my warm-up by practising my kicking, all sorts of emotions were going through my head. My last home game with Bath, win or lose. I didn't want to hold anything back.

I wanted us to get an early score, and we did. One of the lads popped a line-out ball to me. I planned on hitting a channel close in, but it was crowded with Leicester defenders, so I hit JJ up the middle. He got over the gain line, and a couple of phases later Banas – Matt Banahan – scored in the corner. It was a perfect example of how our attacking structure worked: we'd have an option on the gain line and another out the back, and Leicester really struggled to defend it. It worked again when George and JJ put Matt over for his second try.

For our third try, their winger Vereniki Goneva showed our winger Semesa Rokoduguni a narrow corridor between him and the touchline. Rocco took it. He'd done exactly the same to Andrea Masi, the Wasps full-back, last season. His footwork is incredible. He then chipped Niall Morris for Kyle to gather and score.

Leicester had plenty of ball, and they had their purple patches. We had to do plenty of dirty work, defending our try line, putting our bodies on the line for most of the first half. We kept our line intact for five minutes after Anthony Watson and Leroy Houston were sin-binned by JP Doyle within a minute of each other, before Leicester eventually scored at the end of the first half. Still, we led 21–10, with three tries from three visits to their 22.

At half-time we spoke about how we were capable of scoring more tries, that it was just a matter of being disciplined. One of our defensive tactics was the 'Green' call, whereby the tackler would get to his feet and try to be a real nuisance, to get through on to the ball, but everyone else would stay on their feet and onside. We knew that Leicester try to feed off mistakes and ill-discipline, by kicking their points or kicking to the corner and using their maul. We realized that if we were disciplined defensively, they'd go through maybe six, seven, eight phases and run out of options, due to their limited attacking game.

The message was simple. Keep doing what we were doing. Trust our attack and trust our defence.

A big screen had been installed in our changing room for that season, and at half-time the video guys put some clips together. The clips emphasized the positive: even though we'd conceded a try just before half-time, we didn't want that to be the overriding thought going into the second half. We complimented each other on some of the things we had done well, and we went back out in a positive frame of mind: *Keep the ball in play; look to attack the gain line and offload out of the tackle; keep the game afloat.* We knew that if we did those things, they wouldn't be able to live with us.

Fordy brought on most of the subs before the hour. One of those was our back-row forward Carl Fearns, a player who always wants the ball. As a scrum-half, that's what you want: forwards showing, putting their hand up, shouting, 'Give me the ball!' Sometimes I just want to hit George, and Fearnsy will get in the way – but you can't criticize a guy for wanting the ball, wanting to get over that gain line.

Shortly after Fearnsy came on, I popped it to him off a ruck around the Leicester 10-metre line. He burst through two tackles and freed his hands to offload to François Louw. I trailed behind François, screaming at him. He told me afterwards that he could see Goneva coming in to make a big hit on him, and knew he wasn't going to bump him: Goneva is a big unit. So he tried to free his hands. Even though he wasn't looking at me, he later said he'd heard me coming from about ten metres away, so he instinctively knew to turn and pop it up without looking.

After I caught the ball, I remember nearly tripping before regathering myself. Out of the corner of my eye I could see a Leicester player coming from my left, and I transferred the ball to my right hand, to use my left hand to fend if I needed to. However, I knew I was so close to the line that he wouldn't stop me, and I was able to scoot over.

Funnily enough, when we'd beaten Leicester 45–0 at the Rec in September, I scored from a similar scenario in a near identical position. But I'm not known for my tries and so I don't have a celebration routine when I do score. Normally I put the ball down and try to stay straight-faced, run back and be ready for the kick-off. But whatever came over me – probably knowing that the game was won at that point – I thought for a second: 'Hang on, I'm going to enjoy this one.' I stood up and threw the ball into the crowd. Looking at the video, it doesn't seem like me, but I'm glad that I enjoyed that moment, and my teammates' congratulations.

The commentator, John Champion, said: 'He's been playing for years and years, Peter Stringer.' He has actually made a few comments about me recently. That week on Twitter, after I signed for Sale, he said something like: 'Great to hear Sale Sharks have signed fifty-seven-year-old Peter Stringer.'

I couldn't wipe the smile off my face as I jogged back to our 22, and a cameraman stayed with me on the pitch as George lined up the conversion. The crowd in the temporary seating in that corner of the ground stood and applauded.

During a game I wouldn't normally do it, but I smiled and applauded them back. What the hell? It seemed the right moment, and why not enjoy it? My last home game. It was pretty special.

George converted again and, within five minutes, scored a try himself after an exchange of passes with Semesa.

I still find it bizarre to recall that I effectively babysat George Ford for an afternoon when he was about nine years old.

His dad was at a training camp as Ireland's defence coach in UL in 2002, and he had two of his three boys with him – Joe and George. They were always hanging around after sessions, and on our down day we did some kicking practice. Fordy asked me to look after George for a while as he had some work to do, preparing for an analysis meeting with the other coaches the next day. We went to a petrol station up the road from UL, where I bought George an ice cream and looked after him for a few hours.

He and Joe were always there at the end of training when we did kicking practice. George would practise his grubbers, chip kicks and punts. When the scrum-halves box-kicked, George would catch and kick them back. When the out-halves practised their goal-kicking, George would be behind the posts, gathering balls with Rala, our bag man. He was an eager kid with incredible enthusiasm for the game; always wanted a rugby ball in his hands. Being in an environment like that, and with Fordy for a dad, would only have helped him.

As a nine-year-old, he was a bit shy, but polite and well-mannered. At sixteen, he became the youngest professional rugby player ever in England when he made his debut for Leicester. By the time he joined Bath from Leicester at the start of the 2013–14 season, he was an extremely mature twenty-year-old. Since then he's been basically running the show at Bath. He's got it all: running game, passing game and kicking game. He's a huge talent. When George speaks, guys respect him, and that's quite rare for a guy so young.

As I discovered when I broke into the Munster team, a young half-back needs to learn how to bark, and he needs to know what he's barking about. And George did that from his first day in Bath.

Of course, when the story came out about me babysitting him and buying him an ice cream, the rest of the squad lapped it up. If George heads off on his own, one of them might say: 'Make sure now that Strings goes with you.'

But he doesn't need, or look for, any babysitting now.

George's try made it 33–10. Three minutes later I was taken off, and the scenario was exactly what I'd hoped for, but never got, from my Munster farewell. A stoppage on the far side of the pitch; a substitute scrum-half waiting to come on; the game effectively over.

I bent down and put my gumshield in my socks to give myself a couple of seconds before I started to jog off. The ovation was better than I could have dreamed of. I pirouetted to wave quickly to all four sides of ground. It was one of the sweetest moments of my career.

I was emotional as I sat down on the sideline. Fordy came over, shook my hand and said: 'Well done. Incredible. Incredible farewell for you. Well done.'

I wouldn't have believed I could have formed as close a bond with any club as I had with Munster, but I was close to crying; in the dressing room I held my head in my hands and shed a tear. François came over and asked: 'What's wrong?'

Micky Young, who hadn't been in the match-day squad, was kind enough to sit beside me and say well done. 'Is everything OK?' he asked.

'Yeah,' I said. 'It couldn't be better.'

As much as you'd love that to happen every single week, you know that such occasions can only occur once or twice in your career, if ever. I never had it with Munster or Ireland. It wasn't to be. Most players never experience a farewell like that at all.

But I did with Bath, and it makes me proud.

Of course, it was upsetting too. I didn't want my time in Bath to end.

A guy from Northern Ireland, Peter Rollins, who manages the Thermae Bath Spa, has been quite ill recently with cancer. Through him I've met his family over the last couple of years. His brother Nigel texted me before the game to say that his eight-year-old son Cal hadn't been well and asked if I had a few minutes after the game to say hello.

I got caught up with TV interviews, and the doctor and physio examining my thumb – I'd suffered a strained ligament – and I completely forgot about Nigel and Cal.

I went back out and thankfully they were still there, so I brought the two of them on to the pitch. Nigel told me that Cal had been diagnosed with a rare form of arthritis, and they were both very grateful that I'd taken time out to meet them.

I said: 'It's not a problem. I enjoy meeting people.' I love those one-on-ones, ten-minute meetings with supporters, seeing what it means to them. It's no sacrifice. It's a privilege that comes with being a rugby player, or a sportsperson.

Afterwards, I texted Mum to ask where she was. Debbie texted me on her way back from the hen party to say she had one per cent left in her battery but that she had watched the whole game on her phone!

I showered, changed, had my thumb strapped and signed a few autographs. I met Mum and Debbie, who had just arrived from the train station, and we headed back to the apartment. We ate some food and the three of us chilled out for a few hours. But I was raging that I had forgotten to record the match. I always struggle to go to sleep after a game, and it would have been nice to be able to watch it back. I stayed up long after them, went to bed at about two and woke up at about five.

I got a text from our video analyst to say that they'd put the game on our club app, so I was able to watch it on my iPad. At around 6.30 I went back to bed for a couple of hours. At last, I could rest easily.

Epilogue: Another Ending and Another Beginning

A major final in Twickenham in May. This took me back to the Heineken Cup final fifteen years before. I was twenty-two then, a little wide-eyed and innocent, somewhat like Munster at the start of their European journey.

We arrived in London early in the afternoon, to stay in the Hilton Syon Park, about three miles from Twickenham. At the stadium we went for our team run – more a team walk, really. It was my first time in the home changing room. I strolled around the gym at the back of the changing room and then put my suit on its hook and my boots and shoes in the compartment under my seat. We walked around the pitch discussing what we were going to do in different areas of the field and then took the bus back to our hotel.

Everyone was excited, and we had a great team dinner. No tears, nothing too emotional – very different from the night before the 2000 final with Munster. We'd won six games in a row. Training had gone well all week. We were going to play our game. We didn't concentrate too much on Saracens. Sometimes you can become too spooked by the opposition. Sometimes you've just got to back yourself to do your own things well.

It was my last night rooming with Kyle Eastmond, my best friend and regular roommate at Bath. Kyle's background is very different from mine. He grew up in a tough area of Oldham. His father wasn't around, so he's had to look after his mum and his sisters, and probably grew up quicker as a result. He was a Rugby League guy through and through, being capped four times for England RL before coming to Union the season before I arrived at Bath. He's incredibly talented and he has quickly made himself very knowledgeable about the game. One of the best-built guys that I've ever seen, too. He's the same height as me but he's ten kilos heavier.

Even though our lives are quite different, we relate to and confide in each other. There's a trust there. He consistently gives me a different outlook and perspective on things, picking up on how people are thinking. He's honest, and he doesn't hold back. At the start he could be hot-headed on the pitch, but he's calmed down. As an inside centre, Kyle is key to our defence and attack. He is like a coach on the pitch, drawing on his League experience. League is a numbers game. Kyle coaches the team on how to hold a defender so as to create space for others. The coaches value his role.

Kyle is naturally good-humoured. You will hear him laughing from fifty metres away. He slags me about my age, my size and my birthplace. Not a day goes by without him singing 'Ireland's Call' for my benefit in front of everyone. He's the chief slagger, but he's serious about the game. Once, when I was speaking to the squad, he said: 'Ninety-eight caps, lads. Fucking listen to what he's saying.'

In all my chats with teammates that week, I spoke of my time with Saracens and recounted a conversation with Mark McCall. He told me: 'Strings, the one way to beat Saracens is to be so patient. You need to have a good kicking game and keep kicking the ball back, kick for kick. Because as soon as you become frustrated with that in your own half, and you try and play, we'll force a mistake, at the breakdown or in the tackle, force a penalty and take the three points.'

When Sarries get into a lead there is no better team at defending it. But they're a different team if they have to come from behind. So I talked about the need to get our noses in front, and take any three-pointers on offer.

There was another thing that played on my mind all week, and I spoke about it at the backs' meeting at the team hotel on the morning of the final. 'Don't wait for a big loss in your careers to motivate you to win something the following year. You don't have to lose one to win one.' Like Munster did. Or, in Munster's case, lose two to win two.

The Bath marketing department had given out Bath flags, and the roads seemed to have turned blue. Seeing people in Leicester and Northampton jerseys with little rub-on Bath tattoos on their faces and with Bath flags, it was tee'd up for a great day.

There were the usual scenes in the Twickenham car park, car boots open and supporters with their sandwiches and flasks. Space was so tight the bus had to wait for people to get out of the way. Fans were banging on the bus, and as we climbed off we were met with a wall of noise. That's always nerve-tingling. Hairs rising on the back of the neck. That got me in the zone. I'd been quite relaxed until then.

We arrived at Twickenham at 12.45, and did some weights beforehand to loosen up. Fordy spoke, reiterating the need to stick to our principles, to the brand of rugby that had got us to this final. George Ford went over our attacking plan again, and Kyle went through our defensive duties.

Only on the bus journey to the ground, for the first time that week, did it hit home how big this occasion would be, in front of a capacity crowd of 80,000. I'd been so wrapped up in my own game I hadn't thought about that.

I didn't want to think about it being my last game with Bath, either.

That reality only really hit me when I came off with eleven minutes to go.

All my worst fears about Saracens had been realized. They kicked downfield, we made a mistake, Owen Farrell scored a try in the seventh minute and we were never ahead. They had a second soon after, and were 25–3 up at the break.

Although we got back to 25–16, Farrell made it 28–16 and so the game was pretty much lost by the time I came off.

From the bench, I looked at the clock – eleven minutes left. I thought, *OK, there's still a chance, twelve points behind, eleven minutes left.* George missed touch from a penalty. Down to eight minutes. Then, dammit, four minutes. 'Unless we get an intercept here or something it's . . .'

The Sarries bench rose as one, remonstrating with the touch judge and the fourth official. The clock in the ground had stopped. I saw the referee signal there was only a minute left. Game up.

Stuart Hooper was sitting next to me. Once the final whistle went, he stood up and shook my hand. 'Thanks for everything you've done for the club and for me.'

'Likewise. It's been great.' More handshakes. Similar words.

We had a big huddle in the middle of the pitch. Fordy spoke. 'Lads, look, it just wasn't our day. These things happen and I just want to say goodbye to two good men here in this huddle.' And he mentioned Paul James and me.

As soon as the huddle broke, I stood on my own and tried to unscramble my brain. I looked at the crowd. I didn't want to talk to anyone for a second.

I saw Mark McCall jogging along the touchline and on to the pitch, coming towards me. As soon as he reached me, he held his arms out, and we hugged for a few seconds. 'Well done, Strings,' he said, slapping me on the back of the head. That was it.

Time to congratulate the Sarries players.

I congratulated all of them. Chris Wyles, who I got on very well with. Kelly Brown wasn't involved, but I spoke with him too. Jamie George, Schalk Brits – another good mate when I was there. I was also good friends with their young centre, Duncan Taylor. He didn't have much of a run in the team when I was there, but has come through and played for Scotland since. Alex Goode. Dave Strettle. Very good friends.

I wasn't bitter. I might have been, had it been another team.

I went to the edge of the pitch, where Debbie was waiting.

My parents were in Spain. They'd booked that a few months before, when I was third-choice scrum-half! It was too awkward to change and there are no direct flights. Dad was gutted. Every day that week he rang and kept apologizing.

Monday.

'I'm really sorry.'

'Dad, you've said this, and it's not an issue. It's not going to affect how I play. It's not going to affect the occasion. I know you want to be there. Look, don't worry about it.'

Tuesday.

'I'm so sorry I can't be there.'

Wednesday, the same. It nearly reached the stage where I said: 'Look, I'll talk to you Saturday!'

None of my brothers could make it, either. That's one of the downsides of making a final at a week's notice. John was flying from Cork to Spain that day. George tried to get flights from Dublin, but he couldn't get off work. And Dave was still in the Cayman Islands.

But Debbie was there with her sister Ciara, and her husband Dominic and their little girl Eliya.

Eliya is three, going on about twelve, very advanced for her age. They had brought her to a game in Bath during the season and Eliya watched attentively for eighty minutes, repeatedly asking questions.

'Why is that man wearing a different jersey to the others?' – the referee.

'What's the score now?'

'Are Bath winning?' Debbie said Eliya was completely engaged in the whole game.

It was the same for the final, but Debbie told me that Eliya became quite upset when we lost, and her main concern was me.

'Will Peter be upset?'

'He'll probably be a bit upset.'

So Eliya said: 'I want to give Peter a card to make him feel better.'

She had a little bag and took out an A4 sheet of paper, and stuck a few hearts on it.

They had come down to the side of the pitch together, but Eliya didn't really know how to approach me because this was a different environment for her. She hadn't seen me in this situation before.

'Don't be upset,' I told her, and she handed me the card.

What do you say to that? It made me smile, and reminded me that there are other things to life than losing or winning rugby matches.

Back in the changing room I took as many photos with the lads as I could, because I knew I wouldn't be in a changing room with them again. Kyle, Stuart, Sam, Horacio, whoever I could grab. I wish I'd taken more photographs over the years.

On the bus back to Bath the lads were having a few drinks, and I wasn't as down as I usually would have been after a loss. Normally I wouldn't have allowed myself to smile, or be happy. I had to punish myself.

But I think we felt – rightly – that we had had a great season. And in my case, this wasn't drink talking. I was moving on, too. This was my last day with these guys. It wasn't the time to mope.

The club had organized a function that night in a rooftop bar and restaurant called Graze, in Bath. If I'd been coming back for pre-season, then Debbie and I might have gone home, but I made the effort to go to the function in Graze. Everyone who worked at the club was there, including all the wives and girlfriends. I knew that was my time to say goodbye to my teammates, my friends, because even though they were having an all-day session in Cardiff the next day, I would be too busy to go. The removal men were coming at 8 a.m. to put all our stuff in a storage unit near our training ground in Farleigh.

Everything was packed except our duvet, Debbie's wedding dress and my wedding suit, which were hanging up for our flight to Spain on Tuesday. Bar a couple of lads who were coming to the wedding, I wasn't going to see them again.

We were there for two hours or so, chatting to a good few of the lads. Very casual and very relaxed. It got to about 10.30. I was tired. Most of the lads had a bit of drink on board. We needed to be up early. I said to Debbie: 'Will we head away?'

'Yeah, let's go.'

I planned my route around the bar, to say goodbye to everyone, to shake hands and give them each a hug. Debbie walked the room with me. It took longer than I expected, and was quite emotional. Debbie became very upset.

All the girls were there, and she's made some really good friends in Bath, like Sara Louw, François's wife. Despite all that he's done in his career and for the club, François has never won a trophy. No silver-ware. No medals. Yet. He had kept making a point of this during the season.

I said to him, sympathetically: 'Another one escapes you.'

'I just don't know what it is,' he said.

I said: 'You're a guy who deserves to win things. I hope your time comes, that you get to lift a cup, and I hope it's here at Bath.'

'Yeah, well, hopefully.'

Maybe it was partly the drink, but guys I'd regarded as stand-offish, or maybe just shy, suddenly began letting their feelings be known.

We continued on our lap to say our farewells.

Ross Batty said: 'Will we see you tomorrow in Cardiff?'

And I said: 'No, I've so much to do.'

'Oh, so this is it?'

Everything began to seem so final. People who normally just have a handshake, including the coaches, put down their drinks and gave us both hugs.

'You've no idea what it means to me to have worked with you for the last two and a half years.'

As a sportsperson, it is always an incredible feeling to receive compliments and good wishes from supporters, but that night, to hear the appreciation coming from my peers, was a humbling and very special moment.

The last person to say goodbye was George Ford. An embrace followed by his kind words, 'You've helped me so much with my game, without knowing it; you have kind of inspired me.'

The goodbyes were making it tougher, especially for Debbie, who was crying by now. I could feel I was about to start crying too. But at this stage, we were by the door. Just suck it up, smile, and get out that door.

We walked down the wide staircase, holding hands and not saying a word.

Eventually I turned to Debbie and said: 'Look, this is the start of a new adventure. Let's go for it. Let's just be happy about it.'

'Yeah,' she said. 'Let's go for it.'

Acknowledgements

Thank you to my parents, John and Aileen, for your unconditional love and unwavering support. Without your constant belief in me I would not have been able to achieve my career ambitions.

To Debbie, your love, friendship, personal sacrifice and support means everything to me.

To my brothers George, John and Dave, for the great memories I have of us growing up and for always being there for me, especially when I needed it most.

To my teammates, with whom I shared the greatest moments on and off the field. Having the same mentality, the same will to win, has meant the good times massively outweigh the disappointments. It is truly humbling to have played with some of the greatest players in the game and to have made lifelong friends along the way.

I would like to thank every coach who has inspired and taught me throughout my career. Thank you for nurturing my love of the game and giving me so many opportunities over the years.

To all the strength and conditioning staff who have motivated me to succeed, to always challenge myself and to continue to strive for more. Thank you to the backroom staff and medics for your help, which has enabled me to play the game at the highest level all these years.

A huge thanks to everyone who made this book possible, especially Gerry Thornley, who helped me get the past thirty-seven years onto the page.

My sincere thanks to everyone who has supported me during my club career in Ireland and in England.

A special thank you to all the Irish supporters who have loyally followed the team throughout my career in the green jersey.

I'm eternally grateful to the Munster supporters, whom I never got a chance to thank and say goodbye to. You inspired and encouraged me to perform to the best of my ability. Your deafening chorus subdued many an opposition. Thank you for always being the 16th man.

Gerry Thornley

I remember Peter's Heineken Cup debut vividly, against Perpignan in October 1998. It was only a week after his Munster debut as a sub against Ulster, and sitting in the Musgrave Park press seats, someone to my left said to me: 'That little fella is going to play for Ireland.' Ever since, I've always admired and liked Peter, and it was a genuine honour to be asked to pen the story of his life and career so far. Thanks to him and Debbie for their patience, time, unstinting help, hospitality and good food!

Thanks also to Michael and Brendan, and all the staff at Penguin. You were genuinely a pleasure to work with.

To 'the team', Yseult and Petria. Without your effort this simply wouldn't have been possible.

To Evan, for his love and for being there.

To Marian, for her love and support.

Thanks to John Stringer, and also to Noel O'Reilly in the *Irish Times* sports department, for the additional proofreading, and to my understanding sports editor, Malachy Logan.

To Patrick, Lisa, the good shepherd 'Shep', Selby et al. in Patrick's Café on Serpentine Avenue; to Gerry, Ian and co. in Mulligan's in Sandymount; to Dave, Lisa and John in Griffin's Bar in Clifden; to all in Café 1 and to Ronan et al. in Counter Culture in Powerscourt Townhouse Centre, thanks for the great coffee, food, table space and wi-fi!

And also to all those who gave of their time to check dates and facts, such as Peter Melia, Peter Scott, Donal Lenihan, Frank Byford, Barry Coughlan, Mick Galwey, Keith Wood, Fred Casey, Pat Geraghty and Nigel Owens.

Thank you very much one and all!

Index